CHRISTOPHER COLUMBUS

Christopher Columbus

JOHN STEWART COLLIS

SD STEIN AND DAY/*Publishers*/New York

First published in the United States of America, 1977
Copyright © 1976 by John Stewart Collis
All rights reserved
Printed in the United States of America
Stein and Day/*Publishers*/Scarborough House,
Briarcliff Manor, N. Y. 10510

Library of Congress Cataloging in Publication Data

Collis, John Stewart, 1900–
Christopher Columbus.

Bibliography: p. 201
Includes index.
1. Colombo, Cristoforo. 2. Explorers—Italy—
Biography. 3.   America—Discovery and exploration—
Spanish. I. Title.
E111.C63   970′.01′50924 [B]   76-48986
ISBN 0-8128-2173-2

Contents

Illustrations and Maps

A Personal Note

I CALL IT A PERSONAL NOTE since it hardly qualifies as a preface. Often an author is asked why he wrote his book. More than one good answer can be given; sometimes, however, there is the simple one overriding all others—namely, that he very much wanted to write it. Such is my own case here. Ever since, in my thirties, I read a remarkable book on Columbus, I had hoped that one day I might attempt to write the story myself. There is so much to enthral. So much grandeur, and misery, and adventure, and tempest, and hardship; such rich reward followed by such appalling disasters. It is a Cinderella story which, continuing beyond the triumph of the ball, falls into disarray and tragedy, though the element of the sublime is never entirely eroded by folly and sin.

Brooding upon this for many years, grappling with the obscurities, the discrepancies, the inconsistencies, and the conflicting schools of thought about so many incidents and motives in this man's life, I have now attempted to set down, as I see it, the shape and the drama.

Drama and shape are there of course, and it is the task of the artist to reveal this. An artist can produce a fine work (as Louis MacNeice did in a radio drama) without bothering too much about chronology or the detailed march of events, and may telescope or falsify some facts for the purposes of his art. I happen to believe that when nothing is sacrificed, neither chronology nor the prosaic facts which belong to the story, the drama need not lose shape and can even gain by that very adherence to the actualities. What we must do is to bestow enough imagination upon the given facts. Take the first voyage. The established facts have been rehearsed many times. Why not bring them into the realm of truth and the realm of beauty?— for unless this is done the reality is not made manifest. The same for the subsequent voyages, especially the fourth (though I'm

5

glad there weren't five) which is far from being an anti-climax.

I have gained a little by recently making two journeys by cargo boat across the Atlantic to the West Indies on nearly the same route as Columbus took. While in Jamaica I had the opportunity to get my bearings right regarding the current controversy over the possible recovery of the remains of the two ships which were abandoned in St Ann's Bay. The story itself is dateless: in a way the story of so many destined men; the knocking at the door that will not open; the hour of triumph followed by tragedy and humiliation; the crossed and crooked destiny that is chiefly character. This is what I have sought to make new.

John Stewart Collis

CHRISTOPHER COLUMBUS

CHAPTER ONE

The Windows of The Middle Ages

I

CHRISTOPHER COLUMBUS was the man who discovered America, we say. It sounds a somewhat parochial statement. Leaving the Scandinavians aside for the moment, we know that America had presumably been discovered thousands of years previously—by its inhabitants, who doubtless entertained the impression that the land belonged to them, if to anyone . . . Still, this chronicle compels me to approach the matter from more or less the same angle.

Columbus lived from 1451 to 1506. Let us try to grasp something of the cosmographical outlook of Europeans during the preceding centuries. We are at once confronted with the curious fact that they were less well-informed than their predecessors. Roughly speaking, from about A.D. 300 to the fourteenth century, learning appears to have got lost. The great writers and thinkers and cosmographers of Athens, of Rome, and of Alexandria were no longer available. This may sound unlikely, if not absurd. How could a man, living in Verona, say in A.D. 300, know more geography than a similar man living there in A.D. 1300? Knowledge which has been written down is not something which can be lost like a parcel or stolen by a thief. We are accustomed to think of information, especially geographical and cosmographical knowledge, advancing from generation to generation; and it would be unthinkable to suppose, for example, that people in the nineteenth century would know less than people in, say, the sixteenth and preceding centuries. But this is what did happen in the ages which we call 'dark'—for there does seem to have been a considerable darkening of the mind for some centuries. Eventually the old learning was recovered and we got the renewed or new learning, and there was a rebirth of energetic inquiry which we call the 'Renaissance'.

Many solid reasons have been advanced to explain this loss of culture and knowledge: the commercial decline of the Roman Empire and the gradual cessation of trade with India, the Persian Gulf, Arabia and the eastern coast of Africa; the Germanic invasions which undermined the unity of life and culture; the splitting of the Empire into Latin West and Greek East; and later the Black Death which took such a toll that it became an achievement to keep alive at all. Wise after the events we can make a list of 'causes' which doubtless did contribute to this cultural shrinkage, but the fainting in spirit and the failure in intelligence are not so easily accounted for, and could not have been foreseen any more than the rising up of spirit and of energetic inquiry which eventually followed could have been foreseen.

As an example of this shrinkage let us take geography—the aspect with which our story is concerned. The scholars of the Middle Ages affirmed that geography could not very well be fitted into the quadrivium—that is, arithmetic, music, geometry, and astronomy. In other words—we can have a bit of music and measurement, but we don't want to know where we are. And very soon they didn't know where they were because they didn't know where other people were.

In the era of the ancients (so much less ancient, so much closer to us than the men of the Dark and Middle Ages) there was a restricted and limited idea of the *Oikoumenē*, or world picture, but it did show a fairly accurate amount of Africa and India and China; but by the fourth century the habitable globe was confined to the northern hemisphere. 'The southern extension of Africa, established by Ptolemy (and perhaps Herodotus), is ignored, and the Nile is again made to cross the Continent from west to east in a line parallel with the Southern Ocean. Egypt is regarded as forming part of Asia and Africa commences only to the west of the Nile. The Ganges flows into the eastern ocean and the Caspian is once more held to be a gulf of the ocean.'* India is everywhere and nowhere (and remained in this non-position well into the sixteenth century, if not longer). In the early Middle Ages the poverty of geographical knowledge is most apparent with regard to the Far East. 'Whereas in the writings of the Ptolemaic era we are furnished with relatively precise information on such topics as the mountains of Central Asia, the characteristics of the

* *Geography in the Middle Ages*, G. H. T. Kimble, Methuen, 1938.

Chinese people and their silk trade with the West, in the centuries that follow the textbook frontiers of Asia are withdrawn to the Ganges, and in everything but name China is unknown.' This window was not opened again until the coming of Marco Polo in the thirteenth century and the publication of his *Travels* in the fourteenth.

So decadent a geography and so narrowed an horizon following upon a period of expanding world-knowledge are surely surprising. Ptolemy's geography had postulated the earth as a sphere and had calculated its dimensions not grossly far from the truth; but by the fourth century geographical thought was no longer moulded on this pattern, and instead of the opinions of Herodotus, Eratosthenes, Hipparchus, and Strabo, the highly unnatural *Natural History* of Pliny, with its decorations and fancies, was much more favoured. After the fifth century, and until the fifteenth (when Columbus arrived), there were only occasional references to the school of Ptolemy, while his *Geography* was hardly ever noticed.

Though Greek scholarship exerted small influence upon Western culture during this period, its actual existence was preserved by the schoolmen in the monasteries. It was not their line of thought but they felt constrained to preserve it, while at the same time discouraging scientific inquiry. Geography was considered important only as a gloss upon biblical themes, and map-making only as a means of giving those themes a habitation and a name, so that they were much happier in fixing the locality of the Garden of Eden or the resting-place of Noah's Ark than in any scientific investigation. Indeed nothing reveals more clearly to us the nature of the mediaeval mind than the cool assumption that four rivers flowed from the Garden of Eden—those four rivers being the Euphrates, the Nile, the Ganges, and the Tigris. Such a 'garden' would have to contain a number of mountain ranges about the size of the Himalayas and a number of forests about the size of the Ituri Forest of Africa—with probably no apple trees.

Such considerations did not trouble the Fathers of the Church who, absorbed in doctrine, closed their minds to everything which they thought irrelevant to the knowledge of God and the salvation of the soul. In a letter to the Bishop of Vienna, Pope Gregory I while ruling that secular study lay outside the field of intellectual endeavour, declared with astonishment that 'a report has reached us which we cannot mention without a blush, that thou expoundest grammar to certain friends;

whereat we are so offended and filled with scorn that our former opinion of thee is turned to mourning and sorrow. The same mouth singeth not the praises of Jove and the praises of Christ.' Lactantius, another of the early Fathers, went further and declared that science is not only false but foolish, and that 'to investigate or wish to know the causes of things' is an appalling waste of time, while St Jerome in his XXII Epistle inveighed against philosophical work as well as scientific, crying out: 'What concord hath Christ with Belial?! How can Horace go with the Psalter, Virgil with the Gospels, or Cicero with the Apostle?'

If we pass in review the various geographical world-pictures during these ages we wonder how anyone could derive a clear idea about anything. No authority was certain as to the extent of any ocean, nor how far the waters were navigable, nor what truth there was in the assertion that on reaching a 'torrid zone' ships would melt in a kind of boiling soup. It was not really definite whether the earth was like a ball, or a pear, or a dinner-plate surrounded by water—you could take your choice from the puzzling maps. Some of the most powerful voices, anxious to adapt knowledge to the requirements of the Christian faith, spoke with great indignation against the 'ignorance and arro-gance' of opponents who took a more advanced view. Thus, in his *Christian Topography*, Cosmas Indicopleustes spoke with sarcasm of those who 'with supercilious air as if they surpassed in wisdom the rest of mankind, attribute to the heavens a spherical figure and a circular motion', an error which he deemed to be as grotesque as the idea that there was an 'Anti-podal land-mass' upon which people actually lived. The whole notion he declared was an old wives' tale. 'For, if men, on opposite sides, placed the soles of their feet each against each, how could both be found standing upright? The one would assuredly be found in the natural upright position, and the other, contrary to nature, would be found head downwards. Such notions are opposed to reason and alien to our nature and condition.' Not only opposed to reason, but opposed to Christian theology, for the Apostles were commanded to go into all the world and preach the Gospel to every creature; but as they did not go to any such place as the Antipodes, it followed that there could be no such place.

If any inquiring layman, impressed by such topography, sought to find 'the four corners of the earth' delineated on some of the maps of the time, he was bewildered. When we today take a look at these maps, or *mappaemundi*, of the Middle Ages, unless we are specialists we are defeated in our attempt to interpret them, we cannot make out which continent is which, and would find it easier to study a Persian carpet for geographical information. The fact is the maps in those days were regarded as works of art rather than of utility. They were very popular and appealed to the people much more than written work, as pictures have always done—and these maps were really pictures. They were highly ornamented, some of the decorations being of human figures or of a presentation of the Garden of Eden or some other biblical fable, the illustration occupying space which, if one thought about scale, would signify about five hundred square miles! 'In the course of centuries,' says George Kimble, 'the *mappaemundi* became more and more removed from reality, for so great was the stranglehold of tradition, classical as well as ecclesiastical, upon the mediaeval mind that rather than accept facts uncongenial to their way of thinking, map-makers not uncommonly preferred to ignore them and in their stead employ imaginative and schematic designs.' Meanwhile the Ptolemaic world-map remained in total eclipse save for a brief period when it attracted the attention of the adventurous Arabs.

There was no real discrimination, or even desire for discrimination, between fact and fiction. Exactitude of statement was not felt as a need: people did not mind a mixture of truth and invention. This attitude was shared by the leaders of thought, and we find that a great authority, a learned Irish monk called Dicuil, while capable of sober statement and even the searching analysis of doubtful assertion, is at the next moment ready to claim that Mount Pelion is two hundred and fifty miles high and the Alps fifty, and that the world is comprised of two seas, seventy-two islands, and forty mountains. Even in the early sixteenth century (after Columbus's first voyage), we find great Portuguese navigators and scientists being at one moment factually exact and then relating the existence of serpents a mile in length, and of Africans who have the faces and teeth of dogs, and tails like dogs.

But, as we know, history is not neat, and there were those who heralded an advancing outlook. The great Roger Bacon paved the way to a more scientific attitude and persistent inquiry in the face of ecclesiastical indignation and disapproval, though he was never explicit enough to become a martyr. Already by the thirteenth century, Adelard of Bath, a great translator, began to ask in his *Natural Questions* things as outrageous as—Why is the earth suspended in mid-air, and how is it maintained? Why is sea-water salt? How do rivers achieve a constant flow?, and so on, to the consternation of the weaker brethren; while his contemporary, William of Conches, became indignantly argumentative with his obscurantist co-religionists who, conceding that 'we do not know how such a thing can be', yet added 'we know that God can do it'. Conches replied, 'God can make a cow out of a tree, but has He ever done so? Explain why a thing is so or hold your tongues.' Strong words for the period, and indicative of a new spirit that was coming and would bear fruit in the fifteenth century when men, however devout in the Catholic faith, became interested in more than scripture, in more than doctrine, and in the geographically unknown. In this respect, as we shall see, no one was more a child of the Renaissance than Columbus.

It could be helpful at this point to devise a map which might serve as a concrete image of what the world seemed like to Westerners in the Middle Ages. First we look at a modern map of the world. Then we contrive to picture what people envisaged before the Portuguese began to explore Africa under the leadership of Henry the Navigator. We cannot do better than draw upon the images of Arthur Helps whose admirably-written biography of Columbus came out in the nineteenth century.

The map of the world being before us, let us reduce it to the proportions it filled in Prince Henry's time; let us look at our infant world. First take away those two continents, for so we may almost call them, each much larger than all Europe, to the far West. Then cancel that square massive-looking piece to the extreme south-east; its days of penal settlements and of golden fortunes are yet to come. Then turn to Africa; instead of that form of inverted cone which it presents, and which we now know there are physical reasons for its presenting, make a scimitar shape of it, by running a slightly curved line from Juba on the Eastern side to Cape Nam on the Western. Declare all below that line unknown. Hitherto we have only been doing the work of destruction; but now scatter emblems of hippogriffs and anthropophagi on the outskirts of what is left on the map, obeying a maxim not confined to the ancient geographers only: 'Where you know nothing, place terrors'. Looking at the map thus completed, we can hardly help thinking to ourselves, with a smile, what a small space, compara-

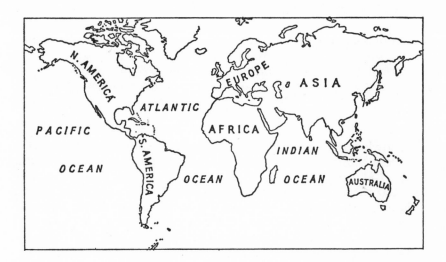

Map 1   An outline of the world as it is known today

Map 2   The extent of the world known in the Middle Ages, before
the discoveries of the fifteenth century

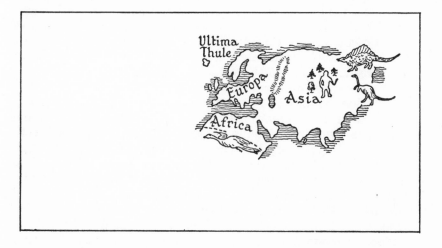

tively speaking, the known history of the world has been transacted in, up to the last four hundred years.

We may think such a commentary too parochial and the map too impressionistic, but it surely gives an idea of what the horizons were at that time, and helps us to appreciate the change of view which was to be effected within one hundred years.

II

Knowledge concerning the water-masses upon which adventurers could not or dared not travel remained fearfully vague until at the close of the fifteenth century Columbus partially lifted the veil by resolutely sailing west. Meanwhile the Asiatic land-masses upon which people could travel began again to exercise the imagination of Europeans. It was Marco Polo who opened the window on the Far East in the thirteenth century. It had been opened in the Ptolemaic era when there was relatively precise information regarding China and the silk trade with the West; but that trade collapsed in the sixth century, and from then onwards till the twelfth century there was scarcely a Latin or Greek work which revealed an immediate knowledge of China. The only people who ventured there were the Arabs, but they set down nothing that was geographically clear. Then Christian travellers began to emulate the Moslems in traversing Asia from the banks of the Volga to the Yellow Sea. The first to go were Christian friars who hoped to gain converts to Christianity and find a counterpoise to the Saracen power. Passionately wishing to spread the Gospel they were ready to believe the wildest legends.

It sometimes happens that a man may attain a tremendous reputation, he may be heard of through extensive kingdoms, he may dwell in gorgeous palaces and command outstanding influence—without actually existing. Such a man was Prester John at this period. He was conceived of as a Priest-King located somewhere in 'the Indies'. He combined the piety of the Apostle with the wealth of a Croesus. For a century or more the quest to find the exact realms of Prester John and to meet the man himself promoted western enterprise into Asia. The fact that he did not exist in no way undermined his influence. Indeed it made it easier for his reputation to grow. He commanded armies and achieved great victories. His lineage increased in splendour and it was found that he was descended from the Three Wise Men, that he ruled over the same nations that they ruled and attained such wealth that he used a sceptre of solid emerald. He addressed letters to kings and potentates, one of which began, 'John, Priest of the Almighty power of God and the strength of the Lord Jesus Christ, King of Kings, Lord of Lords', claiming that he was the greatest monarch under heaven as well as a devout Christian, and rehearsing the millioned glories of his territory which flowed with honey and with milk. In 1221, when news came that he was fighting the Moslems and sweeping away their power, the Pope sent two friars, Plano Carpini and William of Rubruck, to find him and assist at the conversion of the Mongols. But now at last Prester John's lack of existence did begin to tell against him, to undermine his influence, and to impede his progress; and eventually the friars fell into disillusionment and finally into disbelief.

But these friars had blazed the overland trail to Tartary. Ten years later two Venetian brothers, Nicolo and Maffeo Polo, on a commercial enterprise, reached Bokhara on the road to Samarkand where, by an extraordinary stroke of luck which affected the history of Western Europe, they met envoys travelling to the court of the Emperor of China, the great Kublai Khan himself, overlord of all the Mongol states from the China Sea to the Crimea. These envoys accompanied them to Peking where Kublai actually received them in person and made them welcome. After a year they returned home with a letter from the Emperor to the Pope requesting that two friars be sent out to tell the Mongols about Christianity—an exceptional mark of respect from the East to the West.

On their return journey the brothers took young Marco with them. In *The Travels of Marco Polo* which he eventually produced, he tells us a great deal about Kublai, representing him as one of the mightiest of earthly kings, as 'the greatest Lord that is now in the world or ever has been'. His presence is felt strongly throughout the narrative; he is made so forceful a character that the very words 'Grand Cham' could be used six centuries later far away in England to denote a personality like Dr Johnson, and in the next century could haunt the dreams of Coleridge with that vision of Xanadu and its stately pleasure-dome. 'In Kublai,' says John Masefield, 'the reader will find enough images of splendour to make glorious the temple of his mind.' It is right that it should be so, that when we think of Marco Polo it is of Kublai Khan that we think, and that for centuries to come this character should be legendary in the Western as in the Eastern world. It is a just reflection by Masefield that 'this king, this lord of lords, ruler of so many cities, so many gardens, so many fishponds, would be but a name, an image covered by the sands, had he not welcomed two dusty travellers who came to him one morning from out of the unknown, after long wandering over the world'.

The Polos took three and a half years to go from Venice to Peking. First to Constantinople by sea, and thence by land through Persia, Afghanistan, Samarkand, Tibet, Mongolia, and on to Peking. They travelled some ten miles a day for three thousand miles, with ox-carts, camels, and pack-ponies. One imagines that it must have been the most enthralling land journey ever undertaken by anyone in all the history of travel. Think of it: soldiering on for three thousand miles at ten miles a day with ever-surprising vistas or appalling conditions. We cannot have this now, but with an effort we can imagine it, for seven centuries later the same kind of caravans and the same kind of people who went this way could be seen. The great French writer, Emile Hovelaque, in the 1920s, could see them a few steps away from a modern railway, telegraph posts, telephone wires, and European hotels and legations. He could behold caravans from a past age still pursuing their way, the weird procession of monumental camels which had left India two years before and had only just arrived after traversing fabulous icy mountains and deserts, the whole thickness of unknown Asia and of huge China.

These camels and their savage drivers, the whole fierce tribe of outlandish men, women and children, fiery-eyed, flat-faced, daubed with black grease, who followed in their train, stirred one's imagination strangely. With them, as in the dawn of dead civilizations, you left the sun-steeped plains of India and Mesopotamia: you plunged into the eternal snows and the glaciers of prodigious mountains, into the unending barren solitudes of the 'Roof of the World', the cruel land eternally beaten by icy winds, the terrible region of desert sands, the 'Tartar Void', along the 'Way of the Barbarians', of the 'Gate of Jade'. We know what the legendary Highway of the Silk was like from Chinese travellers and from Marco Polo.

In the seventh century a Chinese traveller called Hsüan-tsang observed that often one could be stopped by a river of sand or by demons in the wind. When meeting such, large caravans were often lost. And five centuries later Marco Polo tells us:

> Peradventure, if at any time during the daytime any persons remain behind on the road, either overtaken by sleep, or detained by their natural occasions, until the caravan has passed a hill and is no longer in sight, they may unexpectedly hear themselves called to by their names, and in a tone of voice to which they are accustomed. Supposing the call to proceed from their companions, they are led away by it from the straight road, and not knowing in what direction to advance, are left to perish.

This phenomenon appealed to the imagination of Milton who referred in *Comus* to 'airy tongues that syllable men's names On sands and shores and desert wildernesses'. There is generally a natural explanation of apparently supernatural occurrences. Hovelaque suggests that

> in reality these sounds are the noise of stones bursting asunder from the daily alternation of frost and scorching heat, the howling of the wild winds in the fissures and crags of the narrow gorges. Everywhere in these accursed regions the powers of evil lie in ambush for man, to whom the least slip, a moment's carelessness, spells death. Nothing has changed since the days of Hsüan-tsang and Marco Polo. During thousands of years these caravans have passed unchangingly through these spaces, led by men identical in appearance with those I saw before me; their fantastic procession issued from the fathomless depths of the mysterious past; they were contemporary with the Pharaohs; their eyes had seen Tyre and Sidon, the towns of azure and of gold, Babylon and the bloody triumphs of the Chaldeans and the Assyrians, the armies of Darius and Alexander, the whirlwind Arab riders, the splendour of the Moghuls; their unvarying procession had crossed the fabulous vanished kingdoms whose very name dazzles; they trailed behind them all the memories of the earth; could they speak they would tell us the secrets of the tombs where dynasties and empires lie asleep.

The romantic appeal of Marco Polo's *Travels* was tremendous; no such fantastic journey had ever before been undertaken or described. There was a further element of great importance, and one which was to have a vital influence upon Columbus. Marco Polo also satisfied the passion for rumours of gold which was so evident amongst the people of the Middle Ages, and especially among their leaders, their adventurers, their prophets. The grandees who surrounded the Kublai Khan, Polo declared, wore suits of cloth of gold with jewels sewn in worth £10,000, while the jewels and gems on the person of an Indian king were 'equal to the ransom of a great city'. He tells how a lieutenant of Kublai, called Hulagu, sacked the city of Baghdad, and finding the Caliph in possession of the greatest store of gold and jewels in the world, was so astonished that such a store of wealth should not have been put to good use, such as paying an army to defend himself, that he shut the Caliph in his treasury, contemptuously inviting him to eat his gold when he began to starve.

Marco Polo's report upon Japan was to become very important historically because of the effect it had upon the dreams of Columbus. 'Chipangu [his word for Japan] is a large island of the East and lies in the high seas, fifteen hundred miles from the coast of Mangi.' By Mangi he meant the nearest point on the coast of China—he appears to have taken no interest in scale, anything would do.

The inhabitants are white, very handsome and of distinguished demeanour [he continues]. They worship idols and are ruled by their own king. They have gold in extreme abundance; it is to be found everywhere. The palace of the Prince is entirely roofed with gold plates, just as our houses are roofed with lead. The halls and rooms are lined with plates of gold, and the windows have gold frames. There are pearls in great quantity and so many precious stones that you have only to bend down and pick them up, and the city of Quinsay, which means City of Heaven, is so called from its magnificence and has no equal in the world. In it are to be found delights of such a kind that a man may dream he is in Paradise. The women in all the streets are so tempting and have such experience in amorous intercourse that a man who has once enjoyed one of them can never forget her.

Marco Polo became a great favourite of the Emperor and was entrusted with many offices in the course of which he travelled no less than thirty thousand miles, at least ten thousand of which no European had previously followed. After some twenty years the Polos persuaded the Khan to allow them to return to Europe. This time they went by sea, a journey which took two years. They sailed down the East China Sea, past Taiwan, down the South China Sea, past Cambodia, thence through the Straits of Malacca between Malaya and Sumatra, across the Bay of Bengal to Ceylon, round India into the Arabian Sea and back to land at Persia. When they reached Venice they were not looking very respectable, and their relatives (those still living) did not recognize them nor accept their claim to be Polos. But this did not trouble them very much, and it appealed to their sense of comedy to be repulsed from their former homes. They let the matter stand for a day or so, and then, before an assembly of guests, they slit the seams of their ragged clothes from which coins, gems, rubies, and jewels poured in profusion. Instantly they found themselves surrounded by friends, while the number of close relatives increased with startling rapidity.

Marco had not written a single word about his experiences, but he talked a good deal, and apparently became something of a loudmouth meriting the nickname of Messer Millioni because he was remarkably lavish with the word million. So it might have ended, and Marco Polo would have been at best but a footnote in travel history. But his luck held. He was thrown into prison after being engaged in a sea-fight between Venice and Genoa. He remained in prison for three years and while there he met a literary man called Rusticiano to whom he dictated the memories of his unique experiences in the Far East, and thus *The Travels of Marco Polo* was given to the world, and the author became an immortal. His place as an immortal was further secured by the fact, as we shall see presently, that Columbus eagerly read the *Travels* and made marginal notes in his own copy—and Chipangu became his goal.

The account which Marco Polo gave can be taken as generally true. But since in those days there was so little discrimination or concern between fact and fiction, another book was even more popular. *The Travels of Sir John Mandeville*, which later was notorious for the amount of fable and falsehood combined with definite fact (including the firm statement that the earth was a sphere), became part of the stock-in-trade of wandering story-tellers who carried a knowledge of it amongst all orders of society throughout Europe. It remains an extremely entertaining volume to this day with the added attraction that .the English edition explores for practically the first time the possibilities of English prose. Though bogus with regard to its authorship and untrustworthy with regard to fact, *The Travels of Sir John Mandeville* combine with Marco Polo in opening the windows of Europe on the East.

III

While windows were being opened on Asia a great effort was
made to open the windows upon Africa. It was from Portugal
that this wave of energy went out. On her death-bed Queen
Philippa gave three swords to her three sons. To Dom Duarte
she gave the Sword of Defence. To Dom Pedro she gave the
Sword of Chivalry. To her third son, Henry, she gave the Sword
of Adventure. He became known to history as Henry the
Navigator. He set up an academy of seamanship at the Rock
of Sagres (near Cape St Vincent) which from a distance looks
like a ship beating out against the waves, a vessel for ever
moving and for ever fixed. This was the focus from which
explorations were planned. They were planned by Henry.
Without a great guiding spirit, nothing of this sort can be really
carried out, nothing significant achieved. Henry was so superior
a person that something of his character has come down to us.
'He was bold and valorous in war, versed in arts and letters,'
says Faria y Sousa; 'a skilful fencer; in the mathematics
superior to all men of his time; generous in the extreme; most
zealous for the increase of the faith. No bad habit was known
in him. His memory was equal to the authority he bore, and his
prudence equal to his memory.' He was somewhat taciturn and
solitary, not always easy to make out. Another chronicler
throws a little beam on him with the observation that he was
'in some things slow, whether it was through the prevalence of
the phlegmatic temperament in his constitution, or from inten-
tional deliberation, being moved to some end which men did not
perceive'. At the same time he had the reputation of never
bearing ill-will against any person, however great the injury he
had received from him. He was a man of intense labour and
study—'often the sun found him in the same place where it had
left him the day before, he having watched throughout the
whole arc of the night without rest'. This great energy was
coupled with singleness of purpose and a spirit summed up in
his motto that the only talent worthy of princes was 'the talent
to do good'. It seems fair to endorse the words of Arthur Helps:

Altogether, whether we consider this prince's motives, his objects,
his deeds, or his mode of life, we must acknowledge him to be one
of the most notable men, not merely of his own country and
period, but of modern times and of all nations, and one upon

whose shoulders might worthily rest the arduous beginnings of continuous maritime discovery.

That discovery was chiefly directed to the circumnavigation of Africa. The existence of India was known to the sea-faring nations of the Mediterranean, though vaguely, for the position of that continent, even after the return of Marco Polo, was wildly conjectural. India spelt riches as well as romance and mystery. The question was—could they reach it by going round Africa? It had been assumed by Ptolemy, and it was still assumed, that the continent extended southwards to the Pole, and that there was no sea passage. Africa was a dam between Europe and India. Yet there were doubts about this, especially in the mind of Prince Henry. There were still traditions that Eudoxus of Cyzicus had, in very early times, sailed from the Red Sea to Gibraltar, and that the Carthaginian Hanno had sailed with a fleet of sixty ships from Gibraltar to Arabia. The purpose of Prince Henry was to make an end to this uncertainty. That was the main resolve behind the establishment of his college of naval science and an observatory at Sagres.

Thus, from approximately 1431 for some fifty years the coast of Africa was explored ever further and further. Many expeditions went out, far more than history relates, since only success speaks. Vague rumour is all we get regarding those who, setting out with hope and resolution, returned defeated and broken or, like the Vivaldi brothers, failed to return at all, their story but a legend on a tombstone in the graveyards of despair. But there was success, and the names of Antonio di Noli, Zarco and Vaz, Gil Eannes, Dinis Dyaz, Lancarote, Ca da Mosto, and Fernando Gomez are associated with the steady discovery of the west coast of Africa.

At first Cape Nam (which means 'not') had seemed the furthest anyone could venture; and there was a Portuguese dictum: 'He who would pass Cape Nam will not return'. But there were those who would not take no for an answer, and the cape was turned. Then Cape Bojador loomed ahead, its name signifying 'the outstretcher', for it was like a flinty arm stretched out to bar all further progress, its perilous rocks and fearful currents seemingly impassable. Many attempts were made in vain and the captains returned disgraced in their own eyes. But Prince Henry encouraged one of them, Gil Eannes, to try again—and he succeeded. Hitherto the far side of it had been imagined as fruitless desert, but Gil Eannes came back with a

barrel of good earth and many plants. And beyond this con-
quered cape, what then? Navigation would soon become impossible, it was held. For the water would begin to boil under
the heat of an intolerable sun and the vessels would be sucked
into fiery gulfs. But explorers went on and returned without
being boiled or burnt. They came back with tales of strange
places, and of people so unaccustomed to the sight of exploring
mariners that they wondered whether the ship was a bird, a
fish, or a ghost.

So the explorations went on year after year down the coast
of Africa, right down to the Cape Verde Islands, on to
Gambia, past Sierra Leone, the Gold Coast, to the Congo. And
still there seemed no end to it—was not Ptolemy right after all?
Then in 1487 Bartholomew Diaz reached the final cape. This
was a very great event in the history of navigational discovery.
But the discoverer was robbed of any emphatic glory, and his
just reward went to another. His story is this: he reached the
limit which had been so far attained in these African explorations. Then he sailed on round the southern extremity of Africa
without realizing it, and cast anchor at the mouth of the Great
Fish River, a little to the east of Algoa Bay. A storm drove him
into the bay where he came upon his companion vessel from
which he had been separated before rounding the cape, and
found that the greater part of the crew had been killed by the
natives. Now he became aware of his discovery and he called the
cape, in remembrance of his danger, 'Cabo de todas los tor-
mentos' ('cape of all the torments'). He then sailed for home
and got back to Lisbon by December 1487, and was received
well. But when, after years of inexplicable delay, a grand
expedition was organized to sail again to the cape, Vasco da
Gama was preferred before him—and Diaz was even obliged to
sail under da Gama in that expedition. Worse than this, Vasco
da Gama sent him back to Portugal after they had reached the
Cape Verde Islands and then sailed on and subsequently
renamed the cape as the 'Cape of Good Hope', which had been
for Diaz a place of storm and of blood. Thus he was denied an
emphatic share in the honour of discovering the maritime route
to India, though it was he, and only he, who first turned the
corner in tempest and violence. Three years later he joined the
expedition of Cabral, the discoverer of Brazil, but was lost in a
storm on May 29th in 1500. Thus perished Bartholomew Diaz.
The great adventurer sank beneath the waves without a ripple
of renown; the laurel and the bays were reserved for his

follower, da Gama, while on the brow of Diaz no laurel, no leaf, nothing save that 'rank weed which roots itself in ease on Lethe wharf'.

Portuguese maritime exploration was not confined to the coast of Africa. The navigators also went far from the shore out into the Atlantic. For approximately at this time the compass (used long before by the Chinese and the Arabs who had every reason to keep it dark*) was rediscovered by European men, who now also laid hold of the invisible principalities and powers that bind the earth in steely bonds. Before this time mariners were obliged to keep the shore in sight, for to lose touch with it meant to be lost upon the endless acres of the unknown waste. They could not afford ever to get out of touch with land, and losing direction lose their lives. Now they could leave the shore, go right out into the forbidding deep, and even in the midst of fearful fog, or blinding tempest, or unexpected currents, yet know where they were, or at least know which way to sail for harbour. They could know this if they had on board a little box with a needle in it—less long than a darning needle. We know all about this today, while losing sight of the strangeness, the greatness, and the triumph of our trophies. It was discovered that a certain sort of stone, a lodestone as they called it, was bristling with a strange kind of life and would attract to itself other minerals, especially little pieces of iron, and make them come to it as if called by a voice, or grappled by a chain, or borne on a current. They found that if they rubbed the surface of this stone with a cloth, and then rubbed that cloth upon a bit of steel it would possess the same property —which was called magnetism. This was interesting but useless. Then they found that, given free play, that piece of steel would be compelled by invisible agents to point always in one direction —to the North Pole. These unseen powers—called protons— moving in their massed millions answer an ultimate law by virtue of which all the substance of all the earth is held in check, and so consistent are they in their ceaseless chase for perfect balance that their play upon the needle is constant and unchanging. We call the thing a compass. If we have it in a box upon a vessel we know we have a guide more reliable than a god. 'It is just possible that one reason why the compass was not in use in Christendom until the fourteenth century,' says G. H. T. Kimble, 'was that those in possession of the secret of

* See G. H. T. Kimble's *Geography of the Middle Ages*, p. 122.

it were afraid to reveal it lest they should be suspected of magic, or that sailors were equally afraid to employ the new device for the same reason!' Anyway, it came as a new and wonderfully freedom-giving thing to the navigators of the Middle Ages, and indeed in any age is a marvel to behold.

The Portuguese sailors could now leave the shore behind and venture far out into the ocean. They explored the Atlantic from the Verde Islands in the south to Iceland in the north. Their farthest venture from the mainland was the Azores, the group of islands approximately a thousand miles west of Lisbon. That was a long way to venture into the unknown, and it is surprising that history has so little to say of the audacious mariners who got there—not even of Diogo de Teive who in 1452 found Flores, the furthest island to the west, the outpost beyond which there seemed nothing save the intolerable vast.

There were other places on the great ocean, imaginary islands, which greatly appealed to them. They were not satisfied with Verde, Madeira, Canary, Flores; they filled the terrible emptiness of the shoreless waves with their dreams and their desires. They spoke of the Fortunate Islands and of the Blessed Islands; of Antilia, an island of refuge from the Moslems, where seven bishops presided over seven cities; of the island named after Saint Brendan who had gone, according to a sixth-century Irish saga, to an archipelago which marked the gates of the earthly paradise; of the island of 'Brazil' whose sands were made of gold-dust. None of these places existed. They were the fictions and fantasies of men who had seen no more than clouds low upon the distant water, or bright-rimmed horizons looking like the entrance into a paradise where all sins are forgiven and all tears washed away.

They did not venture west beyond the Azores—or, if so, no expedition ever returned. That marked the ultimate of their endeavour. It was their real Ultima Thule. The rest was the unknown, and did not call to them; the void was to be avoided. But the unknown did call to one man, and called unceasingly. So we come to Christopher Columbus.

CHAPTER TWO

The Coming of Christopher Columbus

I

BEFORE 1931—which is four hundred and thirty-nine years after his discovery—it was still possible to dispute about the origin of Columbus, his birthplace, even the year of his birth. In fact seven towns in Genoese territory contended for his cradle, while both Corsica and France preferred claims. Imprecision in biographical detail opens the door to the ingenious and the sentimental. And when nothing is certain anything can be advanced by clever and able men who are often more untrustworthy than fools. Witness the case of Shakespeare where poverty of material provides scope for those who are able to produce wonderful 'proofs' that he never wrote a line of the plays. Thus it is not in the least surprising that theories have been put forward proving that Columbus was born in Galicia and Catalonia as well as in France and Corsica. He has been identified as a Catalan pirate called Colom and as a Scandinavian mariner called Scolvus. It need scarcely be added that some 'authorities' insist that it was not Cristobal Colon of Genoa who was the discoverer but quite a different person.

Happily the *Raccolta Colombiana*, edited by Cesare Lollis, gathered together and published an exhaustive collection of documents which were republished in Genoa in 1931 in a folio edition with facsimiles entitled *Cristoforo Colombo: Documenti e prove della sua appartenenza a Genova* (Documents and proofs of his Genoese citizenship). Among these papers there are many items which are not subject to question—especially the notarial records. Thus there is a record of 1470 in which Cristoforo Colombo recognizes a debt he owes a certain Giacomo del Porto, and the codicil of the Admiral's will drawn up in 1505 in which the same Giacomo del Porto is named. Again, there are his friendly relations with Nicolo Oderigo, the Genoese Ambassador in the Court of Spain to whom he entrusted a copy of the royal

27

certificates granting privileges; or his letter of April 2nd, 1502, to the Bank of San Giorgio in Genoa in which he made the city of Genoa the beneficiary of one-tenth of his revenues from the Indies; or the clauses in his last will and testament referring to Genoese friends. These are amongst the incontrovertible facts on public display at the Genoa Exposition of 1950–51.

It is good to have that amount of foundation at any rate, as it is good to see Columbus's house in Genoa. This year, after walking down Via Dante to Piazza Dante, I looked round when in the vicinity of the Porta Soprano, for the house of Columbus —could it still be there after five hundred years? I made a false approach at Piano de S. Andrea and gazed down at one of those romantic old streets so narrow that someone on a balcony at the top storey could shake hands with someone on a balcony at the opposite side of the street. But I was looking in the wrong direction and had overshot the mark. I made an enquiry. 'La casa verde,' a man said, pointing to a house almost completely covered with green creepers. And there it was, under the shadow of immense modern buildings given up to insurance and banking. The creeper covered the walls and even the roof of Columbus's house—keeping his memory green. The door and front part was clear of leafage; a door reeking with history and old time, now for ever closed: and for ever open to the wayward images of all visionary minds nourished by the remembrance of things past. Above it was the legend:

Nulla Titulo Dignior

Heia

Paternis in Colombo

Pueritiam

Primam Juventam Transegit*

The modern Genoese are keeping the memory of Columbus green in an additional way. At Piazza della Vittoria there are the Giardini 'Le Caravelle' where, built with flowers, are facsimiles of his three ships, the *Santa Maria*, the *Pinta*, and the *Nina*— and three anchors in a row in another bed. Very impressive. No other city has done this, and I think we may venture to accept him as a genuine citizen of Genoa. Columbus always thought

* No one worthier of fame, Columbus spent his boyhood and youth in his native country.

warmly of the city, not least during his last years, as we see by his will. The port of Genoa cannot have altered in its general contours, and it is hard to think of anywhere more suitable for the birthplace and the boyhood of a great sailor. The port is backed by mountains, misted in the morning, sharpened in the twilight, heightened and solemnized as night falls, and at all times, one imagines, a most welcome hand-shaking sight to home-coming mariners returning from the infirm mountains of the sea.

Columbus was born in 1451. It is worth mentioning that this was just one year before the birth both of Leonardo da Vinci and of Savonarola, since those mighty names indicate something of the spirit of the age. (By a strange irony it was also the date of the birth of Amerigo Vespucci!) Henry the Navigator died in 1460 when Columbus would have been nine years old. His father was a master weaver and the son of a weaver, and had married the daughter of a weaver. There were four brothers, of whom Christopher was the eldest, and one sister. We know nothing of the sister, and one of the brothers died early. The two surviving brothers remained very close to Columbus all their lives.

The personality of Christopher might have been put before us in a living picture by his son Fernando. But we only get a sort of identikit image of him. We learn that he had a commanding presence, that he was tall, with a long face, ruddy cheeks, an aquiline nose, and light grey eyes, and that early in life his hair turned white. This last item is substantiated from many quarters and certainly suggests exceptional hardship and disappointment. But we are not given, as surely Fernando could have given us, any personal touch which brings a character to life—no enlightening incident, no remark kindly or cruel or humorous, which might bring him before us. None of the portraits are trustworthy. The portrait given in this book from a sixteenth-century artist appeals to me because it suggests something of the poetry, the melancholy, and the single-mindedness which did belong to him—though there is less to indicate his physical stamina and the core of practicality without which we would never have heard of him.*

Columbus does not step fully into the light of history before he arrives in Portugal in 1476. Then we have basic documents to rely upon, coming from Columbus himself, his son Fernando,

* Said to be the oldest portrait and to have been made by a Florentine painter who actually saw Columbus in person.

and Las Casas. Before that time there are some facts, but they are sparse, and little is to be gained by biographical sentences beginning—'it is very likely', or 'it is almost certain', or 'we can be sure', or 'probably', or 'all the evidence suggests' and so on—for to allow ourselves any leeway is to allow ourselves too much. Columbus himself was so unforthcoming regarding his youth that it was thought he must have something to hide.

Salvador de Madariaga made out an elaborate theory that Columbus was a Spanish Jew converted to Christianity—a *converso*—at this era of the Spanish Inquisition. Salvador de Madariaga was so able a writer and wrote so formidable a book that his idea can seem to be plausible. But it runs counter to the general tenor of Columbus's life at all important moments, while Madariaga's claim that Columbus was descended from a line of Catalan Jews became inadmissible after the publication of the documents at the Genoa Exposition of 1950–51—not guessed by de Madariaga whose book was published in 1940. It is perfectly possible that Columbus may have been enriched with some Jewish blood, but he was a Genoese, not a Spaniard, and it is pure speculation to maintain that he was a *converso*. Salvador de Madariaga's tactics in advancing his case are as unconvincing as his clever book on *Hamlet* in which he makes out the hero to be a shallow egoist.

This is not to say that he is alone in supposing that Columbus was a *converso*. A book called *Sails of Hope* by Simon Wiesenthal has recently been published in which the author advances the view that Columbus, a Jewish convert, embarked on his first voyage financed not by the Crown but by other powerful Jewish converts. It was a secret mission to seek a place of refuge in Asia for the persecuted Jews of Spain. As Mr Wiesenthal writes soberly and unsensationally it is all the more surprising that he should lend himself to this kind of thing. The book is a curiosity. If a door is left ever so slightly ajar, it is wonderful what can get into a house.

There is not a shred of evidence for his theories. His book consists of inflated supposition and is riddled with factual error. Moreover, there is one psychological fact which rules out the supposition that he was a Jew. One can easily draw up a whole list of traits about anyone and call them Jewish, though they could apply equally well to many races stretching from Ireland to India. But when a man is found lacking in the main characteristic of a given race, we cannot easily suppose that he belongs to that race. The Jews are realists to a man; they know the composition of things; they know the score, as we say; they are always on the *qui vive* against being deceived, and they do not deceive themselves. Their grasp of reality is not canny so much as positively uncanny. And, as we shall see throughout the whole story of Columbus, it was precisely in this characteristic that he was totally lacking.

II

Apart from knowing that Columbus was the son of a weaver in Genoa, we learn nothing of his early childhood. And nothing of moment about his father, his mother, or his sister. There are claims, unsubstantiated by evidence, that later he went to the University of Pavia, though some who prefer these claims also say that he 'went to sea' at the age of fourteen or fifteen. It doesn't matter: all real education is self-education: he knew what he wanted to learn and learnt it. His chief needs were maths and geometry, cartography, cosmography, and Latin which was essential then for the study of any book on cosmography. We do know that he mastered what he needed in this line before abandoning the family business and taking to his nautical career.

Roughly between 1465 and 1479 he went to many places as a Genoese merchant mariner. He was caught up in the enormous bustle of maritime activity of the great Genoese maritime trading companies. Genoa still had trading branches in the whole Mediterranean area under the private control of great ship-owners such as the Di Negro and Spinola families. The trading of these marine merchants was not limited to the Mediterranean basin but extended to the west coast of Africa which, as we have seen, had been opened up by Prince Henry the Navigator, and also to England and Flanders through the great port of Lisbon. Columbus was to claim later, 'Wherever ship has sailed there I have voyaged', for he was given to splendid statements. That he did go in many directions is certain, including England, Ireland, and even the Azores; and it is almost certain that he reached Iceland (still the Ultima Thule in those days). Whenever factual evidence is scanty or conflicting there is a type of biographer who will deny practically everything, and even when some document impedes his negatives will simply declare it a forgery! Thus it is not surprising that it has been denied that Columbus ever went to Iceland, and there has been controversy about it carried on into this century. Simple biography can scarcely breathe in such an atmosphere, and I contend that there is no reason why we should not believe Columbus when he asserted that he had been to Iceland. But there are those who go to the other extreme and declare that not only did he visit Iceland but knew all about Eric the Red and the subsequent Scandinavian discoveries and settlements by Leif Eiriksson in Greenland, and, furthermore, received from that quarter special information which made it possible for him to discover America.*

Many mariners in the Europe of those days sailed in many directions—in the Mediterranean, by the coast of Africa, in the North Sea and the Atlantic. Many seamen. What we are dealing with here is one man. A man without position, without money, without any show of outward power. Yet in all the western lands this one man alone had the vision and the force to change the history of the world. No one else stepped forward to do it: no one from Greece, no one from Arabia, no one from Spain or Portugal, no one from France, no one from England, no one from Ireland—the country that stood upon the last ledge of earth before the fearful waste which so appalled the inhabitants that the undertones of their terror echoed on into the twentieth century in the works of the dramatic poet John Synge. We are dealing with one man of humble origin who yet could enter the courts of princes and the palaces of kings and say, 'I want three ships, under my command, to sail out into the unknown west', and get them. It was in keeping with the character of this man that he should have regarded a certain passage in Act II of Seneca's *Medea* as having an apocalyptic message for himself, and to have given his own translation of it:

There will come a time in the long years of the world when the Ocean Sea will loosen its shackles and a great part of the earth will be opened up and a new sailor such as one who was Jason's guide, whose name was Thyphis, shall discover a new world— and then shall Thule no longer be the last of lands.

The question is always asked—where and when did Columbus first determine that to sail into the setting sun across the Atlantic would bring him to Asia? As soon as it was grasped by seamen that the world was a globe, as soon as they began to think of this as a fact rather than just an accepted theory, many

* See Appendix.

of them must have posed the question as to what would happen if one took a chance and tried to join the East by sailing West. There must have been a good deal of discussion about this. But nothing came of that talk. Lots of people in all periods have good ideas and do nothing with them. It is very difficult to do anything about anything: few people think it worth the effort to overcome the inertia and opposition of the world—fewer still have the force to do so. I think of Columbus as practically born with the idea that was to rule his mind; that just as some musicians seem to come into the world with a knowledge of their destiny and equipped for it, so Columbus had fore-knowledge of what he would one day accomplish. Some exceptional souls do have this foreknowledge, and in his case it would explain his extraordinary behaviour at times. Certainly it is clear that his idea plagued him, gave him no rest, and set him apart. Indeed, throughout all this man's life we can discern no rest, nor happiness, nor spark of humour, nor human touch. Aloof and melancholy, with the single-mindedness of genius, he nursed his vision, and fed it with anything that supported it, from any source, whether from a contemporary geographer or a Greek philosopher or a Father of the Church—especially the last, for as one of the most devout Catholics of the age, he was not only unwilling to question a Father or a biblical prophet, but wished to emphasize the truth of the 'subtle shining secrecies writ in the glassee margents of such bookes'. Indeed, after his enterprise had proved successful, he actually declared to his Sovereigns: 'For my voyage to the Indies I had no help from reason, mathematics, or maps of the world—it was but a fulfilment of what had been foretold by the Prophet Isaiah.'

That was bombast of an unsavoury kind, for he desperately needed, and sought, intellectual support from any source he could find. But he never minded being marvellously inconsistent, and was equally ready to declare emphatically, 'I have spoken and treated with learned men, priests and laymen, Latin and Greeks, Jews and Moors, and with many men of other faiths'. He had mastered, he claims, all the geometry and astronomy necessary to him, and had attained proficiency in drawing maps, and then goes on to say, 'I have seen, and truly I have studied, all books—cosmographies, histories, chronicles, and philosophies and other arts for which our Lord with provident hand unlocked my mind, sent me upon the sea, and gave me fire for the deed'. He habitually spoke of himself as a man 'called' to perform a mission, and that was not bombast for he felt it profoundly, and it certainly did give him fire for the deed. He never looked closely into what he said at any given time, a contradiction never troubled him. Thus he was fond of claiming that he was descended from an illustrious stock of seamen and that there were admirals amongst his ancestry. His son, Fernando, realized that there was no evidence for this, but says that he didn't like to ask his father to give any names. In another mood Columbus would glory in his humble origins and declare, 'After all, David first tended sheep before becoming King of Jerusalem, and I am the servant of Him who raised David to that high estate'.

The proof that Columbus studied very carefully anything that threw light or information upon his idea, is the fact that he made emphatic marginal notes in the books that appealed to him. In company with the educated men of his day he believed the earth to be a sphere: he underestimated its size: he over-estimated the size of the Asiatic continent. The further Asia extended eastward the nearer it came to Spain. The ancient geographers had more or less supported this view: Aristotle and Seneca and Strabo thought that a ship might sail 'in a few days' from Cadiz to India (though they had no real idea where India was!). Marco Polo and Sir John Mandeville confirmed the exaggerated idea of the extent of Eastern Asia.

Two of the books which influenced Columbus most were Cardinal Pierre D'Ailly's *Imago Mundi* and his *Cosmographia*. The Cardinal (1350–1420) was one of the most remarkable men of his time, a university teacher of the highest distinction, a powerful prelate, a cosmographer and astrologer. In 1400 he prophesied a French Revolution likely to occur about 1789; he made the cool calculation that if a man walked at a steady rate of twenty miles a day he would go round the world to where he first started in four years, sixteen weeks, and two days. (He did not deny that this would include walking upon water.) He supported Aristotle and Seneca on their estimation of the proximity of Spain to India. This was just what Columbus wanted to hear, and he made a special note of it. Indeed, he was ready to accept the impressive Cardinal's ruling on all sorts of things—on the geographical situation of the Garden of Eden, on fables of lion-bodied men and dog-faced women, of monsters and salamanders, of giants and pigmies, of sea-serpents that 'kill and devour large stags'.

The circumstantial minuteness which the admirable Cardinal bestowed equally upon the fabulous and the scientific belonged to the spirit of the times with its marvels and bestiaries, while the testing of assertion with evidence was not yet required. We are told that Marco Polo was afraid of exaggerating (perhaps because of his earlier nickname as Messer Millioni). He need not have worried. His *Travels* were seldom queried. Columbus did not query them at all. The marginal notes in his personal copy bear witness to the stimulus which the book gave him. He was thrilled by the rumours of gold and the wealth of the great Khan—for he shared the passion for gold so marked at that period. And Marco appeared to support the calculations of another favourite of Columbus—Marinus of Tyre—as to the extent of Asia.

It is not easy for a twentieth-century person, surrounded by one-inch maps covering most of the earth, to realize the measureless vagueness of mediaeval cosmography. What is really astonishing is the extreme feebleness of Marco Polo in this respect. He goes to China, he takes three years to get there, he stays for fifteen years, and he returns by sea, another tremendous journey down the east coast of Asia till he finds the water-gap between Malaya and Sumatra, after which he can cross the huge Bay of Bengal to Ceylon at the foot of India. Yet he made no maps! Of course it has been claimed on his behalf that he probably did make maps which have been lost. We are at liberty to suppose this, but there is no proof. It is just as likely that he didn't care much for geography. He was in many ways a stupid and lazy man. Fancy not keeping a really detailed day-to-day diary of his almost incredible travels! He cared nothing for culture, he was wholly incurious and remained ignorant of the most elaborately cultivated civilization that has ever existed—the Chinese. He never sought to post himself on this, though he had every opportunity.* And he does not seem to have been in the least particular regarding geographical facts. Thus he says that Chipangu is fifteen hundred miles from the mainland, though it is only one hundred. He claims that there are seven thousand and four hundred islands in the Sea of Chipangu, though there are only five. So why should he bother about maps? He sailed back accompanied by five other ships. He was a passenger, no seaman, and could relax with no call upon him to enquire at any particular time where he was during his long voyage—even if anyone could have told him anything really accurate.

* See the striking section on this in my brother Maurice Collis's *Marco Polo*, Faber & Faber.

At least he might have cleared up where India is. But he did nothing of the sort, with the result that the term India was used in the most extraordinary way. Columbus seems to have thought that it was a few miles south of Chipangu. 'The end of Spain and the beginning of India are not very far distant. It is evident that this sea may be crossed in a few days with a good wind.' That choice item of geography comes from Cardinal D'Ailly, and was underlined by Columbus. Marco Polo, who had sailed the whole way from Japan to India, completely failed to correct these enormous errors. It is amazing that in an atmosphere of such cosmographical murkiness Columbus could have derived certainty about anything. Yet we must see how inaccuracy and vagueness and error made it easier for him to convince himself with regard to a single calculation and become obsessed by it. And we shall see that, in spite of D'Ailly's absurdities and Polo's ineptitude, his calculations as to when he would strike a mainland happened to be accurate!

III

In 1476, at the age of twenty-five, Columbus arrived in Portugal and to some extent comes into the light of documented history.

There is more than a touch of drama in the manner of his arrival which, in the general poverty of attested incident in the early part of his life, has been eagerly seized on by some biographers. In those days there was little emphasis upon nations as we think of them nowadays; you were not so much an Italian or a Spaniard as a Genoese or a Venetian or an Aragonese, and since each sought commercial monopolies there could be fighting between them if they clashed in their occasions. The term pirate or corsair could be freely exchanged, and often there were battles between rival commercial 'houses'.

In August 1476 a Genoese merchant fleet in which Columbus was serving was attacked by a pirate called Coullon the Elder, flanked by thirteen ships. This was no romantic scrap. There was terrible slaughter. The ship upon which Columbus was fighting had got fastened to an enemy ship by a grappling-iron. A fire broke out on both ships and the crews were obliged 'to jump overboard to die the faster'. But Columbus managed to seize an oar, and by means of its support succeeded in gaining the land which was six miles distant. Such is the story, and if we do not look too closely into that six miles, we can accept it. It has been hailed by more than one biographer, and especially by Salvador de Madariaga, as a key moment in the life of Columbus—his trial by fire and water from which he emerged a reborn being and, putting his 'madcap years' behind, dedicated himself to higher things. It could be. Unfortunately we know nothing about his madcap years, and can only speculate about his thoughts at this moment. It is as likely that he had no thoughts at all just then while he chokingly fought his way towards shore, and then after utter exhaustion gradually regained his strength. The spiritual turning-points in our lives are seldom terribly obvious or accompanied by outward drama.

So we now find Columbus in Portugal, residing at Lisbon, a cosmopolitan port which was at the very centre of mercantile activity. What did he do there, if no longer at this period a seaman? Generally we dare not ask this kind of question concerning the early period of Columbus's life, the obscurity of which he himself enjoyed darkening still more. We do know, however, that he took a post as navigator-agent in Lisbon for Genoese trading companies. We know this because in 1904 (!) a notarial document was discovered authentically establishing that he paid a visit in August 1479 to Genoa to settle his accounts with the Centurioni Company which had sent him to Madeira to buy a consignment of sugar. In the ordinary way such a fact about a biographical subject would be intolerably boring. But for us, dealing with Columbus, it blooms like a rose, it glitters like a gem amid the desert sands of biographical guess-work and inexactitude.

It was at this period that we know also that he married, and we actually know whom he married. She was a young girl he had met at Mass at the Convento das Santas, called Dona Filipa Perestrello e Moniz, of noble birth, whose mother was related to the Portuguese royal family, while her father had been a Governor of the island of Porto Santo. In the era of romantic biography she was described as 'a noble Portuguese lady of surpassing beauty'. Others, reacting against this, have claimed that though of noble birth she was a plain husband-hunter since the family's finances had dwindled. The fact is we know nothing of her: no likeness, no revealing gesture by word or deed, nothing. She emerges from the shadows as the wife of Columbus and then after four years returns to the shades of death. 'It pleased God,' says Las Casas in the manner natural to him, 'to take his wife from him, for it was proper that for his great enterprise he should be free of all cares.' This was not before a son, Diego, was born to them in 1480, a fact which Diego himself was kind enough to confirm. Perhaps a ray of sunshine did fall upon Columbus for a few years.

But there can have been no inner peace for him at this time, if ever at any time. He was about to enter into one of the worst periods of his life. He had spent fifteen years under the oppression of a great thought which would not let him rest, but which he was powerless to translate into action. He had made his calculations: and were there not so many hints and omens that he was on the right track? Sailors told him of driftwood discovered with wonderful carvings unknown in Europe; of bamboo that could hold four pints of wine between one knot and the next; of exotic pine-trunks; of two corpses washed up on the island of Flores in the Azores who were surely Chinese (they were Laplanders); of two more found on the west coast of Ireland at Galway, again with features indicating an Eastern land. These were his messengers; these were the signs and answers that he sought and found. But it was nerve-racking to hear about them and yet be powerless to undertake that western voyage, while all the time aware that the Portuguese year by year were getting closer to the goal of reaching the end of Africa and thus finding a sea-route open for commerce with the East.

Two things helped at this time: the encouragement of the Florentine philosopher Toscanelli; and Dona Filipa's family connection with important people at Court. Paolo dal Pozzo Toscanelli was a prominent Florentine physician and philosopher who was also a good mathematician and astronomer who in his late years (he was now eighty) had taken up cosmography and drawn a map which caused so much interest that he was invited by the King of Portugal to develop his ideas. This was the monarch who stood at the focus of all naval enterprise in the tradition of Prince Henry the Navigator. Toscanelli made haste to reply. He had formed the opinion that Marinus of Tyre, Pierre D'Ailly, and Aristotle were right in estimating that the ocean separating Spain and Asia was not more than four thousand miles, and that Marco Polo had come nearer to the truth than Ptolemy. 'You will observe,' he wrote in his letter to the King, 'from my map that the distance from Lisbon to the city of Quinsay amounts to twenty-six espacios [3,930 miles] and the distance from the Isle of Antilia to Chipangu is fifteen hundred miles.' Again, he speaks of a map made by his own hands, from which you should begin to make the journey ever towards the West, and the places you should reach and how far from the Pole or from the equinoctial line you ought to turn, and how many leagues you will have to cross to reach those regions most fertile in all kinds of spices and jewels and precious stones; and think it not marvellous that I call West the land of spices, while it is usually said that spices come from the East, and whoever navigates Westward in the lower hemisphere shall always find the said places West, and whoever travels Eastward by land in the higher hemisphere shall always find the same land East.

It is a strange document, this letter. Most audacious for the period, and true in some respects. At the same time an imaginary map without a single correct geographical fact, and the bold calculation of fifteen hundred miles from an island which did not exist to Japan which existed six thousand miles beyond the position indicated! It did not impress King John and his advisers.

It did impress and delight Columbus who heard about this letter and wrote to Toscanelli who replied promptly and amiably, summarizing his assertions, enclosing another map, praising Columbus for his intelligence, and encouraging him in his quest. 'Be assured,' he wrote, 'that you will find mighty kingdoms, and bring joy to the Princes that rule in them if you open a way for them to become acquainted with Christianity and instructed in our religion and all our sciences.' Columbus was enormously stimulated by this contact. He had been thrilled by Marco Polo's estimation of Eastern extension; and it is clear from his long notes written in the margin of his copy of D'Ailly's *Imago Mundi* that he attributed decisive importance to the assertion that Europe and Asia accounted for about two-thirds of the earth's surface, a fact which indicated that the ocean between Spain and Asia should clearly be navigable. And now here was a learned man, held in high esteem in Florence, the consultant of kings, who supported his view and encouraged him to take action.

Yet Columbus never mentioned Toscanelli if he could help it, and in the years to come in all his letters and papers passed over his name in silence. Many things have been held against Columbus, and rightly so; and this is one of them. He was a secretive man, and in this case secrecy was fairly natural. He did not want others to be inspired by Toscanelli—for someone might steal a march on him. And in the years to come he could not bear to share the honours with any man. Moreover, he didn't get the idea from Toscanelli: it was his idea long before the Florentine philosopher thought of it—and it was the Lord who inspired and guided him.

This Toscanelli episode has caused a good deal of fuss among biographers. There are those who even contend that Columbus had no correspondence with the Florentine, and when confronted with the letters they simply dismiss them as a forgery or fabrication. If Toscanelli existed and did write to the King there was one man above all others in the Iberian peninsula who would have known about it—and that was Columbus. For years and years, obsessed with his great idea, he had sought anything that supported it, and turned blindly from anything that questioned it. Living in Portugal, and through his wife in touch with people at Court, he was bound to hear of Toscanelli. The exchange of letters between them must have encouraged him a great deal. This was exactly what he needed, an eminent scholar, a dabbler in cosmography, who would confirm him in error. In history we find most often that the best servant of energy is error and ignorance. Comprehensive knowledge, sober analysis, temperate reflection, prudence, caution, the careful weighing of geographical statements—these would have been useless qualities for Columbus at this time, for then he could never have made the enormous mistake that led to his enormous triumph.

He is also supposed to have had a 'Toscanelli chart'. There has been much debate about this. Did he or did he not have Toscanelli's chart to guide him? The question is idle. Toscanelli was an old man of eighty who had never travelled a mile on the ocean and whose navigational activity had been confined to a short swim in the Bay of Naples. And what is a chart? It is a sea map. A land map can give us roads and fields and rivers and mountains, but a map of waves is not much good, and all we can have are islands and currents and winds and depths and the determination of latitude. Toscanelli was totally ignorant of these things in relation to the Atlantic Ocean. We can be certain that Columbus devised his own chart in so far as he could possibly do so—though when you undertake a journey into the unknown you don't exactly refer to a map!

The second thing which helped Columbus at this time was his marriage. Filipa Moniz Perestrello was noble on both sides of her family. On her mother's side she came from the powerful family of Moniz, in close touch with the Crown. From

her father's side she came from the Italian Palestrellos of
Piacenza, one of whom had settled in Portugal under King
John I. But now the family were no longer well off; Filipa's
mother was a widow of modest means, and her second
daughter as well as her first married a commoner—so the
plebeian antecedents of Columbus offered no obstacle. This
was in 1479 or 1480. The couple went to live in Porto Santo (a
small island off Madeira), and for the next four years appear to
have resided there and also at Lisbon—the definite facts being
very sparse. However, we do not need a neat row of facts to
prove what is perfectly obvious—namely, that thus connected
with an aristocratic Portuguese family, Columbus was in a
position for the first time in his life to meet influential people.
Thus his knowledge of the Toscanelli letter to the King, and his
own subsequent correspondence with him, become less of a
problem, if problem there is. Above all of course, it would
scarcely have been possible for him to have achieved audience
with the King without the aid of such connections. And it is at
this point that Columbus steps from the almost impenetrable
shades of the first thirty years of his life into the clear light of
history. It was in 1484 that his interview with King John II
took place.

It is easy to write that down, and it has often been written
down easily by biographers. Wise after the established event we
take it without surprise. But really it was an astonishing
achievement to obtain this interview. What was his record?
A Genoese weaver's son, a vagrant, possibly a pirate, a seaman
wandering across the waters, a man without a ship of his own,
often in penury, often little better than an outcast, his countenance ageing, his hair grey; powerless, nameless, deedless,
hopeless in the eye of authority. Then he is practically washed
up on the shore of Portugal and becomes a humble chart-
maker. The next thing we hear is that he has married a lady of
noble birth. 'Forasmuch as he lived an upright life and behaved
very honourably, and was a man of such fine presence,' says
his son, Fernando, 'and Dona Filipa held such converse and
friendship with him that she became his wife.' A beam of light?
Yes, though faint and flickering. But how little it helps us.
There is always about this man a tragic splendour and an
enthralling mystery—and ten years of darkness lay ahead of
him even then. So—he was quite unknown as a person of any
consequence—yet the monarch gave him audience. We try to
visualize him, but we cannot do so, and we cannot hear his

voice, there is no record of its quality. But he gets in at the gate. What did he have with him to urge his case and overcome the doubters? Not special knowledge, not a commanding intellect, not a reputation as yet for navigational skill. He just had some private personal force. In the years to come he often spoke of the fire that burned within him at this time. Did that flame declare itself in his face? Did his obvious sense of mission— hinting at a strange foreknowledge—make them at least give him a hearing? No word that he uttered at this time has come down to us, nor any light touch that might soften the melan- choly of those mists. What then was the force that brought him out into the light of history at last? He was like Wordsworth's Toussaint; he had great powers in earth, air, and seas that would work for him; he had great allies, his friends also were exultations, agonies, and the unconquerable nature of the missionary mind.

Anyway, by whatever means, and however facilitated by his wife's family, he came to the Court of Portugal and had audience with the Sovereign, John II, in 1484—that is, four years after his marriage. But he does not step into the light of documented history as a hero on the way to glory. Far from it. After all his years of planning and hoping and scheming and dreaming, he met with total rejection. It is not known exactly what he said to the King. 'He appears before us as a man of amazing eloquence,' says Wassermann, and surely with justice if we may judge from the best moments in the great letters and expostulations which he wrote after his voyages, 'and though indeed this gift was innate in him, what must have been the feverish, splendid vehemence of his speech when it was first given him to speak in such an exalted place, of his purpose and his mission, and everything depended upon the Sovereign's Yes or No.'

Yet eloquence and splendid vehemence were not what was called for on this occasion except at discrete moments in his discourse. A quiet, cautious, temperate, modest preliminary marshalling of his geographical beliefs would have been essential—after which blazing conviction might have carried the day. But Columbus was the sort of man who, at such a time, would have made every mistake in the book. Men of genius who have risen from humble origins are prone to be unbearably boastful, over-proud, and indeed intolerably cocksure, and to expect others to consider it a privilege to listen to them. We have no record as to how Columbus collected his thoughts on this occasion, or whether he collected them at all or just hurled them at the King, expecting that that was all he had to do. We get some indication of the scene from a book called *Decades of Asia* by Joam de Barras (known as 'the Portuguese Livy') published in 1552, and written in 1539. He writes:

> As all men declare, Christovao Colon was of Genoese nation, an eloquent man, expert, a good Latinist, and very boastful. Since at the time the Genoese navigated for the purpose of commerce, he satisfied his nautical inclination and sailed over the seas eastward and westward for a very long time. Seeing that the king, Don Joao, frequently ordered the exploration of the coast of Africa with the intention of going by that route to reach India, it occurred to Christovao Colon, having read a good deal in Marco Polo who spoke of the Kingdom of Cathay, and the mighty Isle of Chypango, that it would be possible to sail over the Western Ocean to this Isle of Chypango and other unknown lands. For, in so far as at the time of the Infante D. Henrique, the Azores were discovered, so there should be other islands and lands to the Westward, since nature could not have made so disorderly a composition of the globe as to give the element of water preponderance over the land, destined for life and the creation of souls. With these fancies, given to him by his continual voyaging and the conversation of men proficient therein, he came to demand of the king Don Joao that he give him some vessels to go and discover the Isle of Chypango by the route of this Western Ocean.

As to the result of this interview, Joam de Barras says:

> The king, as he observed this Christovao Colon to be a big talker and more boastful in setting forth his accomplishments, and more full of fancy with his Isle Chypango, than certain of what he spoke, gave him small credit. However, by virtue of his importunity it was ordered that he confer with Don Diogo Ortiz, Bishop of Ceuta, and Master Rodrigo and Master José, to whom the king had committed these matters of cosmography and discovery, and they all considered the pleas of Christovao Colon as vain, simply founded upon imagination, such as things like that Isle of Chypango of Marco Polo.

This is a curious tone for an historian to adopt half a century after Columbus had made his first voyage. But Barras was Portuguese, not Spanish or Genoese, still unaware of the full

implication and significance of the discovery, and unwilling to
pay tribute to Columbus. The reference to Marco Polo is
significant. Polo, as we have seen, was widely read, but he was
regarded with suspicion by the 'authorities', and he was
considered more as an entertainer and teller of tall stories than
a truthful traveller. It was a mistake for Columbus to have
brought him in since Chipangu was considered a figment of
Polo's imagination. He was regarded merely as a merchant, not
an authority to be invoked at the Court of Portugal. No doubt
Columbus also based his arguments on the respected
'authorities' of classic antiquity, the Bible, and the Fathers. He
must have drawn upon his favourite Pierre D'Ailly with his
Imago Mundi. He would have called upon Seneca and Pliny.
He would have used Roger Bacon and the prophet Esdras. He
would not have clung to consistency—even hailing Aristotle
and Ptolemy at points—for he himself was not in doubt. 'We
may be certain,' writes Salvador de Madariaga, 'that when
challenged he grew excited and hot—a fact for which we have
ample evidence from the Portuguese chroniclers—and that he
was apt to shift his argument according to the particular yarn
from Madeira, or calculation from Ptolemy, or prophecy from
Esdras, which happened at the time to be uppermost in his
mind.'

Salvador de Madariaga assumes that his presentation was
vague, for he was too self-assured to be specific. 'What could he
do but be vague? It must have been a torture for him to have
to remain there before the King, fumbling about degrees and
widths of water, when right within he was as clear and as
determined—and as hot—as the sun. And we fancy we can see
then his freckled white skin redden with his inner fire, his eyes
flash lightning-lights and his voice burst out in peals of thunder,
more noisy than intelligible.'

We may fancy whatever we please. History is silent. But we
do have a summary from Las Casas which runs,

> Columbus proposed his affair to the King of Portugal, and what
> he offered to do was as follows: that by way of the West towards
> the East he would discover great lands, islands and terra firma,
> most happy, most rich in gold and silver and pearls and precious
> stones and infinite peoples; and that, by that route, he intended
> to come upon lands of India, and the great island of Chipango,
> and the kingdoms of the Grand Khan.

Did he say nothing about Iceland or Greenland or Vinland, and the significance of that? Apparently not, according to Las Casas—though surely this would have been more interesting than the opinions of Esdras or the Fathers of the Church. But all we know is that there is no record that he mentioned the Scandinavians on this occasion—if on any occasion.

As we have seen, the King was sufficiently impressed to set up a board of inquiry (as we would call it) composed of Don Diogo Ortiz, the Bishop of Ceuta, and Master Rodrigo and Master José, whose authority he was accustomed to rely on in geographical matters. And of course the board turned down the project with the well-worn, time-dishonoured words—'It cannot be done'. But the sheer conviction of Columbus still troubled the King, and he sponsored a navigator of proved merit, called Fermao Dulmo, to attempt to discover the Isle of Antilia and what lay beyond, though at his own expense—but if successful suitable titles of honour would be conferred on him. He sailed from the Azores, but finding nothing turned back. Morison maintains that departure from the Azores meant facing the westerlies, and could not have succeeded—a mistake eventually avoided by Columbus. Apart from the condition of winds, Dulmo could scarcely have made it, lacking the drive, the psychological force, the inner certainty, the fanatical dedication of Columbus. More force was needed than could be derived from a borrowed idea.

Even if the board had not turned him down, Columbus himself put further obstacles in the way. He demanded from the King extraordinary privileges to match his extraordinary merits. He desired to be appointed 'Admiral of the Ocean Sea'. He was to be made perpetual viceroy of all the islands and terra firma which he might discover, and to have a tenth of the revenue accruing from his discoveries, and that besides being an admiral he must be made a knight with the right to wear golden spurs. He demanded these titles before the King had even considered sponsoring the expedition. His son Fernando comments, 'Being a man of generous and lofty thoughts, he would covenant to his great honour and advantage, in order to have his own reputation and the dignity of his house conform to the grandeur of his work and of his merits'. That was the son's apologia for the father's folly and greed and passion for power. What past penury must have lain behind such mad demands. What humiliation and suffering, what dreams and delusions of grandeur when he, a man without any 'house', without any supporters, a nobody sitting in the corner of taverns listening to the rumours of seamen, nourished his dream day and night in the awful isolation of the unsuccessful man who yet feels the certainty of mission and the bonds of destiny. To change all this with one leap to Admiral of the Ocean Sea—nothing less would satisfy him. He must at once have golden spurs as a first necessity for a voyage into the unknown.

For a brief period in Portugal the sun had shone and a great door had opened for him. Now the door was closed, and the light at home went out also, for his wife died at about the same time as the door was shut. Again he was without money or position. He was obliged to leave the country, for he had contracted debts while negotiating with the King, and now fled from Portugal with his little son Diego. He was cast out. He was not defeated. Here was a force that could not be destroyed, a fire that could never be quenched. He would go to the King of England, or the King of France, or the King of Spain—they would be compelled to listen, he would never abandon his dream.

CHAPTER THREE

Knocking at the Door

I

IT WAS FORTUNATE that Columbus did not know that he had now to face eight terrible years which would test all his courage and all his endurance. First he went to Palos where he rested at the Franciscan priory of La Rabida, and left his son, Diego, in the care of the friars. His next move was to Seville, a great commercial city in which there was a Genoese quarter. There he fell in with a Florentine banker called Berardie who gave him some financial assistance and also introduced him to two wealthy and important dukes. It is extremely obscure how he managed to make that initial contact with the banker, but it is a fact, and because there was something impressive and convincing about Columbus, he was introduced to the grandees upon whom he also made a strong impression.

There were two powerful dukes in the case. The first who showed interest was the Very Magnificent Don Enrique de Guzman, Duke of Medina-Sidonia. He was so interested in the commercial possibilities of Columbus's ideas about a western approach to the East, that he actually undertook to provide a fleet for that purpose. But the Duke at this time became involved in a quarrel with another duke which was so serious that the Sovereign contrived to make him leave Seville. Then Columbus turned to the Count of Medina-Celi who owned a whole merchant fleet. This duke housed and protected Columbus for two years, surely a very notable fact, and according to Las Casas, he ordered three ships to be built for Columbus's enterprise in his own shipyards at El Puerto. But nothing came of it.

Columbus was with the Duke of Medina-Celi in the years 1484 to 1486, and it was at this time that the last stronghold of the Moors, Granada, after eight hundred years' occupation, now seemed likely to be regained by Spain. 'In the name of Jesus Christ, Saviour and Redeemer of the World, on the fifteenth

47

day of the month of April of the year 1485 of our Redeemer's
birth, the illustrious and famous King Don Fernando with his
host very marvellous and very beautiful, sallied forth from
Castile to wage war on the Moors.' The Duke's attention was
deflected from Columbus, and he became involved in the
campaign. His initial impulse to sponsor the expedition
evaporated and the offer was never renewed. There are grounds
for those who claim that Columbus was never really willing to
be sponsored by any dukes, and would be satisfied only with
royal backing. However this may be, the dukes, impressed by
the force of his personality, by his 'singular grace', were willing
to bring him in touch with the King and Queen of Spain who
would certainly listen to him if only on the strength of such
an introduction.

More than one biographer has considered that Don Quixote
throws light upon Columbus, that in fact Cervantes may even
have been inspired by him. It is not a resemblance which we
can take very far. Cervantes represents his hero as being two-
thirds mad, which seems to me to detract from the work since
madness is not a proper subject for drama because it robs the
work of universality. Moreover there is so much that is utterly
farcical in *Don Quixote* that often the work is not truly comic
or truly tragic—though in the end the hero becomes more
human since Cervantes relented over Don Quixote just as
Dickens relented over Pickwick and Ibsen relented over
Peer Gynt. Columbus was not mad, nor extravagantly farcical.
But the element of boundlessly optimistic delusion belongs to
both of them. Las Casas remarked that Columbus often spoke
of Chipangu as if he had the place in his pocket. And just as
Don Quixote had only to be given a little encouragement to be
filled with delusions of grandeur, so Columbus, when made
much of by these dukes, felt that at last his true merits were
appreciated and that it was now merely a question of royal
patronage. And there was a real element of knight-errantry in
Columbus. He was an intensely devout Catholic. Part of his
programme was to win back the Holy Sepulchre from the
Saracens—no less. That was one of his dreams, most solemnly
contemplated and declared. By sailing west into the setting
sun he would arrive in Asia to find fabulous treasure (which
would be handed over to him in exchange for a few beads) and
with which he would raise armies to recover the Sepulchre.
Don Quixote himself could scarcely compete with such a man.
And he had more in mind than that holy task. It was his mission

to bring the message of Jesus Christ to Asia. This messianic aspect of his motive-power was very strong, for he did see himself as the fulfiller of biblical prophecy, and never hesitated later to quote chapter and verse from the Bible as a gloss to his ambition. His lust for the acquisition of gold held a central place in his heart, but he persuaded himself that gold was the main means by which souls could be won for Christ.

Anyway, in 1486, through the influence of the dukes, Columbus was enabled to put his ideas before King Ferdinand of Aragon and Queen Isabela of Castile—'their Catholic Majesties' whose marriage in 1469 had united Spain by consolidating the anarchical dukedoms into a national whole. Ferdinand was a formidable character, equally master of himself whether in the jousting yard or in the field of diplomacy, registering on his countenance at critical moments neither gladness nor gloom at anything that had happened or was happening. Not an easy king to approach. Queen Isabela was by no means his shadow, but a great queen in her own right. It is notable how the office of queen is highly suitable for remarkable women: all those qualities which make women more human than men—whether for good or ill—can be fully deployed, and we see something that seems larger than life, as in the cases of Elizabeth I of England, Catherine the Great of Russia, or the Dowager Empress of China. Queen Isabela was not a character on the same scale but there was a fullness about her which has preserved her name in history. Ruthless and cruel she may have been in the religious manner of the age of the Inquisition, but this also went with an intense consciousness of her duties as queen. Her personality has come down to us in the clear image given by her secretary, Fernando del Pulgar—'She was blonde, with blue-green eyes, a gracious mien, and a lovely, merry face; most dignified in her movements and countenance; a woman of great intelligence and great wisdom'. The part which she played in the story of Columbus was absolutely crucial.

Columbus's first audience with these Sovereigns was in 1486 in the city of Cordova where they were temporarily holding court. It is not surprising that he arrived at a very inopportune moment, for that is the way of life when we knock on doors at a critical moment in our careers, whatever the aim may be: the person in the room has gone away, or is ill, or has become bankrupt, or is taken up in some pressing duty, or has enlisted in some campaign. So it was now. As we have seen, the eight hundred years' war against the Moors was reaching its climax.

When would Granada fall to the Spaniards? That was the question which was uppermost in the thoughts of the monarchs at this time. The state treasuries were empty, and the royal pair were hard pressed on every side. It was scarcely the right moment for an unknown seaman to come forward with an uncertain oceanic enterprise. 'It was as if,' to quote Morison's just comment, 'a Polar explorer had tried to interest Lincoln in the conquest of the Antarctic about the time of the Battle of Gettysburg.'

Nevertheless he was granted audience, and he did hold their attention. Las Casas refers to the 'singular grace' which belonged to him and which the Lord 'had granted him for his ministry' (as if he were a priest) which induced others 'to see him easily with love'. Certainly he made an impression. He always did on these occasions. No one knows what he actually said at this interview, but it is a fact that he made an impact upon the Queen, if not upon the King. She was disturbed by him. 'From the beginning his grave demeanour, his passionate eloquence when he spoke of the mission that God had bid him fulfil, moved the Queen to confidence and sympathy.' She felt his will-power, and sensed something in him that was genuine knowledge, though she did not understand what it was she sensed. The general attitude towards him was mockery. He treasured her support. In the years to come he did not forget it. 'Everyone made mock of my project,' he eventually wrote to her. 'Your Majesty alone gave proof of faith and loyalty, inspired, surely, by the light of the Holy Spirit'—for he became prone, later on, to uttering himself in this monstrous manner.

It was the Queen who insisted that his plea should not be rejected offhand, but that a junta should be formed to consider his theories and assertions, and pronounce judgement. So once again he was handed over to a commission. In the meantime the Queen granted him a small allowance for immediate necessities—a retaining fee shown in the records of the Treasury of Castile as having been paid in May, July, August, and October of 1487, and in June 1488.

This commission was convened by the Queen's confessor, Fra Hernando de Talavera, later Archbishop of Granada, a powerful and saintly man. It was a junta composed of divines and cosmographers, though there was not much opposition in those days between the cleric and the scientist; they were not yet departmentalized, and indeed the ruling of a cleric on physical matters commanded most weight, and no one cared to dispute an assertion, whether regarding the centrality of the earth in the astronomical scheme, or a belief as to the geographical position of the Garden of Eden, and it was the Head of the Church who, high above all Sovereigns, could 'grant jurisdiction' for this king or that king in Christendom to possess newfound lands, say a bit of Africa or a row of islands such as the Canaries.

It is doubtful if the conference could ever have got under way without the approval of the sternly orthodox Archbishop of Toledo, the Grand-Cardinal of Spain, who after anxious deliberations reached the conclusion that the proposals of Columbus contained nothing contrary to Holy Writ, and that indeed they could find support in the words of the prophet who declared, 'The ends of Earth shall be brought together and all peoples, tongues and languages shall be united under the banner of the Saviour'. Even so, the weight of clerical opinion was almost wholly against Columbus. They ranged against him the Psalms of David, the views of Chrysostom, of St Hieronymus, of St Gregory, of St Basil, of St Ambrose, of St Paul, of St Augustine, and were so carried away by the imperatives of the Fathers as even to question once again the roundness of the earth and to quote the protestation of St Lactantius:

Is there anyone anywhere so foolish as to think that there are Antipodeans—men who stand with their feet opposite to ours, men with their legs in the air and their heads hanging down? Can there be a place on earth where things are upsidedown, where the trees grow downwards, and the rain, hail, and snow fall upward?

Doubtless there were many 'shades of opinion' among the members of the commission, some secretly deploring the obscurantism of the clerics while deploying their own brand of bigotry and pedantry. Why should they listen to a Genoese adventurer whose ideas ran counter to the experience and opinions of previous mariners? Such conferences differ little from age to age. This one would have been particularly heated and acrimonious on the biblical gloss, since belief was so enormously important and disbelief so dangerous. Somehow the members of this commission come before one's imagination with unpleasing clarity, a formidable-looking body with their gorgeous robes and imposing titles of learning and divinity and law, concealing then, as at all times, the pedant and the bigot, the fool and the savage.

Las Casas, himself a bishop, said that the greatest difficulty confronting Columbus was not that of teaching new things but of unteaching old things; not of advancing his own theory but of eradicating the erroneous convictions of the judges before whom he had to plead his cause. Dr Rodrigo Maldonado, who was a city counsellor at Salamanca where the commission assembled, wrote, 'I was among those who held audience with Columbus with regard to his project. All of them declared it impossible, but he defiantly insisted that it was possible.' He stood up to them valiantly. Another contemporary, Pietro Bembo, in his *History of Venice* says that Columbus claimed

> that it was naught but a vain fiction of the ancients to believe that no more than two parts of the world were habitable: for it would be absurd for God to have created the world and to have left the greater part of it useless, as it would be were it to contain no men; and further, that what writers refer to as the Ocean is not a vast empty expanse, but rather is filled with islands and inhabited lands.

Much of this was sound. It helps us to understand why the Grand-Cardinal of Spain, whom people called 'the Third Sovereign', held him in great esteem, observing that 'this foreigner' was 'wise, a fine conversationalist, and a sound thinker'. It also serves to correct the assertion made by some biographers that Columbus did not attempt to make out his case in a reasonable manner, but confined himself to the insistence that he must be regarded as one inspired by God, quoting Isaiah as his John the Baptist. He faced them with courage and conviction on whatever ground he thought right as the occasion demanded.

It is not known how many times Columbus appeared before the junta. They were in no hurry to come to a decision. Months passed while they 'deliberated' and 'considered' and 'gave full attention to the matter'; years passed—five in all! This was the worst period in the life of Columbus. He had suffered much already in the cause of the idea which overruled him. But now his campaign became almost intolerably hard to bear. Las Casas compares the suit of Columbus to a battle—and justly so, 'a terrible, continuous, painful, prolix battle'. And, again, he says, 'All this delay did not go without great anguish and grief for Cristobal Colon, for he saw his life was flowing past him wasted, to judge of the days he would need for his sovereign and enduring work'. Worse even than this was the distrust of his truth and disdain of his person in consequence, which is 'as painful and detestable as death'. He was to face, as other heroes of mankind have faced, in its extremest form, before and after Hamlet's soliloquy, the proud man's contumely, the law's delay, the insolence of office, and the spurns that patient merit of the unworthy takes. Would he ever break through, he wondered. And to all missionary minds which are over-boastful, and even to those which are modest, the inner doubt, the dreadful unexpressed question comes—'Is it possible that, after all, I am a charlatan?' And practically everyone is plagued at an early age by the fear that he will be thwarted and never succeed in becoming his true self. This is most acute for the man of genius. Six months of despair about this left Dickens a damaged man; years of it destroyed Carlyle beyond redemption. Columbus never really recovered from the strain on his mind during this time; it fed his monomania and nearly ruined him at the most critical moment in all his life.

Time was running out. He knew that his idea was in the air and that at any moment someone else might carry it out. (And indeed he was right: unknown to him, and independent of him, Martin Behaim, a German, was attempting to find supporters for the very same adventure.) What was he to do? He knew that the Queen was still well-disposed towards him, but it was terribly difficult to gain further audience with her. Not only was the war with the Moors, coming to a head in Granada, claiming all her attention, but a plague broke out in Malaga where she had gone when the city was taken, and the Court moved to Saragossa, and then to Murcia, and thence to Valladolid, and then back to Cordova. In a state of intolerable suspense he followed her from city to city and camp to camp. He composed petitions. He drew up nautical reports. He sought interviews with powerful dukes and knights, but his lack of response from the commission told against him, and he was avoided by those who had previously helped him, and followed only by cranks and failures and parasites and crooks. Sometimes he met with respect and civility, but more often with the smooth smiling face of insincere sincerity, while yet others regarded him as a dupe, a braggart, a clown, a babbler of fantastic astrology, a mischievous fortune-teller, a beggar seeking favours, even a foreign spy. In this darkness one light did shine upon him—a loving woman of humble origin, Beatriz Enriquez, became his mistress and gave him a son, Fernando, who wrote the life of his father in the years to come. We know little about Beatriz (Fernando always kept silent about his mother) except that she did not marry Columbus, and all we learn from Columbus about this attachment is that it led to sorrow and some obscure load of guilt which he carried to the grave.

The extent of his despair at this time can be gauged by the fact that he renewed negotiations with the Court of Portugal, and received a surprisingly amiable reply from King John II: 'To our most special friend Columbus: we have seen the letter that you wrote to us. We desire greatly to see you'. Further, he assured Columbus that he enclosed 'our safe-conduct so that you may have naught to fear from our judicial authorities'. Such a letter speaks volumes for the impact Columbus made upon the Portuguese Court in spite of everything, and now King John, doubtless aware of the negotiations with Spain, thought it worth while to take up the matter once more. But having arrived in Lisbon, Columbus came in for another disappointment. No sooner had he got there than Bartholomew Diaz returned from Africa to announce that he had rounded the Cape. The possibilities which this opened up caused the King to set aside for the present any further plans he might have entertained regarding the Atlantic adventure. It is true that he made no great haste to send another expedition down the coast of Africa, and it was not till four years later that Vasco da Gama made the discovery of Diaz thoroughly known and accepted. Columbus was terribly alarmed, for he was not to know that King John would be so dilatory, and doubtless expected that there would be rivalry very soon between Portugal and Spain in this area, and that his Atlantic enterprise would be shelved to meet the emergency, and that he would face further opposition and derision.

He hurried back to Spain. When a man reaches his blackest and lowest hour and feels that things can get no worse—then they do get worse. So it was now for Columbus. He had as yet received no definite ruling from the commission, and there was still hope that after the delay a favourable decision would be reached. But time passed and still they deliberated (if they deliberated at all) while he sank into increasing frustration. The position was very dark. Late in 1490 it grew darker. Talavera finally sent in the report. The committee 'judged that the

promises and offers of Cristobal Colon were impossible and vain
and worthy only of rejection'. The enterprise was 'not a proper
object for Royal Authority to favour'. It was an affair 'that
rested on such weak foundations, and which appeared uncertain
and impossible to any educated person, however little learning
he might have'. Six counts were drawn up against the scheme:
first, a voyage to Asia would require three years; second, the
Western Ocean is infinite and perhaps unnavigable; third, if he
reached the Antipodes he could not get back; fourth, there are
no Antipodes because the greater part of the globe is covered
with water according to St Augustine whose ruling was not
open to question; fifth, only three of the 'five zones' are
habitable; and sixth, so many centuries after the Creation it
was unlikely that anyone could find hitherto unknown lands of
any value. It had taken the learned members of the junta four
years to draw up this illuminating survey.

Though the commission had turned him down, the Sovereigns
did not wish him to consider the verdict final. The Queen had
always been sympathetic to Columbus. There is little question
about this; she did have an intuitive understanding of his
essence; in modern terms she knew he was not phoney. She was
responsible for a small retaining fee which was paid to him at
first; and for a royal order, a sort of free pass addressed to
mayors, magistrates and other officials, requesting them 'to
provide Cristobal Colon whatever city, town, or village he
might enter, with good free quarters'. The cost of board was not
included, but it was a wonderful order to possess. And, according to Las Casas, the Sovereigns even informed Columbus that
his enterprise might still be considered at a more propitious
time. That was something, but—'more propitious time'? This
meant victory over the Moors. The war had lasted for eight
hundred years, and might be coming to an end—or it might
not.

Again time passed—days, weeks, and months. An outcast
from fame and fortune, he did not know where to turn. The
machinery of life, of day-to-day living, was breaking down;
immediate cash was running out—for the retaining fee lapsed.
The details of his life at this time are not known to us—indeed
at any time are not known: what he had for breakfast, what he
talked about when not talking Atlantic Ocean, what he thought
about when not thinking Atlantic Ocean. But we are told that
now he was reduced almost to beggary. His cloak was in holes.
His breeches were unmended. There was a wild look in his eye

such as to draw jeers and derision from children in the street. A man of infinite dreams, of unboundaried pride in apocalyptic visions of glorious kingdoms in the West to which he pointed with prophetic finger—he now sat, a lonely, hopeless figure, in the corner of obscure taverns, lost and estranged from all the world. And so we lose sight of him.

II

He comes before us again in the summer of 1491. He called for the second time at La Rabida, a monastery ever ready to succour the outcast or afflicted. 'The beggar who in a state of exhaustion prayed for bread and water at the gate of the Franciscan cloister, saw himself at the end of his hopes,' writes Jacob Wassermann of Columbus at this time. 'He was no longer young, probably near the end of his forties at least,* his hair completely grey, his face lined; he had grown acquainted with so much humiliation and bitterness, and done so much fruitless work, squandered so much enthusiasm, experienced so much contempt and rejection, that it seemed to him enough to lie down and die.'

The friars did not recognize him. He had changed so much in the five years which had passed since he had brought Diego to them. Who was this tall, gaunt man, so poorly dressed, but with the manner of a grandee, and with such spiritual torment in his countenance? They asked him who he was, and he replied, 'I am called Cristobal Colon. I am a sea captain from Genoa, and I must beg my bread because kings will not accept the empires that I offer them'.

It is unlikely that he used those exact words: we cannot suppose really that he could have come out with a phrase of such classic economy and appeal. It does not matter. For when any man has put forth sufficient force to create a legend or a myth, and thereby becomes one of the heroes of mankind, then mankind focuses upon a simple image which is yet more profound in that very simplicity of outline than the fumbling dross of actualities. We reject the dross in the name of truth. When Lincoln made his celebrated Gettysburg speech, he had a miserable audience, few heard him, and fewer still bothered to listen. But we reject this actuality as ultimate falsehood, for we know that in truth he spoke to an immense audience spell-

---

* Ten years out. Wassermann, a great impressionist, was often reckless with facts.

bound from generation to generation across all the nations of the western world.

Our characters create our destiny throughout life to an astonishing extent. This is particularly true of great men—two-thirds of their circumstance being character. At this moment in the career of Columbus, his character, what the man was, his essential being, created the circumstances which launched his ships. Perhaps not wholly: there had to be the element of luck: surely luck must also preside, and the unlucky are obliged to stand down. It happened that the prior of the monastery, Fra Juan Perez, who had offered Columbus hospitality as long as he liked to stay, had once served in the Treasury, and also had been the Queen's Confessor, and though a recluse from affairs of State and the pomp of courts, was of course receptive to the impact of Columbus. He invited a monk called Antonio de Marchena, a man of outstanding cosmographical studies, also known to the Queen who thought most highly of him, to meet Columbus and hear him talk. They were all surprised at his knowledge, his speculations, his tales of strange experiences and omens, his eloquence, his lofty bearing, his firm faith in a mission to perform, his arguments, his maps, his calculations, his certainty of the possibility of the voyage.

They were so enthralled that they invited a third person to join them—a sea-captain from Palos called Martin Alonso Pinzon. He had been to sea from the age of fifteen, and now had become a recognized captain in the expert community to which he belonged. He had sailed in the Mediterranean and to the Canaries and down the coast of Africa. He had served in the war with Portugal, and had proved himself as brave in battle as he was skilful in the arts of nautical enterprise in peace. Uncomplicated, reliable, straightforward, sensible, downright, respected, he was the sort of man who in a roomful of people would be the most noticeable and sought-after. Quite an inspiration to others without being inspired himself. In short, he was a strong character. Columbus had a character weak enough to be inspired from time to time. It was fortunate that these two men should meet. Columbus needed a supporter of exactly Pinzon's type and quality. Pinzon needed a man inspired enough with an idea to interest kings and get official backing for a great adventure. He saw nothing unusual in the aims of Columbus. He may or may not have believed in Chipangu and the riches of Cathay and the legend of the Grand Khan, but as a seaman he would have responded to Columbus's theories of

'land beyond', for if a group of islands such as the Azores
existed, why not others further west, why not the lands of
Marco Polo? He would have been interested as much as Perez
and Marchena were by the fiery conviction and calculations of
Columbus, and very impressed by his contact with the Queen—
and further, by the fact that he had sent his brother Bartholomew to put the project before Henry VII, King of England,
and Charles VIII, King of France. He would want to join this
venture.

The discussions between these four men, Perez, Marchena,
Pinzon, and Columbus went on night after night, at last reaching a point when it was decided that 'something must be done'
to re-open negotiations with the Sovereigns. It is a documented
fact that they did thus meet, and did thus discuss negotiations
which had seemingly closed. Without being fanciful we can very
well see them sitting there in the dim light of a mediaeval
lantern. Not a very impressive sight. But that is the kind of
thing we see when the turning-points in history are occurring.
No pomp or panoply. Everything quiet. For the seeds are
underground where dwell the roots of power. 'A small group of
men in Russia, eight years before 1905, and twenty years before
1917, met in a dingy room, with an iron stove in the corner,
some paper, a printing machine. A drab little group, a sorry
party. What were they doing? What could they do? Yet they
were more powerful than the Romanovs and all their heedless
pomp.'* So here. In that room at La Rabida enough force was
being generated for the performance in one year's time of a deed
which would change the geographical conceptions of the Middle
Ages, and unleash lethal energy across all the lands beyond the
western sea.

The prior, Fra Juan Perez, sent a moving letter to the Queen.
The details of the letter are not known. A strong letter from her
former confessor would certainly impress the Queen, and if the
letter contained, as is supposed, some reference to the overtures
to the Kings of France and England in lieu of Spanish rejection,
this would certainly have made her consider re-opening negotiations—which in any case she had been careful not to close
conclusively. She sent for the prior, and having spoken with him
she sent a message of hope to Columbus. This was followed by
a summons to Court, and enough money was sent for him to buy
a mule and to get clothes suitable for the occasion.

* See my *Marriage and Genius*, p. 197. Cassell, 1963.

So, providing himself with a mule, servants to accompany him, and silk clothing, he rode to Santa Fé in the Vega of Granada, where the Court then lay in camp. This was December 1491. Nothing could be done at once. There was a crisis, of course. Granada was on the point of falling. Columbus must wait. Granada did fall to the Spaniards, and Columbus joined in the rejoicings with as much patience as he could muster, and took part in the royal procession which entered the reconquered city on January 2nd, 1492.

Now, at the age of forty, he was at last within reach of his goal. When the processions and thanksgiving services were over he was received by the Queen again, and once more a commission of scholars and theologians was convoked. There was actually more discussion about St Augustine's view as to the impossibility of sailing to the Antipodes; but when the matter was finally referred to a Royal Council, it was conceded that an experienced seaman of the fifteenth century might know more about the Atlantic Ocean than a Father of the Church six centuries earlier.* The Sovereigns were won over at last, and were to admit later on, 'What you announced to us came to pass as if you had seen it'. This supports the assertion by Las Casas that when Columbus 'had made up his mind he was as sure that he would discover what he did discover, as if he held it in a chamber under lock and key'. After some further delay Talavera was instructed to treat with Columbus and grant him a fleet of three ships for the enterprise. His long battle was over, and he had emerged victorious.

At this point we come to the strangest moment in all his story. 'It is extraordinarily striking to observe,' remarks Jacob Wassermann, 'from the detached point of view which the long completed cycle of events enables us to take, how a great man's star draws him, as though by a never-failing magnetic force, to his appointed end: whatever he does or whatever he fails to do, every error, every neglect, every apparent defeat even, does actually and inevitably bring him nearer to the hour of fulfilment.' Yes indeed: words most true and just. But at this moment in the life of Christopher Columbus there is something so queer, an error of tact and of tactics so enormous and so unnecessary that it appears to have no positive part to play.

* 'It is difficult for us to realize the extent to which the men of the Middle Ages rested on venerable "authorities". This is one of the things which differentiate the period almost equally from savagery and from our modern civilization.' *The Discarded Image*, C. S. Lewis, Cambridge U.P., 1964.

He had won his long campaign: he had been granted ships and equipment under royal authority for his great expedition of which he was to be the captain. All that was necessary now was to get the ships built, the crews enlisted, and the officers chosen —of whom Alonso Pinzon would naturally be the foremost. But no sooner had he got what he had been fighting for than he made haste to throw it all away.

He was not satisfied. He demanded more. Greater recognition must be given to him than being just the leader and captain of the expedition. He had already astounded the King of Portugal with such demands, and by such tactlessness had ruined his chances. Now he did not hesitate to make the same mistake again. He informed the Sovereigns that he would not undertake the journey unless the following demands were granted: he was to be knighted, to be a don; he was to be appointed Admiral of the Ocean Sea; he was to hold the position of Viceroy and Governor-General over all islands or continents that he might discover and occupy for Spain; he might claim a tenth part of all treasures—pearls, diamonds, gold, silver, spices, fruits, and other products found in the lands under his jurisdiction and brought back to Spain; and finally the inheritance of all these rights, titles, and dignities was to remain with his family in perpetuity.

These demands astonished the Sovereigns. The Queen was very embarrassed after all the sympathy she had shown him, and all the hope she had given him. Ferdinand had always regarded Columbus with coolness, referring to him as 'that pauper pilot, promising rich realms'. He was dismissed from the Court. The royal sponsoring of his project was withdrawn. And he was obliged to leave the city.

It is certainly an extraordinary fact that Columbus should have preferred total failure rather than receive anything less than those grandiose titles and emoluments. The most crucial time in any great man's life is when he is *knocking at the door*. Everything depends upon getting that door to open, whether his goal be in the field of action, or the field of art, or the field of scholarship, or the field of science and experiment, or the field of politics. In those hours the man's character is tested in two ways: whether or not he understands the unimportance of being humiliated, and whether he realizes the importance of tact in tactics. Throughout his life Columbus often showed that he could be prudent and cautious: and he could display the cunning of a peasant and the secretiveness of a spy. And he had that species of courage that, holding by an inspiration, endures all things for it, and in hoping all things overcomes all things. How then could he throw his victory away? We are compelled to assume that he saw himself in a messianic light. 'My time is not yet, but my time will come,' he had said to himself, as other destined men have said in their days of darkness—'Forget the worthless, lying mob, and lay aside thy doubts!' And when at last the hour did come for Columbus he thought that tactics were no longer necessary. Innocent of self-analysis, he saw himself as the instrument of God for bearing the message of Christ across the sea to the Indies; and then with vast resources in gold and treasure he would be instrumental in making another crusade to Jerusalem. 'Humility showed me the little that I counted for,' he said later with towering pride, 'but knowing the great message that I bore, I felt myself equal of both the Crown of Castile and the Crown of Aragon.' A knight-errant completely enslaved to biblical hyperbole, he would declare: 'I took upon myself the mission of messenger, announcing to these Sovereigns the new heaven and the new earth of which our Lord speaks in the Apocalypse through the mouth of Saint John, as before He had spoken through the mouth of Isaiah'. And, as we have seen, when attention was drawn to the plebeian nature of his birth, he proudly declared, 'Let them call me by what name they will, for after all, David first tended sheep before becoming King of Jerusalem, and I am the servant of Him who raised David to that high estate'.

At this final meeting with the Sovereigns it never occurred to him that his demands could destroy him. He had such an intense feeling of destiny (almost as if he had foreknowledge of what really did happen) that he was at that moment victim of some kind of mania that blinded him to the practice of prudence and to the taking of that tide in the affairs of men which leads to fortune. Now, having been dismissed, even if he had second thoughts he was in no position to compromise. He must leave the Court and the country. And so, humiliated without being humbled, deposed from an imaginary kingdom which he had not abdicated, pierced with thorns that formed no crown, he must depart again from the palaces of kings and once more become a wanderer across the earth. He took to the open road with his mule and his servant. Once more a penniless outcast and discredited prophet in the eyes of the world, where was he going? Where could he go? To the King of France, to the King of England, offering empires and realms of gold? Not possible really, for his brother Bartholomew had now sounded those monarchs and received a dusty answer.* No, this enchanted knight-errant was surely riding with his dreams into oblivion. He rode on—four miles, six miles, eight miles. He crossed the bridge at Pinos . . . There is a commotion on the road: the sound of swifter hooves behind. He is being overtaken. Who is this? A voice cries out:

'I am a captain of the guards. Are you Cristobal Colon?'

'I am.'

'A message from her Majesty the Queen: she orders you to return to Court.'

What extraordinary and unlikely thing had happened? The fact is that Columbus, though not conscious of it, had some powerful allies at Court. The foremost of these was Don Luis de Santangel, the Finance Minister. He was a *converso*, and certain members of his family had suffered grievously under the Inquisition; but in spite of this Luis de Santangel remained one of the most powerful men in the kingdom; and being immensely rich was greatly respected. A man of commanding personality and penetrating intelligence, he had become indispensable to the Sovereigns on account of his knowledge of the intricacies of finance. His existence at this time, and in this place, was central to the career of Columbus. History does not dwell upon him: but without him history would probably have nothing to say about the discoverer. He had formed the opinion that there was something in the idea that Asia was quite within navigable reach of Spain, and if this really were so and it was Spaniards who first went that way, it would bring great prestige to Spain as well as the possibility of immense commercial gain. If the man who had introduced the idea, Columbus, was mistaken, it would matter little what promises and agreements had been made to him, since he would return a discredited dupe if he returned at all; while if he were right then surely he would be entitled to grandiose titles and rewards. It was a gamble that should be taken, and at once before Portugal or some other nautical power got in before them. As for finance, no vast sum was needed, and if necessary he would raise it himself. He put some or all of these considerations before the King and Queen. A rapid decision was made. They would take the risk, fetch Columbus back, and grant his conditions. Hence that captain of

* There is controversy over this regarding dates. Francis Bacon refers to Bartholomew's journey but says that he was captured by pirates and did not reach Henry VII till after the agreement with the Spanish monarchs.

the guards despatched to overtake him on the road that would
have led him out of history, and to return him on the road that
would lead him into immortality.

Since seeing is believing let us look at these Articles of
Agreement (sometimes called Capitulations, but I think that
translation gives a false impression), which were in truth drawn
up and signed in April 1492, at Santa Fé, in the Vega of
Granada.

I   Cristobal Colon, Don, wishes to be made Admiral of the
Seas and countries which he is about to discover. He desires
to hold this dignity during his life, and that it should descend
to his heirs.
This request is granted by the King and Queen.

II   Cristobal Colon, Don, wishes to be made Viceroy of all the
continents and islands.
Granted by the King and Queen.

III   Cristobal Colon, Don, wishes to have a share amounting to
a tenth part, of the profits of all merchandise, be it pearls,
jewels, or any other things, that may be found, gained,
bought, or exported from the countries which he is to
discover.
Granted by the King and Queen.

IV   Cristobal Colon, Don, wishes, in his quality of Admiral, to
be made sole judge of all mercantile matters that may be the
occasion of dispute in the countries which he is to discover.
*Granted by the King and Queen, on the condition, however,
that this jurisdiction should belong to the office of admiral, as
held by Don Enriques and other admirals.*

V   Cristobal Colon, Don, wishes to have the right to contribute
the eighth part of the expenses of all ships which traffic with
the new countries, and in return to earn the eighth part of
the profits.
Granted by the King and Queen.
Santa Fé, in the Vega of Granada.
April 17, 1492.

If kings and queens could at any time be allowed to indulge
a sense of humour, these Articles might yield a degree of comedy
with the stipulations regarding continents and islands which as
yet had no existence save in the imagination of the adventurer;
a bill drawn upon the future with ceremonial solemnity, without
thought of what it might lead to. And, in addition, there was

a commendatory letter, or pass, intended for presentation to the
Grand Khan, Prester John, or any other oriental potentate in
whose territories Columbus might arrive:

Ferdinand and Isabela to King Blank—The Sovereigns have
heard that he and his subjects entertain great love for them and
for Spain. They are moreover informed that he and his subjects
very much wish to hear news from Spain. They send, therefore,
their admiral Cristobal Colon, who will tell them that they are
in good health and perfect prosperity.

This crediting the unknown ruler of an unknown country with
anxiety for the welfare of unknown monarchs, could also be
read as high comedy if the protocol of royalty could ever be
interpreted as such.

But the whole thing is so unlikely that it could only belong
to history. This *volte face* of the Sovereigns would seem too
extravagant to be possible. Yet there it is. They had chased
Columbus away (and who could blame them?)—and then they
called him back. They had decided to have no more to do with
his dreams and his demands—and then they finally gave in,
point by point, granting him everything he asked, even that he
contribute a share in mounting the expedition in spite of the
fact that he didn't possess a cent!

III

The town of Palos was to be the port of embarkation, and a
royal requisition demanded that the municipality of Palos
should provide two of the vessels. On May 23rd, only eleven
days after his departure from Granada, Columbus was in a
position to call a meeting of the authorities and citizens at the
Church of St George and to read to them the royal demand.

Yet all this was only on paper. To bring it into actuality was
no easy task. Columbus had not yet overcome the forces of
inertia. Especially Spanish inertia—even under royal command.
He was to experience in action the Spanish aphorism in terms
of evasion: 'To be obeyed, but not carried out'. The order was
dutifully obeyed but no one attempted to carry it out. And
apart from the initial dilatoriness in preparing the ships, there
was the difficulty of obtaining crews for such an expedition. The
mariners of Palos knew nothing of the Genoese 'foreigner', and

his project seemed to them crazy. The recruiting situation became so critical that he was obliged to resort to a court order of a 'safe-conduct' granted to prisoners in the local gaols who might be prepared to join the crew. This was an extraordinary measure and a most desperate provision, indicating the general horror in which the proposed journey was held by sailors who had heard, over and over again, about adventurers who had sailed into the unknown never to return. The order was addressed to the criminal administration of the Kingdom as a whole, and it stated:

> We hereby give security to all and sundry persons who embark with Cristobal Colon, that they shall be subject to no loss nor punishment in respect of their bodies or their possessions, for any crime that they may have committed up to this day: and this shall hold good for the duration of the voyage until their return, and for two months thereafter.

This order has pleased the more romantic of Columbus's biographers, since it gave them scope to relate how the most infamous company of ruffians presented themselves—highwaymen, pirates, escaped convicts, thieves, murderers, coiners, branded felons from the whole kingdom. More cautious historians have estimated that no more than twenty-five out of a hundred men came under this head—if that many. For the prior of La Rabida, Juan Perez, as anxious as anyone in Spain to see Columbus successful, prevailed upon the Pinzons to save the situation. It is not clear exactly at what stage Martin Alonso Pinzon and family agreed to join Columbus (it cannot have been at the outset, for otherwise Columbus would not have been in this difficulty) but we know that when he did join him he provided two caravels and had no great difficulty in raising crews, since he was so well known and respected in the locality.

Pinzon did this while still acknowledging Columbus as the leader of the expedition, which was to lead to difficulties during the adventure, and to unseemly lawsuits afterwards; but it is obvious that at this crucial time Columbus could not have done without Pinzon's financial resources and his influence at Palos in the recruiting of crews. It is as unthinkable that Columbus could ever really have managed without Pinzon at this stage. Later on, the Pinzon family tried to claim that Martin was the real instigator of the enterprise and that therefore the inherited financial rewards should go to the Pinzon family. Such a claim

was monstrously false, for in order to get the royal sponsorship
a fanatic was called for, and that was just what Pinzon was not,
though he possessed a cluster of virtues in which Columbus was
lacking. If Pinzon had possessed enough conviction to carry him
across the Atlantic he could easily have made the journey with
his own ships. He needed Columbus to spark him off. But to
achieve the means for setting sail Columbus certainly did need
Pinzon.

The lawsuit which was held in 1507 helps to put us in the
picture at this time. 'The inhabitants of Palos,' declared a
witness, 'all thought that Columbus, and anyone who would
sail with him, were marked for death.' The participation of
Pinzon made all the difference. Another witness testified: 'If
Martin Alonso had not given two ships to the Admiral he could
not have gone through with the expedition, for no one knew
him, and he would not have found men to go with him.' Pinzon
knew how to get recruits. 'To some he said that they would be
raised above their poverty; to others that they would find
houses with tiles of gold; to some he offered good fortune, and
for every man he had pleasant words and money; so that with
this and the general trust in him, many people followed him
from the towns.' Thus Columbus was saved from having to man
his ships with too many recruits from Spanish prisons.

There were three ships for the expedition: the *Santa Maria*,
the *Pinta*, and the *Nina*—now so well known to history.
Columbus was in command of the *Santa Maria*, Pinzon of the
Pinta, while the *Nina* was commanded by his brother, Vincente
Pinzon. These ships were called caravels, the name denoting a
swift, long, and narrow ship with one deck, a fender-beam at the
prow, a flat poop, three masts, usually three-corner sails (lan-
teen), and a few crossyards on the main and fore masts. The
Santa Maria was the largest of these vessels, but they were all
much smaller than one would expect, and each of them could
have fitted comfortably onto a modern tennis court.

They sailed from Palos on August 3rd, 1492. On August 2nd
there occurred one of the dark chapters, though not as yet the
darkest, in the black history of that race whose work in commerce, in art, in philosophy, and in science, shines with a bright
particular glory. This was the expulsion of all Jews from Spain
who had not accepted Christian baptism. The suffering caused
by this exodus would have been under the eyes of Columbus as
he travelled from Granada to Palos. But his thoughts were not
with them. His mind moved always along one single track, and

as he travelled to Palos he fixed his gaze upon that which he could not see, and not upon those things which he could see. On the night of August 2nd he ordered that all hands should confess their sins and take Communion. Then just before sunrise the three ships upon whose sails the cross was painted, went toward the open sea, rounding the promontory on whose heights stood the monastery of La Rabida, twice the scene of his lowest hours in humiliation and rejection.

It is said that all the population came out to witness their departure. It may have been so. We cannot be sure. These great moments are so seldom seen in their significance by a concourse of onlookers. Nor can we picture this in our mind's eye as the dramatic hour when the ships sailed out into the unknown. For they were first sailing to the known, to the Canary Islands some nine hundred miles south off the coast of Africa; because Columbus dared not go near the Azores for fear of encountering the Portuguese. And when they reached the Canaries after nearly a week's sailing, the *Pinta* had a mishap, and broke her rudder! After this delay there was a calm which held up the expedition for another three days. It was not till September 6th that the little fleet really set out from the Old World, and even then on account of a further calm the mountain peak of Tenerife was still in sight of the mariners until September 9th when at last it sank beneath the water and left them nothing but the ringed horizon. In thirty-three days it was all over. They had reached land just as Columbus said they would. The mighty deed had been accomplished. The destiny of whole continents, the reformation of social forms, the closing of the door of the Middle Ages, had been decided upon and histories unwritten were written; while a scorned and rejected fool was hailed as hero and sage, a deluded fortune-teller stepped forward as inspired prophet, an obscure Genoese weaver turned seaman became the Very Magnificent Lord Don Cristobal Colon Grand Admiral of the Ocean Sea.

CHAPTER FOUR

Far from Shore

WHEN I FIRST REALIZED that Columbus had taken only a month and a few days to cross the Atlantic, I was surprised, for I had expected it to be much more.* But it did not seem a short time to those involved. Indeed there were moments when they felt that they were sailing into eternity.

When at last sight of land had disappeared, they must all have felt afraid—even today that is a fearful moment for any sailor setting out alone. And what would Columbus himself have been feeling then? All the boastfulness, all the bombast, all the heady conviction with which he had carried the day, would have gone from him at this moment. Immense relief would have mingled with immense anxiety. This was the moment when his truth was to be tested. He was standing now on the edge of his destiny; he was no longer the dismal suitor but the man given official sanction to prove his point or fail and fall with all his life in ruins. His thoughts at this time would have had no biblical or mystical gloss: the nautical and geographical aspect would have wholly engaged him—was he right in his calculations? As yet it was all theory, all speculation, no one had ever passed this way before, there was no guarantee that D'Ailly or Toscanelli or any of his other favourites were more correct in their assertions than Ptolemy. That they could possibly be erroneous to the extent of ten thousand miles, and that the enormous error would not actually matter, could not have crossed his mind; but he must have needed all his courage to face the testing days now before him. And this was just the kind of courage that he did possess.

In his journal of the voyage, after an opening invocation to the royal family, Columbus says that he proposes to make a

* For a map showing Columbus's voyages, see p. 150.

daily report of all events and experiences, a chart for navigation, and so on. Then he adds that in order to do these things and 'carefully watch my course' he would find it essential to abandon sleep. He ends the introduction to his log with those words. He would abandon sleep. There is no evidence as to how far he succeeded. But that resolve brings the man before us—so much iron endurance, so much proud isolation, and so much determination to trust no one, but to keep watch through day and night!

We take the story up now again after September 9th when land had passed from sight. The three ships were not all of equal speed. Pinzon's ship, the *Pinta*, was the fastest—an unfortunate fact which Columbus was powerless to avoid. The *Santa Maria* was the largest, though, from the replica which we can see in Barcelona harbour today, it seems amazing that it was deemed fit to face oceanic storms. Comforts and conveniences were almost totally lacking. The Captain-General and his men lived in very close quarters; the entire crew slept on deck, only Columbus and the first officer having cabins in the forecastle. Even the cooking was done on deck in a wooden fire-box protected from the wind by a hood. The diet of salt meat, hard tack, and dried peas was washed down with red wine of which they had a large supply—enough to give each man over two litres a day for more than a month. (The empty barrels could be used as extra ballast in a storm, if filled with water.) The total number of crew including all three ships was between ninety and a hundred. The *Santa Maria* had thirty-nine, and this included a Hebrew interpreter, a Fleet Secretary, a Royal Commissioner charged to look after the Crown's interest in the share of the revenues, and one Court adventurer. Add to these the complement of boatswains, caulkers, able seamen and ship's boys. Each caravel had a surgeon. But no priests had been enlisted. However, this did not mean that there were no religious observances. Far from it. At all times seamen have been the most religious of men, and on each of the vessels sailing into the unknown ocean a boy intoned at day-break:

> Blessed be the light of day
> And the Holy Cross, we say

after which the crew recited the Lord's Prayer and the Ave Maria. At sunset all hands attended evening prayers, the boy lit the binnacle lamp and sang:

God give us a good night and good sailing;
May our ship make a good passage,
Sir Captain and Master and good company.

Then all hands again said the Lord's Prayer, the Creed, and the Ave Maria. And as these ships sailed westward into the night the turning of the hour-glass was marked by the chant:

To our God let's pray
To give us a good voyage,
And through the Blessed Mother
Our advocate on high
Protect us from the waterspout
And send no tempest nigh.

The devout Columbus, who had brought his breviary with him from the monastery of La Rabida, may have superintended at these rituals, but he gives no hint of it and may have held aloof. These religious observances, held in the cathedral of the sea, are most touching to us in our own day when enormous technical mastery cuts into our sense of mystery and super-natural fear—though not our fear of natural ills following upon unnatural acts in fouling the waters of the world.

The first ten days or so of this voyage were most smooth and happy. All went well. The temperate breezes, the balmy air in the glad confident mornings, put all the sailors into high spirits, and when on September 15th they saw in the night 'a nosegay of fire fall from the sky into the sea four or five leagues away' they took it as an omen of good fortune. Their captain too was influenced by the agreeable tidings in the air, and reached an almost lyric strain in his log: 'The weather is like April in Andalusia,' he wrote, 'there is nothing lacking save the sound of nightingales'. And when the dolphins were at play around the *Santa Maria*, Columbus (who believed in mermaids) seems from his journal to have been in as happy a mood as Oberon who had 'heard a mermaid on a dolphin's back, Uttering such dulcet and harmonious breath, That the rude sea grew civil at her song'.

As they proceeded Columbus announced to the crew the distance covered each day. And each day he falsified the mileage. Thus throughout the journal (or log) we find such entries as, 'He continued his course westward for fifty leagues and reckoned only forty-seven'; or 'during that day and night they made more than fifty-five leagues but the Admiral reckoned only forty-eight'; or 'the Admiral continued in his course, and since it was calm made twenty-five leagues, but he reckoned only twenty-two'.* He had calculated that the distance to Japan was three thousand miles. (It is twelve thousand.) If he failed to reach Japan after three thousand miles, he wanted to have some mileage in hand—though faked—in case the crew became restive. So he announced false figures throughout, and makes no bones about it in his log. But it is hard to see what he could have gained by such small alterations: instead of 25 he put 22: instead of 55 he put 47—and so on. That is to say that after twenty days sailing he would only have in hand, as it were, about eighty to ninety miles. What good would that do him in a three-thousand-mile journey? Well, he could claim to have in hand a few more days' sailing before the crew had a right to be really anxious. That would be something. But it does seem a fairly useless ruse. And even if he got the Pinzons to join in the deception (as is supposed) then, in the absence of telepathy, they could not have put down the same figures in each ship.

Though Columbus was prepared to travel that distance before striking land, he was also ready to be agreeably surprised at achieving this much sooner. Throughout the journal, from quite early in the voyage, there are continual rumours and 'signs' that land is very near. But Columbus was seldom misled at first into thinking that they were near the mainland, and generally took the 'sign' to be in relation to some island or islands. 'I take the mainland to be somewhat further on' is one of his entries (on September 16th). He considered that this was a little too soon for Japan. But he was ready to believe in the islands. He said that he would 'sail between them' and on the return journey would visit them, but now would 'press on to the Indies'. Actually there were no islands whatsoever anywhere within four hundred to a thousand miles.

In this same early period in September there was a very anxious moment for Columbus. This was a sudden unexpected variation of the compass needles. They should have been pointing east of the true Pole, but they were found to be pointing to the north-west! It is exceedingly difficult for us today to realize how disquieting this must have been. The compass had only recently been discovered. They could rely

---

* The journal is in the 1st and 3rd persons because that is the way it was eventually presented by the editors.

upon this extraordinary finger to guide them truly, for it was linked to those laws laid to the foundation of the earth. But now it was failing them! The steersmen became really agitated, fearing that the fundamental laws of nature were changing and that they were entering on a new world with new laws—a world in which anything could happen and in which they would surely perish. No doubt Columbus was disquieted too when he saw the finger swerve from its established truth. But he was always equal to occasions when there was an element of mystery which could be dealt with in a secretive manner. At dawn he took a sight on the North Star when there was no longer any deviation, and then advanced an ingenious theory to account for the phenomenon of variation—namely, that it was caused by the North Star moving round the Pole. In his log he represents himself as giving the seamen a lecture in magnetic variation. They would not have understood a single word he said. And that was just what suited him. A great practical sailor, one of the greatest, he was also furtive and cunning, and enjoyed the exercise of power through the bewilderment of simple souls.

Presently another thing frightened the crew. One morning they found that the ocean had disappeared. In its place they saw a colossal field of yellow corn. The ships were moving through amazing meadows. On all sides there stretched long-drawn virgin vales of verdure. The sailors were horrified, for this must be seaweed and there could be shoals and rocks below, or they might be closed in and stopped—not wedged in Arctic ice as some lost ships had been, but stuck in weedy bonds in these forever exiled pastures. But they soon cheered up. The ships were seen to glide with ease through the unimpeding plants. It was indeed a species of seaweed, well known now as the *Fucus Natans*, which constitute the immense plains of the Sargasso Sea, and which at one time occupied a space in the Atlantic equal to seven times the extent of France. There is not so much of it today, but on the way to the West Indies, after the Azores, it always appears, though less as plains and meadows than as yellow rugs, carpets, mats, and small clusters—even so, surprising. The sailors soon found that there was nothing to fear. Each ship could cut its way through the substance without difficulty or clogging; and soundless too; the ship a silent plough upon a soil-less prairie. There were no submerged shoals or rocks, only the unmeasured fathoms below the endless canopy of weed.

As they sailed on they were always seeing signs of land. Nearly every day there was some good sign. Even as early as September 17th Columbus was so elated by various auguries as to write: 'Whence I trust that the high God, in whose hands are all victories, will very soon give us land'. On the 18th 'Martin Pinzon called to the Admiral from his ship to say that he had seen a great flock of birds flying westward and hoped to sight land that night'. And to the north there was a great bank of clouds 'which is a sign that land is near'. On the 19th boobies were seen: 'birds not accustomed to fly more than twenty leagues from land'. Again, on the same day, 'a little rain fell without wind, a sure sign of land'. On the 20th a tern was seen: 'a river bird, not a sea bird'. Then, 'two small land-birds singing'. On the 21st a whale turned up: 'a sign that they were near land, for whales always remain near land'.

It is curious, and indeed pathetic, the way they take these things as messengers of hope. Curious, because they had no evidence as to what they were claiming. They had no means of knowing how far birds or whales might stray from land. All their previous voyages had been either close to the coast of Africa or France or the British Isles, or perhaps as far as Iceland. They had no experience as to what held good far out, since no one had been that far before, or if so had not returned. And even if the generalizations were broadly true, the trouble about nature is that there is always the exception which disproves the rule. The last time that I was somewhere in the same vicinity, at least a thousand miles from Cuba, a most beautiful little bird declared itself. I do not know its name, but a neater article I have never seen, a patch of yellow and some flashing green, a piece of winged perfection. But it had no business there. It was out of order. Its presence was untenable.

On September 23rd the men grumbled because of the one-way wind. (By avoiding the Azores, Columbus had by chance hit upon a westward trade-wind, more or less constant, though not as good as if he had sailed from further south.) When the sea was calm and smooth again the crew grumbled, saying that as there were no heavy seas in these parts no wind would ever blow to carry them back to Spain. Later, the seas suddenly rose up very high without any wind, and this astonished them. The journal, as edited by Las Casas, having given those facts, goes on, 'The Admiral says at this point, "I was in great need of these high seas because nothing like this had occurred since the time of the Jews when the Egyptians came out against Moses who was leading them out of captivity" '.

That is a much-quoted remark. We may give it what gloss we choose, but I think it could be read at its face value, and that he really did mean that he took it as a sign from Heaven in his favour. At one moment he was the expert seaman, the practical and the cunning captain; at the next his mind would move in madly messianic and providential lines. But how he could have discerned the faintest factual resemblance between a high wave in the Atlantic and any biblical story, is not easy to fathom.

On September 25th there was a communication between Columbus and Martin Pinzon about a chart which Columbus had sent over to the *Pinta* a few days before—a chart on which, it seems, were drawn certain islands supposed to be in the area. Pinzon maintained that they must be near these islands now, and Columbus replied that he was of the same opinion and that the reason they had not reached them must be that the currents had driven the ships north-eastwards. Having reached this conclusion the Admiral asked him to return the chart, which he did on a line. This was another incident not wholly free from the element of comedy. No one had ever gone this way before. No one knew anything about it. Every step was totally unknown, unmapped by any living soul. Yet they solemnly exchanged and studied an imaginary chart of these uncharted waves.

That same evening Martin Pinzon called out from the poop of the *Pinta* that at last he had sighted land! Not just an island, but their destination, Chipangu itself. Yes, indeed, it was true, and the crew of the *Nina* climbed the mast and rigging and confirmed that it was land. Then all the crews of all three ships saw it—a high dark wall of land like Tenerife, in all the splendour of the substantial flinty earth. Columbus was overcome, and falling upon his knees gave thanks to God. Martin Alonso and his men chanted the *Gloria in Excelsis Deo*, and then the crew of the *Nina* did likewise. In the morning they would go on shore. When morning came the land was no longer there. It had disappeared. It had all been an illusion, a sham; those pretentious stones of earth were no more substantial than the flying vapour or the false mountains in the congregation of the clouds. The ships must still pursue their way, still the centre of the everlasting circle.

They had now been out of sight of land for about seventeen days. That is not long. But for them it was long enough to suggest that they were coming to the end of their lives. The situation was very alarming. Every indication that they were approaching a mainland, or even an island, had proved an hallucination. There was no guarantee of any limit to this unmeasured waste of waters. To realize what it was like for these men, in this place and at this time, is not wholly possible: it is partially possible—if we give the matter our attention. We have to take away from our minds all knowledge of the existence of North America and South America, and in place of that we simply put water with the hope that we may possibly arrive somewhere, at some time. We have been told that the world is a sphere, but that is only a theory, no one has proved it by going round. With blank misgiving we face a void: we face the totally unknown. For these men it would have been much more than misgiving: it would have been terror. Not all the time of course, but many moments of wretchedness at the thought that they would uselessly and surely die.

Let us make no mistake. This was not a difficult journey. It was not painful. It caused no acute suffering and no death. They did not meet with a single storm. The journey could in no way compare with the terrible journeys of other daring men when fortune did not always favour the brave: not poor Scott, not most of mighty Magellan's wretched crew. And it was short. But as a sea voyage it was unique in recorded history. It was undertaken by men who had no definite knowledge concerning the conformation of the world. It was therefore not only physically but metaphysically terrifying. This crew was composed of ordinary seamen of the Middle Ages, not more educated than seamen at any time—perhaps rather less so if we remember the recruitment. They knew nothing of Ptolemy or Tyre, of Esdras or D'Ailly, of Augustine or Roger Bacon. They could see that they were going steadily downhill, over the edge of an everlasting slope, and with a wind behind—how could they ever return? The outlook was appalling. They really did feel themselves to be poised on the brink of the cosmos. Like Milton's Satan, 'pondering his voyage', they were on the edge of an illimitable waste without bound or dimension in which time and place were lost and chaos held eternal anarchy threatening the traveller with utter loss of being. It was worse than that for these simple mariners because the air was getting hotter every day; and had they not heard rumours of how at a certain point the atmosphere became too hot for existence and that you could be burnt alive on board or boiled alive in the sea? And had they not heard of fearful monsters of the deep who could swallow a whole ship, and of sea-serpents half a mile long who with a single stroke could shatter it to bits?*

It was natural that the sailors should begin to ask themselves what they had let themselves in for. Who was this captain leading them to disaster? Was he simply a madman, who had cast a spell upon them so that they must obey? They dared not ask him questions or plead with him. He knew he was not loved. 'I am not soft of speech,' he admitted, 'I am commonly thought harsh.' He was so unapproachably aloft, aloof, standing on the forecastle of the *Santa Maria* from dusk to dawn, his sleepless, steadfast gaze upon the West—'drunk with the stars'. Yes, that phrase has come down to us from Las Casas, and it does much to put the man before us as the great force he really was, the will bent in the determination of one single firm resolve. 'Such a man, spiritually isolated, spiritually unapproachable, must have had a stimulating effect on the wills of the rough, simple characters around him', says Wassermann. 'In him the terrible enigma of the whole expedition stood embodied and visible: the close association of life on board ship had not let a solitary ray of light into that mysterious entity; he was dragging them into a world other than theirs, a world that was no world. Despair was as futile as revolt, since in the last resort all depended upon him: they believed him favoured by Heaven, and possessed by a magic that made him more powerful than any mortal man had ever been.' The question was—how long could that spell be expected to last, when would it break?

The ships kept fairly close together. The fact that the *Pinta* was faster than Columbus's *Santa Maria* could have raised a problem if Pinzon of the *Pinta* had wanted to forge ahead and become the first discoverer, as it were. But of course there was no fear of this happening on the first voyage. The last thing any of these sea-captains wanted was to lose sight of the other two. Especially at night—and it was moonless until the beginning of October. It was a comfort for the crew of each ship to be able to see the others—little lights in a great darkness. Even today when we cross the ocean and see another ship on the horizon, or passing fairly near, we are enchanted and call our friends— and all gaze at it with delight. Today, when we make the journey, the experience is wonderful without being alarming. After all, to contemplate the ocean, from the vantage-point of

---

* Theobald, author of *Physiologus de Naturis XII*, mentions whales mistaken for islands upon which sailors landed and lit a fire—whereupon the whales dived and they were drowned. (See *The Discarded Image*, C. S. Lewis.)

a corner in a smallish boat, is the one ultimate experience we
have left still by means of which we can restore our sense of
infinity and face the mystery of existence. Not just of human
existence but of the whole thing. As we gaze across the alien
heaving hills of senseless wave and foaming crest, stretching to
the beyond, and to beyond the beyond, and, as we well know,
far, far beyond that—we can make nothing of it. Yet we are
elated by it: and if we are crafty enough to get so close that we
can ride upon it at our will—then, Chichester-like, we would
rather die than go craftless through our lives. Thus speaks your
twentieth-century man. Not so in the Middle Ages. Not so these
men far from shore in 1492. Think of night-time for them.
Certainly the three ships' crews would have longed to see each
vessel: for one ship alone to withstand the concentration of
isolation would surely have been too much to bear. The blackness of night upon the inky vast around them; the bleakness of
their fate in the seeming hopelessness of their quest, would have
been intolerable alone!

It is September 26th now, as still they press forward towards
the West. 'The sea was like a river and the breezes sweet and
very gentle.' The next day the same good conditions favour
them. On September 29th the log, as given by Las Casas, reads:

He kept on his westward course and made twenty-four leagues,
reckoning only twenty-one. All day and night they were held up
by calms. They saw a frigate-bird, which makes the boobies
disgorge what they have eaten, and eats it itself. This is its only
food. It is a sea bird but does not settle on the sea, and does not
fly more than twenty leagues from land. . . . The breezes are very
sweet and pleasant, and the Admiral says that nothing is missing
except the song of nightingales.

(A repetition of his phrase earlier in the month.) On from
September 30th to October 6th, in some good weather and some
more expectation regarding imaginary islands. Flying fish also
began to appear, which from the prow of a vessel look as frail
as dragon-flies or like fish-ghosts, though if they land on board
they are found to be most substantial and look like toy aero-
planes. This was a genuinely good sign indicating the vicinity
of the West Indies—had they realized it.

On October 6th Martin Alonso Pinzon thought it would be a
good idea to change course from due west to south-west as it
seemed likely that they were missing Chipangu. Columbus took

no notice of this suggestion until twenty-four hours later a great flock of birds came from the north and flew south-east. This did seem a conclusive proof that they were making for land in the vicinity, and he altered course accordingly. On October 8th the atmosphere was most homely. ' "Thanks be to God," says the Admiral, "the breezes are as sweet as in April in Seville, it is a pleasure to breathe them, they are so laden with scent." ' On October 10th we get:

> He sailed west-south-west, making ten miles an hour but sometimes dropping to seven and sometimes rising to twelve, and in the day and night together they went fifty-nine leagues, which he counted as no more than forty-four for the men. Here the men could bear no more; they complained of the length of the voyage. But the Admiral encouraged them as best he could, holding out high hopes of the gains they could make. He added that it was no use their complaining, because he had reached the Indies and must sail on until with the help of Our Lord he discovered land.

Thus, in a few bland words, Columbus mentions the most critical moment of the voyage. The crew had been becoming more and more on the point of mutiny for some days now, and he was well aware of it. But Columbus chose to be reticent about this in his secretive way, and had it not been for the lawsuit held twenty years later we would know very little about what happened. Eyewitnesses of course always disagree with one another; but it is agreed that the crew at last could bear it no longer, and did say, 'While he is drunk with the stars, let us seize him and throw him into the sea', or some such words. Columbus had become aware of this mutinous mood and mutterings. But he didn't know what to do—for he was no man of action in the sense of being able to make swift decisions. Then Pinzon, bringing the *Pinta* alongside, came to his help, shouting, 'String up half a dozen of the men and hang them: and if you can't I will'. This greatly alarmed the crew of the *Santa Maria*, and order was restored for the moment.

We see Pinzon the sensible, forthright, decisive, strong man taking a strong line. And with success. But obviously with only momentary success. Should such discipline be carried out ? That would depend upon Columbus. And he would see the necessity of prudence. To attempt to carry out such an action would be incredibly rash. To get sailors to hang sailors at such a time, in such a cause, in such a context, might well be impossible, and if carried out would create an appalling atmosphere. Columbus procrastinated—we shall see this tendency often in his career. He told the men that they had already reached the Indies and would sight land in two days. Both captains acted well. The man with the strong line was right for the moment and weak in terms of the outcome. The man of procrastination was right in terms of the outcome and weak for the immediate crisis. Each needed the other badly at this time. Pinzon needed support rather more because he was incapable of the inspired audacity of 'We have reached the Indies and will sight land in two days'.

After this, next day (October 11th) as they sailed on they saw a good many small indications of land; nothing sensational, but genuine—the branch of a tree in flower, a piece of carved wood, a plank. 'At these signs all breathed again and were rejoiced. That day they went twenty-seven leagues before sunset, and up to two hours before midnight had gone twenty-two leagues and a half.' When the crew of the *Santa Maria* had assembled at nightfall for the singing of the *Salve Regina*, Columbus told the men to keep a special watch for land from the forecastle. At 10 p.m. Columbus saw a light, but he was too uncertain about it to call out. Then one of his seamen also saw it, but caution against any more false alarms prevailed and no signal was given. 'The caravel, *Pinta*,' (the log) 'being swifter and sailing ahead of the Admiral, now sighted land and gave the signals which the Admiral commanded.'

The first man to sight land definitely was a sailor called Rodrigo Bermajo. Now, a very unfortunate and invidious promise had been made by the Sovereigns to the effect that the first man who sighted land should receive a pension for life— small but adequate. Invidious, since all the men would have deserved it just as much as the man on the fastest ship and at the best look-out position—and in any case two or three men might all claim to have been the first. If any such award was to be made it obviously should have gone to Columbus himself— though he would have the least need of it. And in the event he ignored the claim of Rodrigo and pocketed the money himself— which was paid to his mistress Beatriz Enriquez de Havana out of the revenue from the slaughter houses of Cordova. But by every legal right it belonged to Rodrigo, who was so bitter about this that on his return he emigrated to Africa and became a Mohammedan. No biographer of Columbus has sought to hide this behaviour: it was too glaring, and, alas, too typical.

They waited till morning, and as the dawn advanced swiftly

as it does in the tropics, a quiet sylvan shore was uncurtained before their unbelieving, believing eyes. The crew of the *Santa Maria* crowded about their captain. 'Some embraced him, others kissed his hands, begging him to forgive them their little faith.' Thus was sunrise on October 12th, 1492. The beach belonged to a small island called by the natives 'Guanahani', at once given a new name by Columbus, 'San Salvador' (Saviour) —which it still bears today.

The three captains—Columbus, Martin Pinzon, and Vincente Pinzon—went ashore in the ships' boats bearing the royal banner of Castile and standards with a green cross. A crowd of natives, quite naked and pale brown, came to the shore and beheld these visitors, some of whom were clad in complete armour! 'Leaping out upon the shore they kneeled and kissed it with tears of thanksgiving, thanking God who had rewarded them after a voyage so long and so strange—Columbus above all, for he was ever one to ponder the meaning of events.'

The rest of the ships' officers and the crews now came on shore and Columbus solemnly 'took possession' of the island in the name of the King and Queen of Castile, and received from the assembly an oath of allegiance to himself as Admiral and Viceroy. 'What tongue can tell the honour given him, the forgiveness asked him, the obedience promised him! They were as if beside themselves, and with tears in his eyes he embraced them all and pardoned them, calling upon them to give the glory to God.'

Neither Oviedo nor Las Casas was present at this scene, but presumably their accounts were gathered later from some of those who were present. It is extremely interesting to find that Columbus does not set down a single word of self-congratulation or emotion at this supreme moment in his life. Perhaps he felt that he could not improve the occasion with any words whatsoever.

CHAPTER FIVE

The New Land

I

So, THEN, they landed on that island which is four hundred miles from Florida. It is a pity that they hit upon such an insignificant island as Guanahani. If its size, and if the approach to it, had offered a similar experience as that of coming upon Jamaica from the east, with the Blue Mountains set immediately behind the shore, that would have made a wonderfully solid and dramatic end to their vigil. As it was, Guanahani is scarcely more than six miles long by three wide, with no mountains or even hills. For all they knew it might have been a lonely little island far from any mainland (as Bermuda is), but they all assumed, quite rightly as it turned out, that it was one of many islands off the shore of a continent.

The officers and crews came on shore and immediately took over the territory, making it out as a free gift to the King and Queen of Spain. They called this 'taking lawful possession of Guanahani, now to be called San Salvador in honour of our Saviour'. The natives from whom they took it watched the proceedings without resentment, for they had not the least idea what was happening. Having not yet arrived at the conception of property they were unable to conceive the idea of theft.

We can imagine to some extent what it was like for the Spaniards to make land here after their long voyage. The explorations down the coast of Africa had so enlarged the knowledge of Europeans concerning more primitive races, that the Arawaks on the island of Guanahani would not have greatly surprised the Spaniards. Can we imagine what the Arawaks saw? I think we can, for in the calendar of nature we are not really a long way removed from them. They would have had no 'idea of the ocean leading after three thousand miles to another land. It would have appeared to them to be just space like the sky. When they saw the three caravels close to the shore

81

on that incredible dawn, it would not have occurred to them that these ships had come across the ocean. They thought the Spaniards were supernatural beings who had descended in winged chariots from the sky. And when they came on shore the seamen would not have appeared to the inhabitants to be normal human beings. True, they walked upright and had two arms and legs, and their faces were human, though terribly pale and bearded. But the whole of their bodies was hidden, even their heads. No matter what the temperature, and here it would have been between seventy and ninety degrees, no European in the Middle Ages would discard any of his clothes—and the three captains we are told came on shore clad in complete armour. The natives seem to have been too stupefied by the appearance of these visitors from the sky to be afraid, and at first none of them ran away.

Columbus had been careful to add to his cargo a number of knick-knacks such as little bells, brass basins, scissors, coins, knives, strings of beads, needles, pins, coloured bonnets, mirrors, and coloured cloth. He can scarcely have hoped to have found the inhabitants of the eastern cities of his imagination with streets of gold, ready to hand over their jewels and spices in exchange for these baubles, but he evidently did expect to encounter some 'tribes' similar to those discovered on the coast of Africa by the Portuguese and Spaniards. It remains a puzzle why he should have expected this, seeing that Marco Polo spoke only of a great conqueror, the Khan, and of the riches of Cathay and Chipangu. Anyway, it was now certainly an advantage to possess these trifles, for when they were distributed among the Arawaks everyone was delighted, considering the baubles to be pearls beyond price, and ready to hand over real pearls in exchange.

Columbus spent nearly three months sailing among these islands here looking for Chipangu. He had no idea where he was; and this simple fact undermines all claims that he possessed any useful chart given to him by mysterious and anonymous mariners who had made previous discoveries of the West Indies. He would have studied a variety of fanciful maps and charts which were entirely useless. Once he had reached Guanahani he realized that this was not Chipangu. So he had two immediate goals: one, to find Chipangu as soon as possible; and the other, to find gold. The importance for him of finding gold can be easily understood. To be able to throw down a few sackfuls of gold at the feet of his enemies in Spain, those who

had jeered at him, those who had spurned him as a futile
visionary, those who had held his cosmographical calculations
in contempt—to have returned with abundance of gold would
be a delicious triumph, and would have utterly floored them. In
the Middle Ages life was appallingly penurious, most terribly
lacking in enjoyment, it was 'nasty, brutish, and short' as the
saying goes. In those days the possession of gold or the finding
of it, was something terrific; and for Columbus, after the
accomplishment of his discovery, to have in addition come back
with gold would have put him in a position of boundless power.
We can scarcely blame him for the feverish anxiety with which he
sought for it on this first voyage, and on each subsequent voyage.

This search deflected him from the goal of finding Chipangu,
and at the same time it muddled him. He did not know whether
to sail west (which would have been the right direction for the
mainland, Florida) or south. He chose to sail south for thirty
miles which brought him to a small island which he named
St Maria de la Concepcion, then looped round past a long island
which he named Fernandina, and then reached a small island
which he named Isabela, this journey being about eighty miles
to the east. Then on hearing of a place called Colba (Cuba), he
concluded that they meant Chipangu, and leaving Isabela
sailed south again some one hundred and fifty miles to Cuba,
and went along its north coast for about a hundred miles.
Finding that Cuba was very unlike his Chipangu and showed no
signs of gold, Columbus now turned back and made for another
large island which he named Hispaniola—where there actually
was a little gold to be found. This last lap from his turning-point
in Cuba to La Navidad in Hispaniola meant sailing east again for
about three hundred and eighty miles. Thus he twisted and
turned for many days (over ninety in all) and for many miles
among these islands, bestowing names upon them as he passed,
some of which have lasted till this day.

II

Let us see what impression he formed of these islands and of the
inhabitants. As we know, he wrote a day-to-day account,
addressed as a kind of open letter to his Sovereigns, Ferdinand
and Isabela. This is called his 'journal'. The original was lost.
But the sum of it was retained by Las Casas and Columbus's son
Fernando. One thing has often surprised readers of this journal

—his response to the beauty of nature. It is generally supposed that Rousseau in France and Wordsworth in England introduced 'love of wild nature' as something new—that, in fact, it amounted to the birth of a new faculty. As usual we go too far. It cannot be true that no one said 'What a lovely view!' before the eighteenth century, and really meant it. However, the claim is probably true that 'a feeling for nature' was invoked for the first time in a travel book by Columbus in his journal—making him in this respect over three centuries ahead of his time. The West Indies were then far greener and fresher in luxuriant vegetation than they are today, and Columbus, after his three-thousand-mile journey on the ocean, was obviously overjoyed by what he came upon as he passed from island to island.

> This island is the most beautiful that eyes have ever seen. . . . It is such a great joy to see the plants and trees and to hear the birds singing that he could not leave them and return. . . . The Admiral says he had never seen a more beautiful country. It was covered with trees right down to the river and these were lovely and green. . . . The wind was very favourable for sailing to this point which I named Cape Hermoso, and beautiful it is. And so I did not anchor in that bay, seeing as I did this green and lovely cape in the distance. Everything on all these coasts is so green and lovely that I do not know where to go first, and my eyes never weary of looking on this fine vegetation which is so different from that of our own lands. When I reached the cape the scent of flowers and trees blew offshore and this was the most delightful thing in the world.

And of another island:

> Though all the others we had seen were beautiful, green, and fertile, this was even more so. It has large and very green trees and great lagoons, around which these trees stand in marvellous groves. . . . The choir of birds is so harmonious that no one could leave this place, but must dwell for ever here.

For the most part the words are artless, the same adjectives repeated, and the same sovereign thought rehearsed again if there has been an interval of a few days. But he makes his impression clear; and there is a lyric note of true gladness here, which is unmistakable. The Admiral has forgotten himself for once. He has forgotten his destiny. He has forgotten his enemies

and detractors. For a few brief hours he has beheld a vision
which had nothing to do with his ambition or his cosmography
or his mission.

And when he beheld the inhabitants of these islands, what did
he see? Something just as wonderful. He was immediately
struck by their beauty, their 'well-built and fine bodies and
handsome faces'. Their colour, 'neither black nor white', much
appealed to him. He was equally struck by their lack of
aggression and the extent of their generosity: 'they did not bear
arms, nor have any knowledge of them, for touching our swords
they cut themselves out of ignorance, and though possessed of
no riches whatsoever, they most graciously gave us all that they
had'. Their innocence startled him: 'They have no knowledge of
evil'. More extraordinary still: 'They do not know how to kill'.
To Las Casas it seemed indeed the primal state of innocence
lost so long ago: 'The Indians approached the Christians as
children come unto their fathers; they were as naked as the day
their mothers bore them, as if they had returned to that state
of innocence wherein our father Adam dwelt'. There was also
great dignity. Columbus gave a remarkably clear account of a
meal he shared on the *Santa Maria* with a young chieftain in
the presence of his retinue. The aristocratic manner in which he
tasted the dishes surprised the Admiral. 'He tasted of the
dishes that I placed before him, then sent them to his people;
he did the same with the wine, which he no more than raised
to his lips. All this was done with wondrous dignity and few
words; his two counsellors kept their eyes full upon him, and
spoke for him and with him most respectfully.' And when later
he met the great chieftain, Guacanagari, and also had a meal
with him, Columbus noted—'From the way he ate, with dignified composure and beautifully refined table-manners, it was
evident that he was of noble birth.'

Biographers have professed to see here the source of 'the myth
of the Noble Savage', which was to enjoy such a vogue in
European literature. If the term myth here is used to mean
something fanciful or untrue, we are entitled to question it. The
noble savage was not a myth. He existed here and there. But
we have this terrible habit of demanding absolutes. At no time
was the noble savage or the noble anything to be found in
abundance anywhere. He was to be found on this island or that
island in the Caribbean. He was not on that island over there,
for he was a cannibal, and this disqualified him as noble, and
rightly so; though, we may add emphatically, his ignobility

could scarcely compete with the savage tortures of the Spanish
Inquisition, and still less with the fouler corruptions and filthier
crimes of modern civilization, the victims of which in their
thousands now look longingly toward remote islands for the
nobility and the simplicity they have cast away.

One further observation from Columbus, made shortly before
his voyage home. He had anchored in a harbour which he named
Puerto Santo Tomas. The Indians touched him by the warmth
of their welcome, bringing gifts of water and bread—'They
bring us cassava bread, and offer us water in calabash gourds
and earthen pitchers of the same shape as those in Castile'. For,
simple as these people were in their way of life, their pottery and
beautifully constructed and capacious canoes gave a good
indication of their artistic skill. Columbus adds, 'And let it not
be said that they give freely only that which is of little value,
for they give away gold nuggets as willingly as they do a
calabash of water; and it is easy to recognize when a thing is
given from the heart'.

It is with terrible sadness that we read these words. They were
written sincerely. They came from the heart. But this did not
deflect Columbus from abusing their hospitality and betraying
their trust. This was the same man who in his journal (or open
letter to the King and Queen), tells how a man in a canoe came
alongside the *Santa Maria*, and how

> I let him come aboard as he asked. I had his canoe hauled aboard
> also, and all that he carried kept safe. I ordered that he should be
> given bread and honey and something to drink. I shall carry him
> to Fernandina and restore all his possessions to him so that he
> may give a good account of us. Then when, God willing, your
> Highnesses send others here, we shall be favourably received and
> the natives may give us of all that they possess.

He was kind to another native for the same motive. The man
had been captured by the crew of the *Nina*. Having observed
this, Columbus sent for him 'and gave him a red cap and some
green glass beads which I put on his arm and two hawk's bells
which I put in his ears. I told the sailors to give him back his
canoe which they had taken into the *Nina*, and sent him ashore'.
This made a good impression, for the people on shore gathered
round him in appreciation of the 'good people' on the *Santa
Maria*. 'It was to create this impression that I had him set free
and gave him presents. I was anxious that they should think

well of us so that they may not be unfriendly when your Majesties send a second expedition here. All I gave him was less than four *maravedis*.' He was particularly pleased with what the natives gave in exchange for baubles: 'they will give all they possess for anything that is given to them, exchanging things even for bits of broken crockery or broken glass cups. I saw one give 16 balls of cotton for 3 Portuguese *ceots*, the equivalent of the Castilian *blanca*'—a copper coin worth the old-time farthing. And when the crew landed on an island where the natives ran away leaving all their belongings behind in their huts, Columbus says, 'I allowed nothing to be taken, not even to the value of a pin'. He expected to reap a reward for this of greater value than a pin.

The unmilitary character of the natives was noted in his journal after the first two days. This appealed to him even more than their generosity. He describes how he went to look for a good place to build a fort.

I saw a piece of land which is much like an island, though it is not one, on which there were six huts. It could be made into an island in two days, though I see no necessity to do so since these people are very unskilled in arms, as your Majesties will discover from seven whom I caused to be taken and brought aboard so that they may learn our language and return. However, should your Majesties command it, all the inhabitants of San Salvador could be taken away to Castile or held as slaves on the island, for with fifty men we could subjugate them all and make them do whatever we wish.

Columbus was fond of the thought of the natives being feeble and cowardly. 'They are so timid,' he said again a little later, 'that a single one of our company can put a whole hundred of them to flight as a harmless jest.' No doubt this was true. Later, the Conquistadors were to be even more of a match for natives. One thinks of Hojeda who got a poisoned arrow in his thigh, and as remedy had white-hot irons pressed to his inflamed flesh, while, scornful of pain, he declined to be held or tied. Such men were to show what an advantage they had over natives, however numerous, who had better things to do than be scornful of pain.

Since we are concerned with historical fact we are compelled to accept that the man who thus wrote to the King and Queen was also the man who responded with such true appreciation to

the attitudes of the inhabitants of the islands which he had come
to pillage and enslave. Shortly before he eventually set sail back
to Europe he had this to say of the people of Hispaniola. 'These
are the most loving people. They do not covet. They love their
neighbour as themselves. They have the most gentle way of
speaking. They have no greed whatsoever for the property of
others.'

All we can say is that the ingenuousness of those words frees
him from the charge of disingenuousness. To give a neat extract
of the Christian virtues belonging to the people upon whom he
was bestowing Christianity by unchristian acts did not strike
him as strange or ironic. And we must realize this—that when
he thought of bringing Christianity to the natives he was
thinking of belief, he was thinking of the faith, rather than of
virtues. When people today talk of religion they are nearly
always talking ethics, blandly or nervously leaving belief alone.
It was very different of course in the Middle Ages. So emphatic
was the importance of belief in the one and only God of the
Christians that virtues, values, morals came second, and could
even be overlooked altogether.

III

Columbus continually found it difficult to get his bearings and
find out where he was. At one point when just off the island he
named Isabela, at a cape which he called Cape Hermoso
(Beautiful), and trying to determine how many islands there
were, he says, 'I did not examine this matter minutely because
I could not do all this even in fifty years'. It is a remark worth
noting by those who think he possessed any map which could
have had any accuracy or been of the slightest use to him.

On October 25th he wrote, 'I am about to set sail for another
great island which must be Chipangu, if I judge rightly from
what the Indians aboard tell me'. (Some natives had volunteered to act as guides.) 'They call it Colba, and say there are
many ships there.' (It was really Cuba.) 'My plan, then, is to go
to the Mainland and to the City of Quinsay (Chankow) to
present the letters from your Majesties to the Grand Khan and
bring back his reply.'

It is at moments such as this in his journal that Columbus is
irresistible. The imperishable Don of Cervantes was also fond of
islands and ready to bestow one upon Sancho Panza, but how

pale were his promises in comparison with the enchantments of
the great original! Here Columbus enters the field of art with
sentences of a sublime audacity unique in the history of travel
literature. He is about to visit, he declares in the course of
October 25th, the city of Chankow—which was nine thousand
miles away—and to call on the Grand Khan, who had not
existed for two centuries.

Arriving at what he thought was Chipangu but was really
Cuba, he was disappointed to find no fleet of trading vessels in
the harbours and no streets of gold. Still, perhaps a little further
inland from the coast of Asia the assertions of Marco Polo would
be verified. He decided to send some envoys, led by Luis de
Torres who had accompanied him on the *Santa Maria*, a gifted
interpreter who was in command of Hebrew, Arabic, and
Chaldaic—just the man to hold converse with the Khan. They
set out but returned in four days without being able to find a
trace of either the capital or the Khan. Instead of that they had
merely come to a village of fifty dwellings similar to what they
had seen before in those parts. Here were no citizens of Quinsay
or Cathay or Chipangu, but more natives such as they had seen
before in these islands, who, on beholding their strange appearance and believing they had descended from the sky, ran out
and touched them and kissed their hands. Their leaders then
took them in their arms, led them to the chief's house and bade
them sit down while all squatted about them in awe, and the
women felt them all over to see if they could possibly be
constructed of flesh and blood.

They returned to the ship without any report of gold, but
they did not come back empty-handed. They did not bring the
hard substance of gold but the soft substance of smoke. By
chance the inhabitants of Cuba had discovered that if they
sucked the burning weeds of a plant called tobacco they got a
soothing sensation; and it was here that the industry of smoking
was first introduced. Columbus's commercial instinct was on too
grandiose a scale to have perceived at this stage that here was
a gold-maker better than gold itself in the long run.

By this time some of the natives of these islands had learnt—
with a shrewdness unimagined by the Admiral—that the best
way of getting rid of him was to name some place where he
would find gold; and while he was at Cuba he was told of a
splendid island where gold was simply gathered from the
beaches in quantities and hammered into bars. This island lay
east of Cuba. So Columbus then sailed eastwards on the north

side of Cuba making for the land which he was to name
Hispaniola. He sailed in that direction at too leisurely a pace to
please Martin Pinzon in the *Pinta*, who forged ahead sensing
that this was a good opportunity to look after his own interests.
Up to this point Pinzon had been extremely helpful and loyal
to Columbus; but now, over three thousand miles from Spain,
he did not feel the ties of discipline, and was weary with
Columbian attitudes. He thought that if he went ahead in his
faster ship he might be able to help himself to gold in a private
capacity. He disappeared out of sight and did reach the island
and did in fact find gold and was enabled to help himself and
his crew to a considerable amount—which Columbus failed to
do, for the amount was limited. The Admiral was utterly
powerless to prevent such insubordination.

He sailed at a leisurely pace because he truly enjoyed this
wonderful new earth that he had found—'it was most marvellous to see the fresh wooded groves, the crystal water, the birds,
and all things so fair that it seemed to him that he would never
be able to sail away. He told his company that it would need
a thousand tongues to tell the Sovereigns of all this.' Moreover,
he was continually looking out for future sites for Christian
settlements. It is difficult for us to realize how big a part
evangelism played in Columbus's enterprise. He not only intended to open up commercial activity through a western
approach, but to acquire so much gold there as to be able to
raise armies to regain the Holy Sepulchre from the Saracens;
and not only that but to bring Christianity to people beyond the
confines of Christendom. In fact he liked to claim that 'the
prime purpose of this undertaking has always been the propaga-
tion and the glory of the Christian religion'—as he reminded the
Sovereigns in his journal on November 28th. And as he sailed
along the coast of Cuba and was enthralled by the beauty he
saw, it is clear that he was lifted up into quite a high mood, and
let himself go in unqualified anticipation on the shape of things
to come, seeing in imagination cities rising throughout this land
witnessing to the power of Spain and the glory of the faith. The
Arawaks seemed to qualify particularly for conversion; they had
no religion, Columbus thought: but in this he was mistaken, for
they worshipped a number of agreeable gods (whose simple
images are to some extent preserved in a museum near Spanish
Town in Jamaica). 'I hold it for a certainty that if we had
sincere and devout Christian believers who knew their language,
they would become converts therewith.' He becomes excited

about this, losing all touch with present reality, and from more
than three thousand miles distance says to the monarchs, 'I
hope that your Majesties will attend to this most diligently.'
There will be no difficulty in the matter at all: 'they know that
there is a God on high, and are convinced that we have come
from heaven. They parrot all the prayers that we recite and
make the sign of the cross.' And when he reached his Hispaniola,
he was in the same exalted mood: 'Let your Majesties be
informed that Hispaniola is as much your possession as Castile;
you need do no more than have a settlement built here. These
people are most tractable, and easily led; they could be made
to sow crops and build cities, and be taught to wear clothes and
adopt our customs.'

Like many complicated men, Columbus was also a simple
soul. He meant no harm. It was merely that his mind moved
in as narrow a passage as the most guileless 'savage'. He was
completely enslaved by words. He said, and he believed, that
he had come to 'save' these natives, and to 'free' them; though
from what he was saving them, and from what he was freeing
them he had no conception. In his eyes these natives were no
more than a bunch of children, not mature enough to have a
way of living of their own. It was clear to him that he couldn't
do them a better turn than introduce them to the Christian idea
of life, and to make them put on a pair of trousers. He wished
them well. He did not know that he had come to exterminate
them. It is less often for the enemies of Christ than for his
followers that the prayer has been uttered—'Lord forgive them,
for they know not what they do!'

IV

On December 4th, 1492, Columbus found himself and the *Nina*
off the coast of what is now Haiti, and he anchored in a bay
which he named San Nicolas and then entered a harbour which
he called Concepcion, for the next day was the Feast of the
Conception of the Virgin, and Columbus consistently preferred
Catholic nomenclature. He still didn't know where he was in his
'Asia'. After Colba had misled him he now heard of Caniba
which really referred to the Caribs (who were the cannibals)—
but surely that was their way of pronouncing Cathay, and on
December 10th he declared (using a person for a place)—'Again
I say, as I have done many times before, that Caniba is none
other than the Grand Khan, which must be close by'.

However, he was again delighted with the country and the wonderful harbours. One spot was so lovely that he named it Valle del Paraiso, the Valley of Paradise, and declared, 'I have never seen anything more beautiful'. What gifts he had in store for his King and Queen! If not sacks of gold, at least lovely islands, especially this one which he now came to and called Spain or Hispaniola, and he erected a great cross on the heights of a promontory, 'as a sign that your Majesties are the possessors of these lands, and especially as a sign of Jesus Christ our Saviour, and the glory of Christianity'. He was careful to establish good relations with the inhabitants when he made landings. He always behaved with a prudence that sprang not only from policy but from his own nature. One day 'a very young and very beautiful girl' came aboard, unclothed and in her right mind. She was quite at her ease. She knew that she was alone amongst men, and understood her power. It was as true then, in that place and at that hour, as it has been since the beginning of time, that beauty always rules, regardless. In the eyes of the natives on shore these sailors were supposed to be gods let down from heaven. They did not see themselves as such, they knew the score too well. But when they saw this girl they saw a goddess—and were awed. So was Columbus. But he felt that, 'in honour of your Majesties', he should improve the occasion with a Christian gesture, and made her put on a dress— though what the stuff was composed of, or looked like on the girl, is not recorded. Thus clothed, she returned to shore.

He felt sure now that he was getting close to real gold mines. Various places were named including one called Cibao, and Columbus at once assumed that this at last was Chipangu. It had been Colba; it had been Caniba; now it was Cibao! This was December, and as Columbus did not contemplate returning to Spain before the spring, he could have another three months of exploration. On December 20th the two caravels were anchored in a harbour which Columbus had named Puerto Santo Tomas. The natives gathered round them in great numbers—more than a thousand canoes! Many came on board the *Santa Maria* bringing gifts. On December 23rd they sailed eastwards to visit the headquarters of a great and very friendly chief called Guacanagari who had invited them. At nightfall on December 24th they were rounding a headland on their way to the place where they would find the chief. The wind had gone down completely and the water was as calm as oil. Everything was very peaceful, and everyone was very tired for during the time in the harbour of Santo Tomas no one on board the *Santa Maria* had been able to sleep on account of the natives swarming over the ship. This peacefulness and lovely nightfall calmness led to disaster. In a few hours the career of the *Santa Maria* came to an end. It would never sail from that headland, it would never move again, and most of its crew were condemned to death within a year.

When the 11 p.m. watch had been set, Columbus retired to his cabin to sleep—which was very uncharacteristic of him. The ship's master, Juan de la Cosa, also decided that his presence on deck was unnecessary, and he too retired. This negligent behaviour led to the helmsman turning the tiller over to the ship's boy. Towards midnight the ship grounded gently, without a jolt, on a coral reef. Though the boy raised the alarm at once the *Santa Maria* never got off that reef. Columbus ordered the master with a boat-crew to immediately run an anchor out astern so as to hold the vessel from inching further onto the reef in the ground-swell. But Juan de la Cosa, for reasons which have never been fully explained, did not do what he was ordered, but rowed to the *Nina*.

> I told him and the other sailors [says the Admiral in his journal] to get in the boat which was towing astern and take the anchor aboard and kedge her off by the stern. The master and a number of sailors duly got into the boat, and I thought that they were carrying out my orders. But they rowed on, making all haste to the caravel which lay half a league away. When I saw that they were saving themselves in the boat and that the tide was falling and the ship in danger, I had the main mast cut away to lighten her as much as possible and see if we could pull her off. But the tide dropped still further and the ship would not move and lay rather more athwart the seas. New seams now opened and the whole hull filled with water. Then the *Nina*'s boat came to help me. The master of the caravel had refused to take on board the sailors who had fled in the *Santa Maria*'s boat and it was therefore compelled to return to the ship.

Why had they fled? From what immediate danger had they sought to save themselves? How could there possibly be such incredible lack of discipline in the obeying of the orders of the Admiral? We can never know about this, for it seems that Columbus alone kept a journal. It is a strange thing that neither Alonso Pinzon nor Vincente Pinzon kept any kind of log or diary or journal. Presumably they could write, and if they had done so and given their account it would have been of priceless value.

This happened many centuries ago, yet it is a curiously clear and present incident to us. One feels that even if Juan de la Cosa had acted properly and a thousand canoes had assisted in an endeavour to pull the *Santa Maria* off the reef, they would never have been able to shift it. It grounded into the reef gently but would then have got stuck there as if grappled with steel rivets or held by hooks, for such is the effect of coral.

It seems extraordinary that if this was ever to happen it should not have happened before. During approximately ten weeks they had been sailing around and between uncharted coral islands—sailing, not steaming which at least allows for swift twisting or reversing. The fact that they had hitherto avoided coming to grief is amazing, either in terms of luck or skill. And distance from shore in an environment of coral islands is no guarantee of safety, since you can be well out from shore and yet come suddenly upon water so shallow that you can see the bottom—a coral shelf invisible until you reach it. But the mystery remains. It is not why Columbus went to bed, but why no anchor was cast for the night, instead of the vessel being allowed to drift along quietly in a small current.

As the ground-swell gradually drove the ship ever further onto the reef, the coral cut holes in her, she began to fill, and it was necessary to abandon ship. In this they were generously assisted by the chief, Guacanagari, who appears to have been really sorry and upset by the misfortune of the Spaniards, and seeing Columbus weep, he also wept, and others with him. He sent numerous canoes out to unload the abandoned vessel, and they did this without the idea of looting ever entering their heads. 'Not so much as a needle was lost,' wrote Columbus.*

Thus at the very moment when he seemed to be within reach of gold, the Admiral was robbed of the flagship, *Santa Maria*, under his command. But when he had got over the initial shock and pain of the disaster he began to regard the matter in the

* The tragedy of the flagship *Santa Maria* claimed a victim in 1972. Fred Dickson, Jr., was in command of 'The Santa Maria Foundation', the aim of which was to bring to the surface relics of the Admiral's ship. There was a good deal of excited expectation and optimism regarding the possibility that such relics could be located and recovered; and indeed the members believed that some genuine relics had been discovered. During one diving exploration Fred Dickson was most tragically drowned.

light of providential good fortune. Since it would be impossible
to take three crews home on two ships he would be obliged to
leave some of them behind. He would build a fortress and
establish a little colony of Spaniards there who in his absence
could make a really good job of gold-mining (he was without
proof of the existence of any mines whatsoever). At the thought
of this he cheered up considerably, for this would enable him to
get the imaginary gold and also return at once to Spain, which
he was most eager to do. And who can blame him for the eager-
ness to report his discovery to his Sovereigns, and to his doubters
and enemies? It would be a terrible thing if Pinzon got back
before him and was the first to tell the tale.

Thus he now began to see the disaster as good fortune, and he
wrote, 'There has been such concert amongst so many events
that in truth it was not a disaster but a great good fortune. Had
I not gone aground here I would not have built a fortress.'
After a long-winded account of why it was 'the determined will
of God that the ship should be wrecked here', he adds in the
journal entry for December 27th that he hopes to find on his
return from Castile a ton of gold collected by the settlers in
trading with the natives, and that they will have succeeded in
discovering the mine and the spices, and all these in such
abundance that before three years the King and Queen may
undertake the recovery of the Holy Sepulchre. 'For I have
before protested to your Highnesses that the profits of this
enterprise shall be employed in the conquest of Jerusalem, at
which your Highnesses smiled and said you were pleased and
had the same inclination.'

While indulging these dreams he was also attending to
practical matters in a shrewd manner equally characteristic.
Those rumoured cannibals proved most helpful to him. They
really did frighten the gentle Arawaks who declared that they
had only one eye and that their faces looked like dogs. Columbus
assured the cacique, Guacanagari, that when the fort was built
they could absolutely depend upon the settlers to protect them
from any enemies. He invited the chief to accompany him to a
spot where he had placed what seemed to Guacanagari a big
stone on wheels, part of it shaped like a pipe. The Admiral
stood beside him and showed some powdery stuff he held in his
hand. Giving this to an officer who put the stuff into a receptacle
in the stone, he gave a word of command; there was a flash, a
loud noise, and at the same moment something was seen to
pass right through the hulk of the *Santa Maria* on the reef. The

chieftain was amazed and horrified, and his people who saw this were so terribly frightened that 'they fell down like dead men when they heard the cannons fired'. Columbus always enjoyed, in an unsmiling way, anything in the nature of dramatic deception in the presence of simple men, and without seeking to give a natural explanation to apparently supernatural powers, he assured Guacanagari that he and his people could be certain of complete protection, and had nothing to fear from their protectors if their presence was appreciated. 'They need no longer fear the Caribs, because the Christians would kill them all.'

Columbus now saw to the construction of the fort, largely built with material from the *Santa Maria*. He appointed two officers whom he felt trustworthy to take command over the thirty-six men who had volunteered to stay. Most of them were from the crew of the *Santa Maria*—and all the convicts were volunteers. After all possible arrangements and precautions had been taken for the benefit of the settlers, the Admiral now prepared for a direct return to Castile, alone with his one ship, the *Nina*. Vincente Pinzon, its former Captain, had remained loyal to Columbus, and now he was obliged to stand down while the Admiral took over his ship. This cannot have been very pleasing to him. We have no record of what he thought or said, and Columbus does not make a single allusion to him. So history passes him over. It was his own fault. A little instrument lay ready to his hand which, had he taken it up, would have conferred immortality upon him. He never noticed it.

CHAPTER SIX

The Return

I

ON JANUARY 4th, 1493, leaving the Christian settlement—or fort—which he called Puerto de la Navidad (Christmas Harbour), Columbus set sail for Spain at sunrise, as at sunrise on August 3rd he had set sail for Chipangu. On January 6th he was very relieved to see the caravel *Pinta* suddenly sailing towards the *Nina* with the wind behind. Fernando says briefly about this:

> When she came up to the *Nina* her Captain, Martin Alonso Pinzon, immediately went aboard the Admiral's ship and began to explain why he had left him, inventing various excuses and false arguments. He said that he had not wished to do so but had been unable to avoid it. Although the Admiral knew that it was untrue and that Pinzon's intentions were dishonest, and though he remembered the liberties he had taken on many occasions during the voyage, he concealed his thoughts and accepted these excuses in order not to imperil the whole enterprise. For all might easily have been lost, since the majority of the men in the Admiral's ship were compatriots of Martin Alonso—many of them indeed being his relatives.

That makes good sense. And his father, in refraining from making an issue of the matter at this time, was surely right. Later, at a more propitious time, he could let Pinzon know what he thought of this, and act upon it—but not now. As for Pinzon, it is not difficult to understand his attitude either. He was thousands of miles from Spain. He was quite uncertain as to whether he would ever manage to return. As he surveyed the vast impediment, the legal obligations to Columbus must have seemed to him then as composed of dust and of smoke. At least he might try and line his pockets. He had heard from certain

'Indians' that he could find gold in the island to the east (Hispaniola). And in fact for six weeks he succeeded in exchanging valueless trinkets for gold, half of which he kept for himself, and half of which he gave to his crew in order to keep them quiet.

There is supposed to be a Pinzon problem for biographers. There are Pinzonians and Columbians exhausting the matter. It is a little unnecessary. Thus, from Salvador de Madariaga: 'Colon's anxiety—a feeling which seems never to have left him—led him to fear that Martin Alonso's plan consisted in stealing a march on him and stealing the glory and benefit in Castile before the arrival of the slower flagship. But the evidence available today warrants the conclusion that Martin Alonso never thought of so dastardly an act.' Of course he didn't; for he could never have thought of so stupid an act. Unless Columbus failed to return on account of shipwreck, Martin Pinzon would have been in a worthless position. If he had turned up in Spain and had advanced a story that he had succeeded and Columbus failed, and was supported in this by his crew, it would have availed him nothing if Columbus had then turned up a week or a month later, since the Admiral and his crew would have contradicted Pinzon. The Sovereigns did not appoint Columbus, for fun, to lead the expedition, and did not confer the title of Admiral upon him, if successful, for fun. Under the circumstances Pinzon would have been open to the charge of plain desertion and treachery. He would have instantly lost everything, and could have been subject to prison or even execution. Failing disaster for Columbus on the ocean, Pinzon could not afford to steal a march on him. He would do so if he could, as we shall see presently, but he did not dare to do so at this stage, so he joined up with his Admiral again, and together they started to sail home to Spain.

After some trial and error, for they had nothing nautically definite and scientific to go on, by virtue of sailing north-east they eventually connected by sheer good fortune with a constant easterly wind (only later called 'trade' wind after it and others had become a benefit to commerce) which would drive them in the right direction for Spain, though so much more north than the journey out that it was nearly on a Bermuda parallel. The constancy of these respective winds, one blowing from the Canaries to the West Indies, and one, further north, from the West Indies to Europe, is a wonderful phenomenon, if we are interested, as we should be (but are not) in the mystery of what

wind is. Nor must I dwell upon it here, beyond saying that the
laying hold of wind in this manner was equivalent to the laying
hold of fuel for motor-activity, as definite as a car being able to
fill up with Esso or Shell—without payment, and with little
fear of the fuel running out. Some writers like to grant Columbus
knowledge of these winds in advance of his time, but that is
ludicrous. He was an empiricist, marvellously fortunate, and a
great navigator, not a magician. Anyway, all went well for
three weeks. Then came a storm the like of which he had completely escaped on his journey out. So it was not to be plain
sailing this time.

Indeed, it happened that he came into a winter so stormy—
especially during February—that hundreds of ships were
wrecked. 'The centre of an area of very low pressure,' says
Morison, 'was passing north of the Azores at full gale strength,
and the caravels had to pass through three weather fronts.' By
February 12th the *Nina*, stripped down to bare masts, scudded
before the wind. It was not just a storm, it was a tempest. In
that part of the Atlantic a tempest can be very dangerous
indeed. The waves can reach 120 feet high (I take this figure
from Chichester) which we can visualize as high as a five-storey
house. As high as the spire of a village church. There are places
in the English countryside, in Dorset especially, when on a road,
or in a village street, one sees green hills on each side so
immediate and so high that they are seen above the church or
the trees. Heighten them, darken them, and make them move,
and you get in your mind's eye the scene around a ship in such
an Atlantic storm. Add to this a raging wind. When we speak of
a man in a rage it is our best way of conveying overpowering
anger. And the awful thing about a tempest or hurricane is the
seeming anger, even fury, of the elementary forces around you.
To scud before the wind is easier said than accomplished in a
sailing boat. Only too easy to be knocked broadside-on and to
see a wave as high as a church, and looking as high as St Paul's,
about to collapse upon you. When in a hurricane the isobaric
system is elongated, it brings opposite winds into play very
close to one another, with the result that great pyramidal
waves rise up capped with clashing crests—a glorious sight for a
safe spectator on a modern steamship. And according to Morison
it was in some such tempest that Columbus now found himself
in his caravel, the *Nina*, which would seem hopelessly unfitted
to survive the holocaust. Pursued by a series of nightmare
pyramids of Egypt, lifted high and then thrown down between

towering waves whose crested cliffs seemed mingled with the clouds, the captain and the crew gave themselves up for lost.

When night came they were alone. They could no longer see the *Pinta*. For three days they had been able to look across and see a companion on the embattled vast. But now in the blackness of the midnight tempest the *Pinta's* light flickered and went out, and when dawn came she was no longer to be seen. They were wholly by themselves, lonely castaways amidst the tumult of the surge.

We may be sure that these hours were the worst that Columbus had ever known. He had come upon a great idea. After years of battling against resistance and mockery he had carried it out. He had tasted the relief of being proved right. To return in triumph would be beyond the dreams of even the great conquerors of the world. Was he now to sink without trace as others had done before him—and in his case as a vain boaster? If the *Pinta* was also lost, no one would ever know what happened, how far the little fleet had gone in their adventure. And if the *Pinta* did get back Pinzon could claim whatever he chose and tell whatever lies most suited his advantage. In the past Columbus had so often, so continually prated about the Lord guiding him, about God using him as the ambassador of Christ, that he began to worry about this. Had his pride offended the Almighty who now might favour Pinzon? This was the Middle Ages and faith meant something not easily imagined by us. The higher powers might be placated by a vow. The Admiral made all the crew draw lots to choose one of their number to perform a pilgrimage to the shrine of Our Lady of Guadalupe in the event of their deliverance. The Admiral was chosen. Twice more lots were drawn, and again one lot fell to the Admiral. Then they decided that they would all make a vow to go in procession, clothed only in penitential shirts, to the first church dedicated to the Virgin which they might find on making land. These vows to some extent gave Columbus courage, because the lot had twice fallen to him. But he admits in his journal that this was hard—'My weakness and my anguish were so great that my soul would not take courage'. His nervous tension was such he confessed that 'the least little mosquito is enough to trouble me'.

This casting of lots amidst the tossing and uproar of the tempest, from a mere practical point of view, would seem very difficult. Then Columbus, not really expecting to be saved, did something else. He retired to write some letters. It is a fact.

These are his words, given by Fernando as written by his father on February 14th, 1493. Feeling that perhaps God now wished to humiliate him and rob him of his glory, he writes to the Sovereigns:

In this perplexity I thought of your Highnesses' good fortune which, even were I to die and my ship be lost, might find a means of turning the victory I had gained to your advantage, and that in some way the success of my voyage might become known to you. Therefore I wrote a parchment, as brief as the exigencies of the time required, saying how I had discovered these lands that I had promised to you, and in how many days and by what course I had reached them. I described the goodness of the country and the manners of the inhabitants whom I had made subjects to your Highnesses, taking possession of all the lands I had discovered. I closed and sealed this letter and addressed it to your Highnesses, undertaking the cost of carriage, that is to say promising a thousand ducats to the man who should present it to your Highnesses unopened. My purpose was that if some foreigner should find it he would be too anxious to obtain the reward to open and master its contents. I then sent for a large cask, and after wrapping this parchment in cloth and enclosing it in a cake of wax, placed the parcel in a cask. The hoops were then secured and the cask thrown into the sea, all the sailors supposing that this was in fulfilment of some vow. And since I thought it possible that this cask would not be picked up and the ships were still following their course to Castile, I prepared another similar package and placed it in another cask at the highest point of the prow, so that were the ship to sink it should float on the waves and be carried wherever the storm might take it.

In the year 1852 a paragraph went the round of the English press announcing the discovery of this cask on the African coast, by the ship *Chieftain*, of Boston (Mass.). The biographer Lamartine has accepted the claim as correct but it was never authenticated. When 1992 approaches there will doubtless be another 'find' presented with all the modern expertise in hoax and forgery, and accepted by thousands with the boundless credulity that never dies.

The sad, poetic humour of this dramatic gesture appealed to the poet Shelley, and it inspired him in the nineteenth century to write messages of exhortation and prophecy for the benefit of mankind, seal them in bottles and cast them into the sea.

Now, it was easy for Shelley to write those messages, but it is astonishing that Columbus could have written a single word while being tossed about in a hurricane. However, we must suppose that he managed it somehow, for he was a man of exceptional parts. And, we may ask, while he was pursuing authorship, who was pursuing seamanship at this crisis? It must have been Vincente Pinzon, his ever-faithful second-in-command. Great navigator as Columbus must have been, he was most fortunate in his officers, and Vincente Pinzon was in later years to be known as the most distinguished mariner of his time. Columbus never mentions him, he utters not a syllable in his praise. But perhaps we may say that as the *Nina* did *not* founder we can attribute its survival as much to the seamanship of its former Captain as to the Admiral.

Anyway they came out of it, and on February 15th they caught sight of the Azores, though it was not till three days later that it was possible to anchor off the island of St Mary, belonging to the Portuguese. Near the harbour there was a chapel seen upon a promontory, and most of the crew (leaving only a few able-seamen on board) went on shore, bare-footed and clad simply in shirts, to make a pilgrimage in honour of their vow. Their appearance, at once ludicrous and alarming, so disturbed the inhabitants that they were set upon 'by the whole town' and secured in prison. These sailors had ventured three thousand miles into the unknown, they had entered upon lands unrealized by any European, they had found themselves among the people of Guanahani who imagining them to be gods had lavished them with love and gifts; and now after passing through appalling tempests they were treated by these Portuguese as dangerous clowns. They were in no position to appreciate the high comedy of this, for seemingly they were promptly abandoned by their Admiral. The weather again had become so terrible that the *Nina* could not retain anchor and was forced to stand out to sea, being unable to return for three days.

Then the governor of the island was in a position to make himself objectionable, or worse. He tried to seize Columbus himself. This behaviour is generally put down to the governor's suspicion that the *Nina* had been trespassing along the coast of Guinea which only the Portuguese had the right to enter. This makes no sense. A Spanish ship would not have sailed one thousand miles from the coast of Africa to the Azores for the express purpose of annoying the King of Portugal. It is plain that Columbus had come up against a petty official imagining that an exercise of power against a Spanish vessel would find favour in his own Sovereign's eyes. Luckily on this occasion Columbus did not restrain himself, and using his full authority as Admiral of his Spanish Sovereigns he achieved an intimidating rage and violently threatened this small man with dire results if his crew were not instantly released. The man was cowed, the prisoners were freed and sent back on board.

Now the Admiral could set out once more for Spain. He aimed to reach Cape St Vincent in about a week (it was a question of 800 miles) weather permitting. But weather did not permit. The *Nina* was overtaken by another storm even worse than the former and the sails were whipped to ribbons. Great seamanship was again called for, and once more Columbus and Vincente Pinzon responded magnificently to the occasion. They were in the midst not only of a storm but of a thunderstorm, and the forked lightning was traced like a musical score silvered on the dark screen of night. It was their worst experience, and again they gave themselves up for lost. On the evening of March 3rd 'the sea raised the caravel in the air, and lightning flashed on all sides'. Thus raised aloft as upon a hill they saw the lights of land. 'We waited for daylight amidst endless anxiety and anguish.' They had been blown so much out of course that now they were practically opposite Lisbon, at the Roca de Sintra. When morning came they made harbour in the Tagus to the amazement of the fishermen seeing so tiny a vessel coming in from so terrible a tempest.

Having anchored in the harbour they were soon observed by a large warship also in the harbour. The captain came over and offensively ordered Columbus to give an account of his presence there. By this time the Admiral had endured a great deal. He was in no mood to be treated in this manner. It had been bad enough to have been exposed to the insolence of the governor of an island in the Azores. He did not choose to forget that he was the Grand Admiral of the Ocean Sea, appointed by his Sovereigns, King Ferdinand and Queen Isabela of Spain. Again greatly to his credit he cast restraint aside and asserted himself with a dignity exactly right for a great man in a small boat answering the bullying challenge of a captain in a big boat. He declared that he was an admiral of the Sovereigns of Castile, and accounted to no one, and that it was the habit of admirals of Castile to die rather than surrender themselves or their men to overbearing demands. This aggressive attitude proved successful. The captain of the warship had been acting in a routine

manner, and finding himself suddenly met by the force of
outrage instantly moderated his tone.

The man who was captain of the warship was Bartholomew
Diaz. Just consider. Here were two great men in a snug harbour
in the Tagus. One of those men had looked towards the horizon
of the West with such intensity of gaze that he could imagine
and then actually reach uncharted shores; and on his return had
sought succour in this harbour from out the very jaws of death
after sleepless nights and days in fearful battle with the
waves. The other man had ventured down the coast of Africa
further than any man had ever gone. Coasting on and on by the
unbending beach he sought the final curve—and found it. He
found that cape: not called by him 'Good Hope', but rather
'Disaster', after the loss of his companion ship. Now anchored
here in the Tagus, these two great seamen came face to face; and
all they could do was wrangle over each other's right to shelter
in a harbour.

Presently King John II of Portugal invited Columbus to visit
him. It was he who had turned down the Admiral, but now he
thought that perhaps he could claim dominion over waters
which though explored by Columbus could yet be claimed
through Papal Bull or otherwise as the property of Portugal.
It is strange enough, not just in the eye of eternity but of
ordinary sense. We may not be amused; and yet we muse: a
man claps upon his head a disc, or crown, assumes to represent
a certain part of land in Europe, and then pointing to an
imaginary meridian upon the far-flung waters of the western
sea, to the horizon and beyond, to the endless, tameless,
nameless waves, says *this is mine*; and certain lands beyond on
that meridian *are mine*. No one laughed. Quite the contrary.
The counsellors of the King assured him that far the best plan
would be to kill Columbus there and then and take over the
property. It was a pleasing thought to King John—but not a
politic one. Instead he extended every courtesy to the discoverer, enduring the chagrin of his own initial failure to
authorize the enterprise, and the Admiral's tactless reminders
of that fact. For Columbus could never let well alone. He must
always improve the occasion to gratify himself. Thus he made
a bad impression on the Court, creating further indignation and
a desire to kill him.

The King received him with friendliness [wrote Joam de Barras,
a chronicler of the period] but was very sad when he learnt that

the natives that came with him were not curly-headed blacks and featured like the Africans, but similar in figure, colour, and hair to what he had been told of them in India. And as Colon told bigger greatness and things of that land than the land had, and this with a looseness of words, accusing and scolding the King for having rejected his offer, this way of speaking made some gentlemen so indignant that, having added their hate of his insolence to the sorrow the King felt at the loss of that enterprise, they offered to kill him and thus prevent his departure for Castile.

Indeed, Columbus was lucky to have been able to set sail for Spain on March 13th, and to have had the *Nina* thoroughly repaired. That he should have spent eight days in Portugal is an extraordinary fact. Apart from the tactlessness and rashness of this from a politic point of view, his tardiness is unbelievable on the personal ground alone of risking his arrival in Spain after Pinzon in the *Pinta*. One would think that his anxiety on this score would have overruled all other considerations. It was but a single day's journey from Lisbon to Palos in Spain, so that the most perfunctory repairs on the *Nina* would have served his turn. Some biographers claim that he sent a message to the Spanish Sovereigns from Portugal, others that he sent it as soon as he reached Palos (there is always this discrepancy in facts!), but no evidence is offered as to how he could possibly have sent it from Portugal. This eight days' delay remains utterly baffling. The chronicler Barras—and others—suggest that he lingered at the Court of King John because he could not forbear the exhilaration of being treated as a grandee and bidden to sit down every time he was in the presence of the King. It would have been very natural to enjoy this gratification at the expense of a monarch who had once humiliated him and scorned his project. But how could he have enjoyed one moment of this if it meant reaching Spain possibly after the arrival of the *Pinta*?

In the event he was unwarrantably lucky. The *Pinta* arrived at Palos on the same day as the *Nina*, but a few hours later. The astonishing fact that the two ships made harbour on the same day would have seemed quite natural to any onlooker on the wharf at Palos—two sister ships making port together. What had happened was that Martin Pinzon had also been driven off course by the storm, and had eventually made port in Galicia near Vigo in northern Spain—that part of Spain where the coast-line is north of Portugal's coast-line. Thus, while Columbus had landed in Portugal not very far from the Spanish port which he had hoped to reach, Pinzon had been forced in a totally wrong direction. Disembarking at Vigo he at once despatched a message to the Sovereigns bearing news of his arrival. He received a reply commanding him to proceed to Palos. This message and reply must have taken several days, after which he had to sail down the whole coast of Portugal and past Lisbon, travelling as it happened then just behind the *Nina*, though not in sight of her. A single day's further delay by Columbus would have put Pinzon in front. Was ever man more fortunate than the Admiral at this time, or a rival more unfortunate? Pinzon half-believed, perhaps wholly believed, that Columbus in the *Nina* had gone down. Even if this had not happened his arrival would create a sensation and give him quite sufficient glory for a lifetime. But when he entered the safe waters at Palos he saw the *Nina* quietly at anchor there! This was a fearful shock. Enough to finish off any man less ambitious and less gifted than Martin Pinzon. In fact it killed him. Worn out by his own battle with the storms, and now deprived of acclamation, he took to his bed and died within the month. That was surely well for him. Had he lived he was a lost and ruined man. He could look to no future. When thousands of miles from base, in strange territories, among fabulous islands like a necklace of pearls in a new morning of the world, it was a natural thing to chance his arm, disregard his superior officer, and line his pockets if he got an opportunity. But he could not expect the Admiral to overlook this now, for he knew his character only too well. He stood no chance at all of accompanying Columbus on a second voyage with a second fleet which would be a great affair. And to have seen that second fleet sail westward without him would have been intolerable, he could not have borne the humiliation and neglect. His essential former services would count for nothing now. He drew a circle and died within the walls of the monastery of La Rabida where he had first met Columbus and explored the future of their convictions and their hopes. 'If ever man died from mental distress and a broken heart, that man was Martin Alonso Pinzon,' says Arthur Helps, surely with some truth. As for Columbus, he entered now, and had the right to enter, days of dazzling acclamation.

II

The Admiral had sent more than a message to the King and Queen announcing his arrival and his discovery. He had sent an elaborate Letter. It was one of the characteristics of this extraordinary man, that whatever the conditions, he always managed to write up his achievements—in contrast to the total literary silence of his fellow captains. And he generally wrote in terms of extreme bombast: 'Thus the eternal God, our Lord, grants to all those who walk in his way victory over apparent impossibilities, and this voyage was pre-eminently a victory of this kind. . . . So all Christendom will be delighted that our Redeemer has given victory to our most illustrious King and Queen and their renowned kingdoms, in this matter. They should hold great celebrations and render solemn thanks to the Holy Trinity with many solemn prayers . . .'

Whatever the King and Queen may have thought of this letter, *per se*, they were delighted with the news. How right they had been, they reflected, and soon forgot that they had long resisted his appeals. They invited him to come without delay to the Court at Barcelona, addressing him as 'Don Cristobal, our Admiral of the Ocean Sea and Viceroy and Governor of the Islands which have been discovered in the Indies'. They urged him to hurry and prepare for a second voyage in case the Portuguese sought to claim jurisdiction in those regions. And in fact there was to be much trouble with the claims of the Portuguese, though warfare was happily avoided by virtue of the Pope acting as a kind of referee and making demarcations on the ocean with the ruling that west of the 'line' would belong to Spain and east to Portugal. If only the Grand Khan had really existed there, it would have been salutary if he had drawn up lines of demarcation in answer to the Pope. Even so, the farce did not impose on everyone. Not on the clear-minded Henry VII of England who in a very English way and with very English wit, coolly observed, 'I cannot find these marks in Adam's will'.

Columbus now 'entered into the greatest reputation', says the historian Herrera, and he underlines the true meaning of *re-putation*: 'it does not consist in success but in doing something which cannot be easily comprehended, which compels men to think over and over again about it'. The Court was at Barcelona, and while awaiting their Majesties' commands, he

stayed at Seville, and his entry into that city aroused un-
restrained enthusiasm and his stories were listened to with
unbounded amazement. Already at Lisbon he had made his
special display. He had produced his 'Indians' with their
parrots and popinjays. What the poor Indians thought of this
'New World' after their appalling voyage, we shall never know
and can scarcely imagine; we only hear of one of them for
certain who managed to survive the change of scene. Now at
Seville they were on show again, their presence immensely
advertising the event and adding authority to anything
Columbus chose to say. And then one of the most important
officers of the royal household had been despatched to convey
the message that the Admiral must come to Barcelona without
delay.

Barcelona is a long way from Seville, and the procession along
the roads and from town to town was truly triumphant. The
people can have had no clear notion of what he had done or
where he had been: they only knew that some extraordinary
thing had happened, and they came out to gaze at the strange
cavalcade. They rode on horses and mules, with Columbus in
the fore. The Indians wore feathers and various ornamental
girdles and aprons of bright stuffs, their ears adorned with gold
pendants, their arms with bracelets, and they had necklaces of
beads. Some carried spears and a few held up oars inscribed with
mysterious runes. Red and green parrots which had survived
the tempests perched on the shoulders of the Indians. Prodigious
shells, glittering quartz and crystals and precious stones were displayed in baskets, while mules brought up the rear heavily laden
with sacks which supposedly contained all sorts of treasures.

Everyone flocked to gaze at this unique cavalcade. While
passing through Cordova, a town which overwhelmed him with
extravagant acclaim, Columbus paused to embrace his mistress
Beatriz and to pick up his sons Fernando and Diego who now
joined this historic procession. On April 30th, 1493, the great
moment arrived when they reached Barcelona. As soon as run-
ners reported that the Admiral was approaching the town,
distinguished merchants came out to receive him, and then the
King's Chamberlain stepped forward to conduct him to the
King and Queen. 'Bells rang out from every tower, carpets hung
down from every balcony, flags and handkerchiefs waved from
every window, and the streets were clamorous with music and
jubilation.' Progress through the streets was slow, and some
armed sailors belonging to the procession had to force a way

through the crowd. At last they reached the palace. 'The
Admiral entered the hall where the Sovereigns, the Infante
Juan, and a great crowd of caballeros and hidalgos were
waiting,' Las Casas tells us. 'Among this noble assembly his
lofty stature, and his air of authority, his noble countenance
crowned with his white hair, his modest smile, gave him the
appearance of a Roman Senator.' As he advanced to make
obeisance, an unexpected thing occurred which may have done
him harm. As he approached the throne and knelt to kiss the
hands of the Sovereigns, the royal pair bade him rise and be
seated on a chair between them. This meant that he was no
longer a mere vassal, but was greeted and acknowledged as
Viceroy of the Indies.

This was the supreme moment in the life of Columbus.
Sitting there upon the dais between the King and Queen,
himself now a don and viceroy, he saw around him in the hall
princes, dukes, archbishops, knights and barons, admirals and
generals, and their attendant ladies gorgeously attired—and all
eyes fastened on him with burning curiosity. It was a captive
audience; and he knew that he could captivate it. He had
written account after account, letter after letter about his
discoveries: he was not tongue-tied when he came to speak it
now before the Sovereigns, the grandees, and all the dignitaries
surrounding the Spanish throne.

We must remember—it is easy to forget this—that all his
listeners were completely ignorant of the existence of North and
South America and of the Pacific Ocean and of a huge area of
islands called today the West Indies. The fabled East, as told
by Marco Polo, was not a New World to their imaginations, it
was a sort of Other World very indeterminate in place and
unreachable by sea until this first great westward voyage. The
ideas of Columbus had been doubted: there was no call to doubt
them now. It was marvellous to be told that those eastern lands
of imagination really did exist and that Columbus had returned
from islands skirting the domains of the Grand Khan. It was
possible for him, sitting there before them all upon the dais, to
mislead them about almost everything—geography, gold
deposits, and the nature of the inhabitants. Not consciously
mislead them: it was just that he had got everything wrong. He
was marvellously confused. He may have used, in fact we are
told that he sometimes did use the term 'New World'. For it
was a splendid thing to be able to say 'I give you a New
World'. But the conception did not really go with the claim

nearest his heart, that he was right about reaching his Chipangu and his Grand Khan: he preferred to be proved right about this rather than to be the discoverer of something else.

However, sitting there on the dais, for one glorious hour he could unfold his fairy tale without fear of caveat. All he had to say was so factual, so definite and detailed as to carry conviction. We know that he could speak well when he chose, and his narrative must have flowed easily from him now, resting as it did upon his journal and his letters. He would have begun by telling them of his journey across three thousand miles of shoreless wave, and how at last one evening they saw that flickering light far off, and in the pale poetic pearl of tropic dawn the curtain raised upon a new glad world with people in it so gentle, so generous, and so innocent that it seemed like entering into the Garden of Eden. And we may be very sure that he would have rehearsed the beauty of those islands, especially the glowing green that had so enchanted him as he passed by baptizing them with holy names. Since this was all so factual his claim that these islands were the outskirts of Chipangu and Cathay—the very words an incantation that lulled the senses— would have gone unchallenged. And when he came to speak of the wealth he had discovered he did not rely upon words alone to tell of his trophies and his spoils. At a sign from him the seven Indians stepped from behind a screen bearing a display of gold before the enraptured Court: in grains and in ore, in dust of gold, in coils, rings, plates, masks, and pendants. Actually there was not much gold to be found in any of the islands, but Columbus had gathered enough to make a good show, and the chieftains had given him many precious things. To the monarchs and the court it would appear just as a sample of boundless wealth in store.

This address to the Sovereigns, together with his exhibition of the trophies, perfectly timed for effect, created a sensation. Las Casas says in summary,

When he had given wise account of all the graces God had given him during the voyage, and of the grandeur and felicity of the lands discovered, when he had displayed the pieces of carved gold and the specimens of gold, some in large nuggets and some in fine grains, and avowed that these lands produced such in infinite quantities; when he had described the innocence and docility of these peoples and their readiness to receive our Holy Faith—as was well proved by the Indians that he had brought thence—then the Sovereigns rose and kneeled, their eyes full of tears, and the choir of the royal chapel chanted the *Te Deum*.

Thus Columbus emerged from his battle with the ocean that had seemed about to swallow him up with all his deeds and hopes, and his battle with the sceptics who strove to wreck his life, into the full light of history, and his name was to become as familiar to the beggar in Denmark as to the serf in Russia and the prostitute in Rome.*

The King and Queen were ready to grant almost anything he asked. They established him in all the rights guaranteed under their agreement drawn up before he sailed. They added further marks of special distinction. The term 'don', a designation confined to noblemen, was granted to him, to his sons and to his brothers. He was saluted as a grandee on all solemn occasions. At banquets his food was tasted for poison—an act indicating an extremity of importance. He rode by the King's side, a privilege hitherto reserved for members of the royal family. He was granted a coat of arms—a wonderful rise in the mind of a plebeian. The Queen, with endearing rashness, wrote to say, 'The more we understand the grandeur of your plan, the more we esteem the wisdom you have displayed, a wisdom we would not have supposed any mortal to possess'. Clearly confirmed in his sense of a divine mission he now began to sign his name in hieroglyphics which have puzzled pundits for nearly five hundred years.

Standing in this supreme position he could now afford to be magnanimous, and perhaps send some message of good will to the dying Pinzon. Incurably vindictive, he did nothing of the sort; nor did any word pass from his lips in recognition of what all the Pinzon family had done in this great enterprise. He would share with them neither glory nor spoil. As we know, he even

---

* In October 1973, in New York, Sotheby Parke Bernet auctioned two small crystal lockets said to contain relics of dust from the remains of Christopher Columbus. Indeed, 'there are small portions of his dust scattered over the world', if we are to believe Frederick L. Benton in his *The Last Resting Place of Christopher Columbus*. 'It is a fact that the Italian Consul, Signor Luigi Cambiaso, Senor Joaquin Montolio, the Dominican Minister of Justice, and Sr Jesús Maria Castello, the Spanish Civil Engineer in charge of the work on the alterations of the Cathedral, each on September 10th, 1877, appropriated a small portion of the First Admiral's dust. Even Bishop Roque Cochia did so. Of the dust so appropriated he sent one portion to His Holiness Pope Leo XIII, a second to the University of Pavia, and a third portion, which he retained for himself, was donated to the Municipality of Genoa.'

secured for himself the grant of 10,000 *maravedis* promised by the King and Queen to the first man who would see land—an act as impolitic as it was mean. The poor sailor who had really seen the light from the *Pinta*—who needed this modest yearly pension so much more than the Admiral would ever do—went to Morocco and became a renegade. An action of this kind spreads far and wide among humble folk and produces a very bad effect. And standing as he did, in so firm a place, there was no need now for Columbus to say 'I told you so' to anyone who had been in the wrong, or to harbour resentment against those who had obstructed him. But even this, calling for nothing more than the simplest psychology and a small degree of tact, was beyond him. This boded ill for the future.

CHAPTER SEVEN

The Second Voyage

I

THE SPANISH SOVEREIGNS were now as eager to launch the second voyage as they had been reluctant to launch the first. They were exceedingly anxious to remain ahead of the King of Portugal's plans and claims. True, the Pope had been so good as to draw that imaginary line from north to south (which ran some hundred miles west of the Azores, marking all to the west of this line as belonging to Spain, and all east of it to Portugal). But the King of Portugal was far from satisfied with his portion of wave, and was making plans to forestall the Spaniards. Ferdinand and Isabela, feeling it essential to confront Portugal with a *fait accompli* irrespective of Papal Bulls, were in haste to get the expedition organized.

The aim of this second enterprise was first, so they declared, the conversion of the natives to Christianity, and for this purpose they sent six priests (who did win one convert after six years, we are told). The second aim was to colonize, for which purpose they despatched one thousand four hundred and ninety-four laymen. The third aim was to undertake a further exploration of Cuba and make sure that it really was part of the Asian mainland. The fleet was to consist of seventeen ships.

The third aim reveals the extreme haziness in the minds of the Spanish Sovereigns as to what Columbus had actually discovered. Was Cuba the mainland of Cathay? If so, then presumably the offshore islands would be under the sovereignty of the Grand Khan, described by Marco Polo as 'the greatest lord in the whole world'. And if so, how about colonization, which in plain words means taking over somebody else's property? Would that greatest lord approve, and if not, might he not be a more powerful opponent than any European rival such as the King of Portugal? Further, even if the Grand Khan received them with civility, how were they to return to Spain with wealth and justify the claim that one had only to go to Cathay to come back laden with gold and precious stones? They could scarcely expect the Grand Khan to exchange a sack of pearls for a string of beads. The Sovereigns do literally appear to have been as careless about this as Columbus himself, and to have been thinking two things at the same time: that there were defenceless people (sitting on gold-fields) whom they could easily plunder, and on the mainland a 'mighty lord' who would be delighted to see them.

The captain-general of this expedition was, of course, Columbus, but powerful executives were needed to organize the preparations. There was a treasurer, Francisco Pinelo; Juan de Soria, Columbus's private secretary, was the chief comptroller and accountant; while the main organization of the affair was in the hands of Don Juan de Fonseca who though a cleric and bishop was also a worldly-wise man of great ability 'especially for assembling soldiers and manning fleets', says Las Casas. These able men did not get on well with Columbus. The Admiral was not a man of affairs and had no real idea how such an expedition could be organized and financed, but at the same time he wished to be consulted about everything, and would stand on his dignity if baulked. He had been made into a magnificent personage by the Sovereigns who had lavished wealth, honours, and power upon him to such an extent that he could appoint whom he chose to act as his administrators in the Indies, a power of patronage which virtually silenced overt opposition. With a title such as the Very Magnificent Lord Don Cristobal Colon Grand Admiral of the Ocean Sea, he was not the man to undersell himself or accept less than his due, and he demanded a permanent retinue of footmen in excess of what was necessary, and became as indignant as King Lear when a reduction in the number was suggested by Fonseca. The latter envied his position, disliked his character, and sought to hamper his activities and disparage his services. Juan de Soria also showed a reluctance 'to honour and respect the Admiral of the Indies as it should be done and as we wish it'—the words used by the Sovereigns themselves as an indication of their wishes in this matter. Such a phrase throws a good deal of light upon the behaviour of Columbus at this time, but it is also noteworthy that the King and Queen had still such a regard for their Admiral that they would not allow anyone to treat him with disrespect, and in fact even in the matter of the retinue of footmen they advised Fonseca to humour him.

This time the recruiting of a crew provided problems opposite to those he had met with before. The difficulty now lay not in the fewness of the volunteers but in their excess. The rage for gold that broke out at that time all over Europe was responsible for this inadmissible dream. A nonexistent El Dorado had been created in the minds of thousands of poor wretches who imagined themselves freed from their misery by the magic of gold, and it is said that many of them in their disappointment at rejection put an end to their lives. Those who were permitted to join literally thought that when they reached the Indies they would instantly be able to fill their pockets with nuggets of gold—for when a crazy idea is in the air, always then the minds of simple men get crazed, and the blind lead the blind and the squinting the squinting.

Unconscious that they were being responsible for the kind of history they had never contemplated, the Spanish Sovereigns wrote letter after letter to Columbus and Fonseca urging speed in the preparation for this second voyage. But it was not easy to accelerate the organization of a fleet of seventeen ships which was deemed a minimum necessity. Apart from the complement of sailors essential for the manning of the vessels, and the force of trained soldiers to be enlisted for their protection, a choice had to be made from men applying as miners, carpenters, shoemakers, farm-labourers, masons, locksmiths, tailors, weavers—some thousand in all. Room had to be found and decisions taken regarding a number of hidalgos, men of noble birth and adventurous spirit who were wild to join the expedition. And though 'colonization' simply meant land-robbery, it also meant, or should have meant, land-development, and for this end it was important to select grain and implements of agriculture, and to bring a considerable number of horses—animals unknown in the Indies. Preparations of this kind inevitably take longer than expected, and if we add to this the weight of inertia, the obstructions of incompetence, and the cunning of self-seekers who supplied barrels of wine that leaked, or substituted some skinny hacks for the formidable steeds that had been paraded before Fonseca, they were quite lucky to be in a condition to sail on September 25th, 1493.

II

Again they sailed first to the Canaries before standing out for the Atlantic crossing. The day they left the island of Ferro behind is generally calculated as October 13th, not that it matters. The voyage was uneventful except for a thunderstorm on St Simon's Eve, after a fortnight's sailing, 'which split a number of sails and lighted those ghostly flares which sailors call corposants on the tips of the masts and yards'.* This is one of the aspects of the phenomenon of phosphorescence. Sometimes a brush discharge of electricity during or in the wake of a thunderstorm will cause a tapering glow to appear on the spires of churches or even the tops of trees. It has been called St Elmo's Fire and has most frequently been witnessed on the main-topgallant mast-heads of ships in open sea. These lampless lights aided by no living hand, gleaming high above in the darkness of the midnight tempest, have a supernatural power to chasten and subdue. We think of Melville's *Pequod* in the typhoon, torn of her canvas and left bare-poled to face the storm; and how Starbuck looking upwards and seeing the three tall masts silently burning like three gigantic wax tapers before an altar, cried out, 'The corposants have mercy on us all!' And Melville, while reminding us that oaths to sailors are household words on most occasions whether in the trance of the calm or the teeth of the tempest, yet adds that in all his voyagings, 'seldom have I heard a common oath when God's burning finger had been laid on the ship, when His *Mene, Mene, Tekel Upharsin* had been woven into the shrouds and the cordage'. Since such an ocean thunderstorm is seldom less than five square miles in dimension, Columbus's fleet of seventeen ships would have been encompassed. The sailors on each vessel would have seen many of the others thus ghostlily emblazoned amidst the riot of the storm, the tip-edged fire fed by no fuel and quenched by no spray.

Before returning on his first voyage Columbus had learnt from the natives of Hispaniola of the islands which are now known as the Leeward Islands (the Lesser Antilles). Accordingly, with his usual nautical skill he made his way there and arrived at break of day on November 3rd. 'All the men were so delighted that it was marvellous to hear their shouts and cries of pleasure.' So writes Dr Chanca who was one of the King's physicians, and, being detailed as doctor to this expedition, wrote an interesting account of it. 'I think everyone had seen enough water!' he declared. The journey, of course, had not been an adventure into the unknown, nevertheless they were so

* *Christopher Columbus: Admiral of the Ocean Sea*, Samuel E. Morison, Oxford U.P., 1942.

exhausted by their privations, says Dr Chanca (though he does not say what those privations were), 'that they all longed most fervently for land'.

The approach to these islands was more dramatic than the former approach to San Salvador, for many of the Leeward Isles look from a distance like mountains sitting in the sea, strange to behold in the muslin mist of dawn. Gazing up at one of them they were amazed to see a waterfall flowing from the highest peak! Was it water, they asked themselves, or a white rock? 'When we got nearer the truth was apparent. It was the most beautiful thing in the world to see the height from which it fell, and from how small a place such a force of water sprang.'

Unable to harbour at the first island, which was named Dominica by the Admiral, they anchored at one which he named Mariagalante after his new ship. From thence to another which he named Guadelupe in remembrance of a pilgrimage of thanksgiving which he had made in Spain after his return from the first voyage (for the devoutness of Columbus was absolutely genuine). But this time they did not find themselves among inhabitants apparently fit for the Garden of Eden. They had come across the Caribs, who, according to Dr Chanca,

> eat the male children that they have [by their female captives] and only bring up the children of their own women; and as for the men they are able to capture, they bring those who are alive home to be slaughtered and eat those who are dead on the spot. They say that human flesh is so good that there is nothing like it in the world; and this must be true, for the human bones that we found in their houses were so gnawed that no flesh was left on them except what was too tough to be eaten. In one house the neck of a woman was found cooking in a pot. They castrate the boys that they capture and use them as servants until they are men. Then, when they want to make a feast, they kill and eat them, for they say that the flesh of boys and women is not good to eat. Three of these boys fled to us, and all three had been castrated.

Since the immediate objective was the fortress at La Navidad in Hispaniola, the Admiral did not linger long at any of these islands, merely bestowing names upon them as they went along —St Maria de la Antigua, Montserrat, St Maria la Redonda, Santa Cruz, the Virgin Islands, and so forth. If sailing along and discovering something fresh all the time was a marvellous experience for the Spaniards, the sight of seventeen ships with huge wings instead of oars was so stupefying for the natives that they made easy targets at first if the Spaniards chose to attack them. However, though afraid of the Caribs and sometimes thinking it necessary to fight them, Columbus was anxious to press on to Hispaniola and meet the gentle Arawaks and his friend Guacanagari who had been so good to him when the *Santa Maria* had been abandoned. That was something to look forward to. The providential wrecking of the vessel meant that he would be welcomed by the men whom he had left in the fort on the island, who would now have achieved a settlement and a *modus vivendi* with the natives, and would have accumulated piles of gold from the adjoining 'mines'. Once in possession of gold and able to ship it back to the King and Queen, his position would be unassailable and his enterprise seen by friends and enemies alike to be the great service to Spain and to Christianity which he so emphatically and boastfully claimed.

They had spent some three weeks passing through these islands as they made their way towards Hispaniola, reaching the off-shore from the fort of La Navidad on November 27th. There they anchored. Columbus expected that dozens, perhaps hundreds, of canoes would fill the bay crammed with Indians coming out to welcome him. Not a single canoe appeared. There was an ominous stillness in the atmosphere. The flagship fired off a cannon, but there was no kind of reply from anyone on shore. The hours passed, and nothing happened. At last a canoe of Indians came to the Admiral's ship, looking for him, and recognizing him by his tall stature, one of them ventured to give him presents sent by the chief, Guacanagari, from whom he had parted on such friendly terms. How about the Spaniards whom he had left behind in the fort, Columbus inquired. They were very well indeed, was the reply, except those who were not terribly well, having died. This was breaking the news gently, for soon it transpired that none of them were very well since all of them were dead.

The Admiral then went on shore to visit his friend the cacique, Guacanagari, who would doubtless explain everything. In order to impress the chief Columbus was accompanied by a retinue of followers as elaborately dressed as if on parade in Seville or Barcelona. Guacanagari was unprepared for this, but he put up a good show as wounded hero who had attempted to save the Spaniards from their attackers. Having a skilled physician with him, Columbus pressed for a medical examina-

tion of the wound pending a prescription for recovery. No
wound was found, and it became evident that even Guacanagari
intended to deceive the Admiral. And the truth of the calamity
'was demonstrated both by Guacanagari and by the corpses of
ten Spaniards which had been found by our men miserably
deformed and corrupted, smeared with dirt and foul blood, and
hideously discoloured, for they had lain out in the open'.*

There had been, as we saw, much difficulty in the recruitment
of crews for the first voyage. Some, not many but some,
convicts had to be recruited. Granted that there may not have
been more than twenty such, the Pinzons would scarcely have
needed them, while Columbus the stranger, the Genoese, would
have had to use them to make up the full complement of his
crew. And we may be very sure that when the time came for
volunteers to stay at Hispaniola, it would have been the
convicts who would have come forward the most willingly. For,
as a convict, there could be no question that it would be much
nicer to remain on an island paradise regarded as gods than
return to Spain and be regarded as the scum of the earth.

This would make a bad foundation for the garrison at La
Navidad. It began to become clear what had happened. When
the Admiral had departed for Spain the members of the
garrison began to give rein to their greed and their lust. The
account which Guacanagari gave to Columbus was that the
Spaniards who had been left at La Navidad took to evil
courses, quarrelled amongst themselves, straggled about the
country, and finally were set upon by a neighbouring chief
called Caonabo who burned the fort and killed the garrison. It
was in Caonabo's part of the country that the gold was supposed
to exist, and that the cupidity and the profligacy of the
Spaniards became so gross as to call down upon themselves the
vengeance of the natives. Guacanagari represented himself as
having endeavoured to protect the Spaniards, being wounded
in the attempt.

One aspect had become particularly clear in the course of
communication with any of the natives: and communication
was possible because Columbus had with him the one surviving
Indian who had gone back in the *Nina*, and had learnt enough
Spanish to become a valuable interpreter. The aspect which
stood out was the sexual one. The Spaniards had each taken, or
tried to take, four women as mistresses. Naturally this enraged

* Guillermo Coma, an Aragonese who went on the voyage and took notes.

the inhabitants more than anything else, especially as the girls may have seemed to enjoy the novelty.

Some light is thrown on this aspect of the Christians' behaviour to the Indians, and on the response, by a complacent account of a personal incident written by one of Columbus's lieutenants, Michele de Cuneo, recorded when they were at the island of Antigua. 'While I was in the boat I captured a very beautiful Carib woman,' he wrote, and had brought her on board the *Mariagalante*, with the Admiral's consent, it appears.

> When I had taken her to my cabin she was naked—as was their custom. I was filled with desire to take my pleasure with her and attempted to satisfy my desire. She was unwilling and so treated me with her nails that I wished I had never begun. But—to cut a long story short—I then took a piece of rope and whipped her soundly, and she let forth such incredible screams that you would not have believed your ears. Eventually we came to such terms, I assure you, that you would have thought she had been brought up in a school of whores.

It is clear that the members of the garrison, with the imbecility which accompanies arrogance and the lack of simple psychology which belongs to insensitiveness, did not know when they had gone too far, whether in snatching gold or girls— and thus cut their own throats. Not one of them was left alive, and the so-called fortress was razed to the ground.

This put Columbus into an awkward position in front of his officers and men. His claim that it had been God's intention to wreck the *Santa Maria* so that a Christian settlement could be secured in Hispaniola while he returned to Spain, was now regarded as so much bombast. Moreover, he had failed to use discretion in his selection of a leader to command the garrison, and instead of choosing a man of outstanding character, had given the position to Diego de Arana, the man most personally connected with him. And he had shown himself as lacking in perception with regard to the character of the Indians, imagining that weakness is a necessary concomitant of gentleness and generosity. The amiability, and the tears, of Guacanagari deceived him into supposing that he was as soft as a marsh mallow, whereas there was steel in that cacique's character by virtue of which he had attained his position in the first place.

After Guacanagari's 'wound' had been exposed as a fabrication it was obvious to Columbus that the chief was dissembling.

What was he to do? Advisers were not wanting in urging him to take a strong line—especially advice from Bernardo Buil who having conducted many heretics to the stake at home was clearly well qualified to lead the monks sent to Hispaniola to convert the 'infidels'. He now recommended that the chieftain be executed as an example to the others. But the Admiral never liked taking drastic action of this sort. In any case it more appealed to his secretive nature to dissemble with a dissembler, and to deceive a deceiver, meeting mendacity with furtiveness, rather than play the strong man of action. He pretended to believe what Guacanagari had told him, sympathized with the suffering caused by the wound, asked him if he could walk, gave him his arm helping him up, and finally invited him to dine on board his ship. By this means, the Admiral reflected, he would also be able to let the cacique observe with what strength of men and ships he had this time come from Spain. He reserved a special thing as a final exhibit, with that furtive unsmiling sense of theatre which he showed at intervals throughout his life. He conducted the chief to a ship where he could display fifty remarkable animals some of whom were nearly six feet in height, with five feet of shining furry body horizontally placed upon four hinged legs slender as stalks and hard as marble. Guacanagari, who had never seen any animal larger than a lizard or a small dog, was appalled at the sight of these creatures, as well he might be. A horseman might have alarmed him even more: when Pizarro later was in Equador with some conquistadors in danger of death at the hands of Indians, he just managed to extricate himself because his attackers were shocked into momentary inactivity by the sight of one of his caballeros becoming *separated* from his horse.

Next day Columbus thought that perhaps he had overdone it. For, going on shore to visit the chief, he found that he had vanished. He had abandoned the 'village' and departed somewhere into the interior of the island with all his subjects and possessions. Nevertheless, Guacanagari seems to have appreciated the Admiral's attitude towards him, for in the months to come, and indeed until the end, he remained friendly with Columbus. There was mutual understanding.

III

There was not much understanding, or respect, for Columbus at his headquarters. By this time we may have discerned certain salient characteristics about him. He was not a man of action in the sense of a strong character who could make decisions and bestow order among those under his command. His genius did not lie in that direction at all. He had inspiration by virtue of which he could launch those ships. And he had great nautical expertise; but that does not qualify him to be considered a man of action any more than skill in other arts. As a man of action who could lead and rule men he had no ability.

The great leader is so rare because he knows what to do and has the strength of character to carry out his decisions. The man of action is confronted with chaos and shambles: the situation is terribly critical: there are a dozen choices and points of view, and the more brilliant his counsellors are with their conflicting and yet convincing theories, the more difficult it is for him to choose a line. But he does choose a line and sticks to it. He makes himself feared. He commands the respect of fear. If it is known that after he has made a decision he will destroy anyone who impedes him, he will meet with few who will take the risk. If it is known that he will even be rash enough to 'cut off his nose to spite his face' few will dare to take issue with him. If he makes the wrong decision he completely disappears; if right he becomes an infallible hero.

Columbus never commanded the respect of fear. The crew of the *Santa Maria* were not afraid to mutiny. When that ship came to grief on the coral reef, Juan de la Cosa defied the orders of the Admiral in the most flagrant manner, apparently neither fearing nor receiving any punishment. When Pinzon decided to desert him and go off on his own in search of gold, he did not hesitate to do so, not anxious about the consequence. When the cacique, Guacanagari, deceived him he took refuge at once in procrastination. If vacillation causes fatal delay it is called cowardice: when successful it is called prudence. The general mass of men like their leaders to pursue one line of action without hesitation. But this was not a policy that Columbus could ever fulfil. Yet for such a man even to desire to be Viceroy, let alone insist upon the appointment, argues a lack of self-knowledge as great as the lust for importance.

When the Admiral and his fleet of no fewer than seventeen ships landed in Hispaniola in 1493 they expected to find a vastly different scene from that which confronted them. They expected a flourishing colony of Spaniards living off the fat of the land, and with those sacks of gold neatly piled up. The fairy-tale expectation about food was as childish as about gold.

Food, of course, comes before everything else, and without enough of it that garrison could not have functioned. Very soon they would have run out of their rations and their wine. The natives lived incredibly simply in comparison with the appetites of the Spaniards: apparently what a Spaniard considered a meal was enough to last a native for a week! It is certain that it was not only their appetite for the women but their voracious demand for food that led to their extermination.

And now this armada had arrived with fifteen hundred men to find no fortress, no single member of the garrison, no gold, and their own food running out (the wine literally ran out, for the barrels leaked). This was an appalling disappointment for those who had set out with avaricious dreams. It might seem that no leader could grapple successfully with such a situation. But that is just where real leaders of men do succeed, and always have done so. The kind of man who could not possibly grapple was Christopher Columbus. Vacillation and procrastination now were fatal qualities. His inspirational genius had brought him to this land. He had the strength to get there. No one else had that inspired force. But as ruler, as Viceroy, he was weakness personified.

A sufficient amount of grain had been shipped over to lay the foundations of agriculture, but the hunger for bread was so great that Columbus actually allowed hundredweights of grain to be ground into flour! Yet there should have been no food problem. According to both Dr Chanca and Fernando the fish were more wholesome than those in Spanish waters. And as for the wonderfully fertile and largely virgin soil, both Fernando and Dr Chanca declared that vegetables could be grown in eight days as against twenty in Spain, while grapes and sugar-cane ripened with extraordinary speed. But Columbus could not organize working parties to prepare the land, and showed himself powerless to deal with the hidalgos who were much too stupid to understand the art of cultivation, declaring they would rather die than soil their hands with soil.

Instead of looking to the future by planting crops and fishing, Columbus relied upon their diminishing supplies and on what he could plunder from the natives; and in the meanwhile spent four months deciding upon a site for a new fort to take the place of La Navidad. Having built this fort, which he called Isabela, he then turned his attention to the project nearest his heart.

IV

That project was the search for gold. He had already sent Alonso de Hojeda with a party into the interior to a region called Cibao where Indians had told him that the main source of gold could be found. Hojeda had returned with a very optimistic report. The following words occur in Dr Chanca's account, and it is rather important to know that he wrote in this vein just on the strength of Hojeda's report.

The captain who went to Cibao found gold in so many places that no one dared to guess the number. Indeed, they found it in more than fifty streams and rivers, and on dry land also. He says that wherever you look, anywhere in this province, you will find gold. He brought samples from many parts from the sand of rivers and from springs on land. It is believed that, if we dig as we know how, it will be found in larger pieces, for the Indians cannot mine, since they have nothing with which to dig more than eight inches deep. . . . Our Sovereigns therefore can certainly consider themselves henceforth the richest and most prosperous on earth, for nothing comparable has ever been seen or read of till now in the whole world. On the next voyage which the ships make they will be able to carry away such quantities of gold that anyone who hears of it will be amazed.

It was not surprising that Columbus was excited about this. If it were really true that such quantities of gold could be found, and pocketed, then all his troubles would be over, the whole situation would be changed. He decided to lead an impressive expedition to Cibao and be present himself at the places where gold was discovered. It was a very critical moment in his career. 'When the column of horse and foot (500 strong according to de Cuneo, for every available man had been rounded up) marched out in battle array, with banners flying and trumpets blowing,' writes G. R. Crone, 'it was more than a brave show to impress the natives. To Columbus it was the prelude to a long-delayed triumph which would vindicate his reputation and secure his future, and he had staked much upon it.'* This was in March 1494.

It was a joy to be on the move out of Isabela and everyone

* *The Discovery of America*, G. R. Crone, Hamish Hamilton, 1969.

was in great expectation, while the beauty of the surroundings raised their spirits more. Having made their way over a mountain pass they set eyes on a valley which according to Las Casas was 'so fresh, so green, so clean, so colourful, so full of beauty, that they thought they had arrived in some region of paradise, bathed and steeped in a deep and incomparable joy'. The expedition passed through many Indian villages with round straw-thatched huts. Fernando says,

> On entering these houses, the Indians whom the Admiral had brought from Isabela promptly took anything that pleased them and the owners showed no sign of resentment. They seemed to hold all possessions in common. Similarly, whenever any of the natives went up to a Christian, they took from him whatever they liked in the belief that similar customs obtained among us. But they were quickly undeceived when they saw that this was not the case.

So Columbus pursued his way inland to Cibao, the 'Stonyland'—for Ciba means stone in the native language. When they got there did they find gold? They found bits and pieces: enough to nourish their dreams and to falsify their claims. They found some: but what they needed was an enormous amount. Then Columbus would be free, then all things would be delivered into his hands, every failure would be seen as success and every folly turned into wisdom. But never! Never was this to be! It would always be round the corner, over the hill, a little further on, not now, not here, not yet!

Nevertheless Columbus was pleased, or professed to be pleased, with the immediate gains in Cibao. He even caused a fortress to be built there as a settlement, and called it Santo Tomas, as a rebuke to those who had doubted his promises of gold. He decided to leave a garrison of fifty men there under the command of Pedro Margarite, a Spanish nobleman. His instructions as to the treatment of the inhabitants are interesting. Margarite was to be good to the natives; he was to be extremely kind; but if any of them stole anything, then they must be chastised—by cutting off their ears and noses. As such a punishment makes 'a strong impression for all to see, the inhabitants of this island will know that the wicked are punished whereas the righteous are well-treated.' No offence was so rank as when a native attempted to help himself to a bit of his own country, such as a nugget of gold.

Having built Santo Tomas and put Pedro Margarite in command, and having half-satisfied himself that his expectations of gold were justified, and that more was to come from the 'mines' in the region, Columbus returned to Isabela. By this time Dr Chanca had sailed for Spain with his optimistic expectations of boundless wealth. The Admiral despatched with him a famous letter to their Majesties which amounted to an elaborate report on progress, assurances of much gold to follow the samples he is able to send, excuses regarding the present discontents in the colony, and a long list of requirements to be sent out to Hispaniola, including cattle and sheep, donkeys and mares, sugar, raisins, rice, almonds, and honey; also quantities of cloth and leather for clothes and shoes; added to which he would appreciate it if a hundred more firearms and crossbows could be sent, together with two hundred cuirasses, and plenty of powder and lead.

Having started infirmly at the outset, Columbus was now in no position to make himself felt as the Viceroy. 'It was inevitable that in the face of so many problems the Admiral should alienate everyone,' says Las Casas. 'To this was added the fact that he was a foreigner and held no fiefs in Castile; he was thus held in little esteem by the Spaniards, especially the highborn, for they have an overweening pride.' It was nothing to them that he was the greatest discoverer and seaman of the age, their birth was more meritorious.

One of the ways of being weak is to be strong at the wrong moment; having too often been too lenient to become too severe. Columbus tended now to become sporadically violent inadvisedly. Thus, suspecting that his chief accountant, Bernal de Pisa, was plotting against him, he threw him into prison and threatened his assistants with death. As he couldn't really follow this up, diplomacy would have probably worked better. Again, 'The Admiral,' says Oviedo, 'had several men hanged and had others whipped, and began to be more severe and more rigorous than he was wont to be. The Admiral was accused of being cruel, in the opinion of Friar Buil who, deputing as he was for the Pope, intervened.' He laid him under an interdict and caused divine offices to be stopped in relation to the Admiral. Thereupon the latter caused the friar's food rations, together with those of his household, to be withheld. The element of comedy in this was not lessened by the fact that Friar Buil had previously been so pained at the leniency of Columbus over Guacanagari.

It was never predictable now whether he would be too lenient or too severe. Shortly after his return to Isabela he sent Hojeda out to Santo Tomas to relieve Pedro Margarite who had expressed distaste for his position there. An interesting incident occurred. A certain chief had offered the assistance of five Indians to carry the clothing of three Spaniards across a river. 'When the Christians were half-way across,' says Fernando, 'these Indians had run off to his village with their clothes and the cacique instead of punishing their crime had taken the clothing for himself and refused to return it.' Now, this was a great indignity to the Christians who did really feel naked without their clothes, indeed lacking identity. The cacique had not realized the fury he would create by taking the garments, and he was soon to pay for the offence. Hojeda caught up with him and cut off one of his ears in the centre of his village, and then sent him with a brother and a nephew in chains to Isabela.

The cacique who ruled on the other side of the river, [says Fernando] relying on the services he had rendered to the Christians, decided to accompany the prisoners to Isabela and intercede for them with the Admiral. The Admiral received him politely and ordered that the Indians with their hands tied should be sentenced to death by public proclamation. The good cacique wept at the sight and their lives were granted him, the guilty Indians promising by signs that they would never commit another crime.*

V

Though the Admiral had insisted upon being appointed Viceroy, he much preferred to delegate authority and be on the move himself. Luckily the Sovereigns had instructed him to make sure that he had reached the mainland of Asia. This provided a good excuse to escape from his responsibilities at Isabela. Indeed, it was high time that he called on the Grand Khan.

* That is the story as told by Fernando. But Salvador de Madariaga ignores his account and in reference to the same incident says, 'The Viceroy suddenly turned ruthless and had three prisoners beheaded in the centre of the square'. He gives this as an example of 'the impulsive outlet of energy on the part of a man who was not a complete master of his own mind and will'. I try to avoid footnotes; but I include this as a single example of the kind of discrepancy regarding fact (and chronology also) which one finds so much in Columbian biography.

He delegated his brother Diego* to act in his place. This brother is described by Las Casas as 'a virtuous person, sober, peaceful, of simple and friendly disposition rather than cautious or evil-minded, who dressed very quietly, indeed almost in clerical outfit, and I do believe that he wished to be a bishop'. One can scarcely imagine a man, with such a list of negative virtues, less fitted to deal with the conflicting interests at Isabela and the intrigues against his brother. But he was the only person that Columbus could trust.

So, on April 24th, 1494, in company with two other ships, he set out from Hispaniola in the *Nina*. Passing the eastern extremity of Cuba he decided to seek the island of Yamaye—Jamaica—because there had been reports that it was rich in gold. They met with a rough reception by the Jamaicans and it was necessary to resist them so emphatically that some of the natives were killed—after which the others instantly became amiable and obsequious. Columbus found no gold, but he said, and it was characteristic of him to say it in spite of his disappointment, 'It is the fairest isle that human eyes have ever beheld'.

Departing from Jamaica, the Admiral returned to Cabo de Cruz and began to sail along the south coast of Cuba, wondering what he would find. To us the thought of this is delightful. Not to know where one is: to be finding islands never known before to any European: a new experience of beauty or alarm at every step—to us this would be an ultimate in adventure. It was not so for Columbus. He desperately wanted to know where he was and to come upon his ever-elusive Chipangu. This journey took five months—four months longer than his voyage from the Canaries to San Salvador. It was a period of exceptional mental and physical trial for him. The danger of running on a coral reef or sandy shoals made navigation a nightmare. For thirty-two consecutive nights and days he had no sleep! Rather than making him sleepy this had the effect of putting him into a state of mystified excitement bordering upon hallucination. Mandeville had told of five thousand islands in the Indian Sea. Now surely he was amongst them, and counting a string of one hundred and four he bestowed upon them the name of 'The Queen's Garden'.

* We have four Diegos to contend with: this Diego, the brother; Diego the son, at this time a page at court; Diego the Indian interpreter of the Admiral; and Diego de Arana, related to his wife, whom he left in charge of the garrison at La Navidad.

The days and nights of sleepless watch did not yet wear him down so much as buoy him up in spirit. He became increasingly elated at what he heard, at what he saw, at what he imagined. He was told that a place called Mangon lay just ahead (on the coast of Cuba). At last he was getting closer to the realization of his dreams and prophecies, for this was Marco Polo's 'Mangi', the name he gave to South China. On an island, by some trick of light conjured by the visiting moon, he beheld three figures clad in white. These were emissaries of the Khan, or prelates of Prester John. The *Nina* suddenly entered waters white as milk. Had not Polo told of a mariner who had sailed through a midnight sea of milky whiteness, spectral and appalling?

The crew looked on with amazement at their Admiral. What was he doing, where was he taking them? Victim of mirage and illusion, enslaved by prophecy and fantasy and dream, he had left reality behind. Having now made sure that Cuba was the mainland of Asia, he decided to return to Spain with these very ships by sailing straight on. This is a fact. It is supported both by his son Fernando and by Bernaldez. Imagining that India was adjacent to Cathay, he intended to return to Spain by way of the Ganges and the Arabic Peninsula, and from there over-land to Jerusalem and Jaffa, when he would again have to put to sea. That was his plan, most solemnly contemplated, and apparently without a thought given to the problem of abandoning his ships at a given place, and subsequently acquiring fresh ones to finish his journey!

However, reality broke into his dreams. He was unable to go much further along the coast. The caravels were beginning to leak in consequence of frequent groundings, the riggings were badly torn, the provisions running out, and the crews getting thoroughly restive. They had gone over three hundred miles and reached the Gulf of Batabano. They went no further. They were less than a hundred miles from Cuba's turning point at Cape Antonio—which is about a hundred miles from Yucatan. It is sad to think that Columbus never discovered America, never the mainland of America; only a tiny island at first, more than four hundred miles from Florida. It is sad to think that now, having once more come all the way from Spain, he failed to go the few more miles that would have reached the fabulous splendours of Mexico. Then he could have done without his Khan and his Cathay. His triumph as discoverer would have been complete and his critics silenced. It was not to be. He had the power to get as far as San Salvador and Batabano—and then he was spent, like a wave with no more force behind it.

Before turning back on June 13th, 1494, Columbus made another of his historic stage effects. Here they were at Cuba. He had decided that it was the mainland of Asia. And having decided this, it must be so. It did not matter to Don Quixote whether Dulcinea had a face like a pig, she was the most beautiful woman in the world since he said so. It did not matter that yonder house was an ordinary inn, it was a gorgeous palace since he conceived it so, just as Peer Gynt would applaud the obscene antics of the Trolls as exquisite dancing and their discordant din as divine music. For Don Christopher Columbus the island of Cuba was the mainland of Asia, and remained such till the hour of his death. And all those around him now must share his belief, and connive at his illusion. Everyone on board the three ships was required to bear witness to this belief. Fernando Perez de Luna, acting notary of the fleet, was instructed by the Admiral to ask, one by one, all the pilots, masters, and seamen to express their opinion and say whether they, like himself, were convinced that they had found the Asian coast. The notary carried this out and questioned all the people involved, and furthermore told them that if anyone should later deny what he now said he would be fined 10,000 *maravedis* and have his tongue cut out, and 'were he a ship's boy or such-like inferior person he would receive a hundred lashes and have his tongue cut out as well'.

Columbus had no difficulty in getting them to agree. They were all very weary and dispirited and so alarmed at the likelihood of this voyage ending in catastrophe, that they were ready to sign anything if it would hasten their return. But no doubt most of them genuinely agreed with the Admiral. Even today, when we go from Montego Bay to the Windward Passage leading out into the Atlantic, with Haiti to the east and Cuba to the west, the outline of Cuba from Cape Cruz to Cape Maisi seems endless and gives no impression at all of being only an island.

The journey back was just as exhausting, for again they had to find their way through the islands and cays because they could not go far from shore in deep water on account of strong winds consistently against them. Sometimes Columbus sought rest on the shore of an island, and from Bernaldez we occasionally get a vignette of interest and charm. One day the Admiral decided to have Mass celebrated on some such island. When the cacique of the region saw him come on shore he came forward with an old man of eighty, and approaching the tall, impressive, and apparently benign figure of the Admiral, took him by the hand; each of them in fact held one hand and thus went with him, escorted by a great crowd of Indians, to a place made ready for the service. After the Admiral had prayed and risen to his feet, the old Indian—in the manner of many 'primitive' men who do not see themselves as in the least primitive, and are ready to preach a sermon to anyone—addressed him, exhorting him not to be lifted up in pride, for like all other men he too was mortal and after death his soul would either ascend to heaven or descend to hell, according to his deeds.

By means of his gestures and with the help of his marvellous interpreter, Diego, Columbus understood the drift and was pleased with it. He answered through Diego that he had come to do no harm to the righteous, following the express wish of his rulers, the King and Queen of Castile. The old man was astonished. 'You obey another ruler?' he asked through Diego. 'Yes,' said Diego, 'he obeys the King and Queen of Castile who are the greatest Sovereigns in the world.' Then Diego told of the marvels he had seen in Spain, the wonderful houses, the great cities, the fiestas, the tourneys, the bullfights, the horses. 'Take me there!' pleaded the chief, though now restrained by his wife and son who protested weeping.

In Jamaica Columbus met with the same pathetic illusion that happiness could be found in Spain just as the Spaniards sought El Dorado in the East. He decided to pay Jamaica another visit on his way back, and this time sailed along the south coast where the natives were found to be very friendly. When the Spaniards were about to leave, a chief came out to the Admiral in a canoe, and in joyful accents addressed him thus:

Friend, I am determined to quit my country and go with you to your rulers who are the greatest Sovereigns in the world, because it is at their command that you march through our lands, bringing them beneath your yoke, as I have learned from your Indians, and because even the great Carib tribe fears you since you destroyed their canoes and took their sons prisoner. For this reason, before you take my lands and domains from me, I wish to board your ships, taking my retinue with me, so that I may go and look upon the great King and the great Queen and see the marvels of Castile, which your Indian tells me are beyond number.

He had learnt about Spain from Diego, whose mental ability and interest in what he saw had doubtless contributed to his physical staying-power, denied his less gifted companions who died in misery. It added greatly to the prestige of Columbus to have as his aide this Diego who conjured up before the minds of his countrymen the marvels of the land whence the Admiral had come. Now, when the chieftain in Jamaica made this request, Bernaldez says,

> The Admiral took pity on him, his daughters, his sons, his wife. He answered him saying that he would receive him as a vassal of the King and Queen of Spain, but that he could not take him along at this time; that he would satisfy his desire another time. They took their leave of each other as do good friends.

There is something touching about both these incidents, and they ring true in the telling. A ray of light plays upon the doleful countenance of this strange knight. Now and again a certain sweetness of behaviour surprises us. He is not predictable, not always consistent—even supposing that anyone ever possesses a character that is always characteristic.

Happy interludes perhaps for a few brief moments. But the whole thing had been a terrible strain upon him. The constant navigational hazards, the tension caused by the failure to find gold in any abundance, and by the everlasting elusiveness of Cathay, wore him down till finally his health gave way, and by the time he reached Isabela he became terribly ill. 'He was seized by a pestilential torpor,' says Las Casas. 'He suddenly lost all his strength, and it was thought that he would not live through another day.' It took him nearly five months to recover.

VI

Having been absent from Isabela for five months and ill for another five, the Viceroy had practically abdicated for ten months, and was in no position to improve his authority. However, during his absence, his brother, Bartholomew, had arrived. He had failed to relinquish certain assignments in France in time to join Columbus on either his first or second voyage, but now accompanying de Torres who was returning, he hastened out to assist him. And he was of great assistance, for he was strong in the very qualities in which his eldest brother was particularly weak. He possessed great executive capacity, the power to make quick decisions, and a ruthless determination to carry them out. He was now appointed 'adelantado', and remained his brother's chief executive, while poor Diego fades into the background.

Bartholomew was not liked by the Spaniards, for here was another case of nepotism; once again a 'foreigner', a Genoese, was put in authority over them. Yet if anyone was capable of saving the colony perhaps he was. But could it be saved? It was raised on hopeless foundations. If there is to be a *modus vivendi* with the people of a country you usurp, there must be a certain amount of giving and taking on both sides. But the Spaniards had nothing to give, and they had nothing to take except the land which they failed to develop. There was no gold to speak of. There were no 'spices', a term which covered many things coveted by Europeans. There could be no 'trading centre' set up, for you cannot trade with people who wear no clothes, and do not want anything. Nor could it be simply a question of lotus-eating, for there was nothing to eat. The Spaniards were terribly hungry, devouring, we must remember, in one meal what would last the natives a week, and at the same time failing to cultivate either the soil or the sea.

The food situation was eased to some extent by provisions sent over from Spain in a succession of shiploads. The Sovereigns still took a sympathetic view of the Admiral's efforts. This was chiefly because of the emphatic promises of a vast amount of gold to follow, as stated in his letter, and strongly supported by Dr Chanca. The King and Queen had still absolutely no idea that this was all moonshine; and that far from Columbus supplying them with wealth from the Indies, they would have to pay heavy sums for the upkeep of the settlement. Before this dawned on them, they made gracious and amiable comments in the margin of his document (or letter) which had been handed to them by Antonio de Torres. Thus: 'Their Highnesses give much thanks to God, and hold as very honoured service all the Admiral has done', 'He has done well', and so on. But they were surprised by one suggestion clearly made in the document, and they wrote in the margin: 'As regards this matter, it is suspended for the present'.

That suggestion was that an arrangement should be made for the regular sending of slaves across to Spain, not only of the cannibals who would be taught a more Christian way of life, but others also, harmless Arawaks taken as prisoner in conflict. The more of them that could be taken the better, he asserts, for considering what quantities of livestock and other things are required for the maintenance of the colony, a certain number of caravels should be sent each year with these necessary things, and the cargoes be paid for in slaves. He touches upon how good this will be for the slaves themselves, rather in the manner in which our modern apologists for blood sports insist upon how excellent this is for the animals themselves, and how we should appreciate that they are really being preserved by virtue of being killed.

This project for the establishment of a slave-trade, so distinctly put forward, did not appeal to the Sovereigns, especially the Queen. Thus it is not even true to say the idea of slavery was taken for granted at that time, for not only were the Sovereigns against it, but Las Casas, an admirer of Columbus, was bitterly opposed to it.

But the Admiral was too obtuse to sense the feelings of the Queen, and this disfavour for his scheme did not deter him from shipping off to Spain, after a pitched battle in the Vega Real when the victory fell to the Spaniards, in the spring of 1494, five hundred slaves to be sold. Thus the policy of shipping slaves across the ocean was initiated until it reached a climax in succeeding centuries when two million African slaves died on the way to America. These five hundred Indians were exposed for sale by auction at Seville. The change of life, the harsh treatment, the overwork, so affected them that they all soon died. Yet ship after ship during the succeeding years was sent back to Spain crammed with these human goods—a futile enough policy even from a commercial point of view, since all these poor creatures torn from their homes and natural surroundings came to the same end as the first consignment. When Columbus discovered Hispaniola it had a population of three million. Ten years later it was not one hundredth part of this. In the end all the indigenous population of the West Indies had been exterminated.

There might have been some point in this if the founder of the religion which Columbus so devoutly favoured had been tyrannical and responsible for a policy of cruelty and greed. But there is little evidence that Jesus was a cruel man. The assertions of his followers may suggest the opposite. Few of his supporters would have claimed that if he had been in the place of Columbus he would have been unkind to the Arawaks or wished to exterminate them.

It is said that what the natives found so terrible about the Christians was not their violence or their greed, but their coldness, their lack of love. They could see a man torn from his girl and put on a slave ship, without any feeling of compassion. How apt, in such a context, is the cry of Lispeth:

> Look, you have cast out Love! What Gods are these
> You bid me please?
> The Three in One, the One in Three? Not so!
> To my own gods I go.
> It may be they shall give me greater ease
> Than your cold Christ and tangled Trinities.*

In no journal, in no letter, has Columbus left any hint as to what he thought and felt, or if he suffered and grieved over this outcome of his policies. His heart is hidden from us for the most part, even if sometimes it appears at an unexpected time, or gleams fitfully in a strange place. He was truly interested in the religion of the natives. At first he thought they had no religion, then he realized that his first impression had been superficial, and he instructed a monk called Ramon Pane to learn their language and record their rites and antiquities. He was very interested in the report which Ramon Pane drew up. But one day he had a shock. Among the 'antiquities' he came upon the prophecy: 'There will come men wearing clothes, who will dominate us and kill us'. The monk then adds, 'They had originally thought that this oracular revelation concerned the cannibals. They now think that it means the Admiral and his company.'

One wonders what Columbus thought when he came upon this. He was probably bewildered, for just as he never knew where he was, he never truly knew what he was doing. But since a man should know what he is doing, we ponder upon how much sense there really is in the exhortation 'Forgive them, for they know not what they do'. Alistair Cooke (the incomparable) draws attention to the story of a native Indian king who was about to be burned at the stake, and how as he felt the fires rise on his body, refused baptism on the grounds that he might then go to heaven, 'and meet there only Christians'. If Columbus had heard this story he would certainly have been unable to

* Verse heading to *Lispeth* in *Plain Tales from the Hills*, Rudyard Kipling, Macmillan, 1965.

brush it aside, since for him baptism was tremendously
important. He would have been pained, and perhaps
bewildered.

VII

By the spring of 1495 the Spaniards saw that they could not
hope to make a settlement and settle down in concord with the
natives—whom they had insulted and robbed too much. If a
second La Navidad was to be avoided they must master them
completely. The Indians having passed from terror to despair
attempted to overcome the intruders by force of numbers,
hoping to achieve victory by ambushes and assassination. But
their numbers were no avail against the superior arms of the
Spaniards—a naked stomach, as someone brutally put it, made
a poor shield against a Spanish bullet. Indeed, on one occasion
(March 24th, 1495) during a campaign which lasted for ten
months, a force of two hundred from the garrison put to flight
an army of natives estimated by Las Casas at one hundred
thousand.

The fire from muskets, however primitive, is sufficient to
overcome hosts of naked men. The Christians also used another
weapon—savage bloodhounds. As soon as a company of Indians
took to flight the bloodhounds (imported from Spain) leapt with
fury upon the backs of the flying natives, pulled them down and
tore them to pieces. This was a greater terror to the Indians than
anything else and in consequence was regarded by the Christians
as their most effective weapon. One of these hounds, noted in
Spain for its ferocious capacities, was sent out as a special treat
for the Spaniards, a dog called Bercerrico, which won a high
reputation for its outstanding skill in tracking down the Indians
and tearing out their guts.

There was one chieftain whom the Spaniards were particularly anxious to dispose of, and if possible capture alive in
order to make an example of him. This was Caonabo, the warrior
who had routed the garrison at La Navidad, and who was still
the most powerful chief in the land. He was a man of resource
and gave a striking example of this when Pedro Margarite was
at Fort Santo Tomas. The natives in the district were treated
with particular savagery by the Christians; they were robbed of
their ornaments and their food, and their women were assaulted.
But there was still a tendency among the natives to regard
these men as possessing supernatural powers, men who had

come down from the sky, and were not subject to death—for many of the inhabitants of this central region had not grasped the significance of La Navidad.

Caonabo decided to prove to them that their foes were as mortal as themselves. As we have seen, the Spaniards were accustomed to be carried across rivers by Indians. One day, when the river between the plain and Fort Tomas was much swollen after heavy rains, a Spanish nobleman waited to be carried across. Caonabo ordered the bearers to test the heavenly status of the man by attempting to drown him. When they reached the middle of the river they let him slip from their shoulders and fall in, and then held him under water until he ceased to struggle. After he had been carried to the bank the local population sat round the corpse and waited to see if he would come to life again. After three days the decay of the corpse at last persuaded them that the Christians had not come from heaven and that the departed spirit had gone to the other place.

Columbus had already expressed his view as to the best method of capturing Caonabo. He possessed some extra shirts in reserve which might come in useful. This was his idea:

Caonabo must be induced to pay you a visit. As he goes naked, it may be difficult to lay hold of him, and if he once slips away it will be hard to apprehend him. You must therefore offer him a shirt and a cloak, a girdle to put round it, and a cap to wear, and thus you may easily seize him. If he will not come to see you, then you must so arrange that you go to him. One of your men must be sent to say that you wish to see him and come to a friendly understanding with him.

Actually, Hojeda went one better than this when an opportunity arose. Instead of shirts, why not some attractive bracelets? Hojeda possessed some manacles, satirically called by the Spanish *esposas* (wives), most finely wrought in polished steel. This metal dazzled the Indians just as gold dazzled the Spaniards. Thus when Hojeda showed these bracelets (or hand-cuffs) to Caonabo and told him that they were a present from the Admiral, and that he would show him how to put them on, the incautious chief fell into the trap and was captured.

There is some sense in comparing Columbus with Don Quixote. But the comparison cannot be consistently sustained. Often it won't wash: at least we cannot whitewash him in this way. The Don believed in the ideal of chivalry above all else. In his nature there was no meanness as also no cruelty. Columbus's plan to ensnare Caonabo was as thoroughly base and treacherous as can be imagined. When the Admiral, gazing towards a West Indian island, cried out 'Behold Chipangu!' it was in the best tradition of Quixotic self-deception; but there were times when he achieved a macabre humour in the perversion of reality foreign to the mentality of the Don. Three hundred and forty gallows were erected by the carpenters in the Vega Real for the benefit of rebellious natives. When someone drew the attention of the Admiral to these things, and inquired about the need for such excess of execution, he showed surprise. 'They are not gallows,' he replied. 'They are crosses. I have instructed crosses to be erected on all roads, for as (God be praised) this land belongs to Christians, and the remembrance of it must be preserved for all time.'

VIII

The main fighting was over and the Indians subdued by 1495. But still the problem remained: what was the justification for the enormous expenses of the colony, the salaries to pay, the provisions that were required to be sent out from Spain? It is a significant fact that at about this time a proposal was made to the Admiral by the cacique of the Vega Real, Guarionex, to the effect that he was prepared to institute a huge farm for the growth of corn and the production of bread, stretching across the whole island, which would suffice to feed all the Spaniards and more. This was an idea which should have appealed to the colonists who sometimes were so hungry that they were reduced to eating lizards and snakes. But nothing was done about this. Bartholomew had been strong and ruthless in 'putting down' the natives, but the putting up of agriculture was beyond him; while Columbus was still fatally attracted by the search for gold. The delusion that he could find it still ruled his mind and was to enchant him for years to come until his life lay in ruins. He now thought that he had found a gold-mine in Cibao: a mine! Peter Martyr actually wrote in his *Second Decade*, 'They found there shafts that had been dug long before. The Admiral thought that he had found in these mines the ancient treasures of King Solomon. It is not my task to decide whether this be true or false.' These imaginary 'shafts' would presuppose the existence of a previous race dwelling there capable of that kind

of technology—of which there was not the slightest trace. That
did not worry Columbus, and to the end of his life he spoke of
how he had found King Solomon's mines—though he had not
extracted from them a single treasure.

Meanwhile gold must be obtained somehow. He now imposed
a tribute upon the whole population of the island. In plain
words, he taxed the inhabitants of Hispaniola for living in
Hispaniola. When they had surrendered the bits and pieces of
gold which they possessed by way of decoration, there was no
more left and they were compelled to wash grains of gold out
of the gravel of streams. This labour was more than they could
bear, and they fled into the mountains. The tax—'irrational,
abominable, and intolerable' as Las Casas puts it—was a
failure. Even when drastically reduced it was still a failure, for
the Indians refused to co-operate in this senseless pursuit, and
tried to starve the Spaniards out of their country. This only led
finally to their extermination.

Meanwhile Columbus became increasingly alive to the
necessity of returning home so that he might report to the
Sovereigns in person. Pedro Margarite and Father Buil (among
others) had already returned to Spain, full of grievances against
the Viceroy whose shortcomings they would doubtless emphasize to the King and Queen, thus undermining the effect of his
own letter and the support of Dr Chanca. They would be sure
to mention the current form which an oath took in the Indies:
'I'm telling the truth, as God may carry me back to Castile!'
Practically everyone wanted to escape from this 'paradise'—
described now by the Admiral himself as 'hell'—as soon as
possible and get back to Spain.

And indeed their reports were so effective that the Sovereigns
became anxious and despatched to Hispaniola a nobleman
called Aguado to look into the problems. He arrived with a
curious document which read:

Cavaliers, Esquires and other persons, who by our command are
in the Indies: we send you thither Juan Aguado, our Gentleman
of the Chamber, who will speak to you on our part: we command
that you give him faith and credence.
   I the King: I the Queen.
Madrid, April 9th, 1495.

It was very humiliating for the Admiral to receive a communication couched in such terms—not one word addressed to

himself personally, his position as Viceroy completely ignored. It throws some light upon the terms used by Pedro Margarite and Father Buil in their report, that Columbus should have received so insulting a missive.

Naturally he was anxious to get back to Spain as soon as possible to give his own account of things. But a hurricane wrecked the ships in which he should have sailed, and it was nearly a year before he could get away. It was not till March 6th, 1496, that he embarked. There were so many volunteers hoping to return on the two ships that they were overcrowded—which makes it the more surprising that Columbus included thirty captive Caribs, among whom was Caonabo, who at last, wasted and miserable, his pride broken down and with no more will to live, died during the voyage.

They returned via the Leeward Islands, first calling at Guadeloupe to see if they could find a rumoured tribe of wild women. They did come upon a group of formidable Amazons; and a seaman was rash enough to pursue one superb naked beauty who 'ran like a deer' according to Las Casas, but when she saw that he was overtaking her, 'she turned on him like a mad dog and embracing him, felled him to the ground, and if other Christians had not come to his rescue she would have strangled him'. After this diversion, having collected more water and provisions, they made for open sea. It was a wretched journey. Columbus failed to locate the right winds and was obliged to beat his way to windward at a terribly slow pace. The length of the time for this voyage had been disastrously under-estimated and the crew became so hungry that the Admiral had some difficulty in preventing them from eating the thirty Caribs—the Christians claiming that the Caribs themselves would appreciate this as the proper thing to do. It took them three months to reach Cadiz on June 11th, 1496.

CHAPTER EIGHT

Trials in Spain

I

THE ADMIRAL was not immediately summoned to Court. He was kept hanging round for over a month. This was humiliating, but it did not bother him overmuch, for he had already clothed himself in the garments of humility. Quite literally so. He claimed to belong, as a simple lay friar, to the Third Order of St Francis—for which no particular garb was obligatory. But now he began to adopt the penitential garment of hair-cloth with the rough surface against the body, and he let his beard grow like a Franciscan. Hardship, sickness, prolonged vigilance through sleepless nights, unrewarded patience, ceaseless anxiety, unmerited misfortunes had exhausted his frame, and those who knew him were now shocked at his emaciated condition, and disquieted by the dark glow in his eyes.

But why the long brown robe drawn together by a cord, so incongruous with the Grand Admiral of the Ocean Sea? It was the very incongruity which appealed to him. An incurable lust for importance and possessions, a passionate greed for gold, ruled his mind, while at the same time a profound piety informed his spirit. How adorable the ideal of St Francis! What unspeakable relief to embrace the vow of poverty and be redeemed from the longing for power! Then, and only then, could one be invulnerable. To humble oneself, to endure insults and persecution without reproach—that would be true armour against the world's harms. It would be 'the joy that is perfect'. He was drawn to St Francis's philosophy of suffering as the way to freedom, and he responded to the fable of the poor ragged men refused succour by the doorkeeper—

If then we do not feel offence at the Doorkeeper but think with humility and love that he is right, that God must have directed him to act towards us as he did; and we stay, wet, cold, and hungry, in the snow and water until the morning, without a murmur against the Doorkeeper, then, Brother Leo, and only then, will our joy be perfect.

It was not just an ostentatious show of humility, as some have thought, that made Columbus adopt what must have appeared a ludicrous garb for a great sea-captain and discoverer, but a profound desire to place himself beyond humiliation. He had known what it was like to be rejected by doorkeepers. He would place himself on a plane beyond their power ever to harm him more.

Yet when word at last came from the Sovereigns summoning him to Court, he decided upon a second triumphant entry! His failure to foresee that this was bound to be an anticlimax is almost unbelievable: but there it is; history records that he prepared for a second acclaim in the streets, a splendid procession with a display of gold ornaments, popinjays, and all the rest of it—though his Franciscan garb was wholly out of place in such a parade. He need not have bothered. No crowds greeted him. The streets were silent. The fact is that in so far as anyone knew about his return at all, it was known from members of the crew, from what they had said and were rumoured to have said; and from what they looked like, 'faces the colour of saffron', worn out by fever they looked like ghosts, ragged beggars slinking through the alley-ways of Seville and Cadiz, their dreams turned into nightmares.

Nevertheless Columbus was received at Court with surprising cordiality. Aguado was not a spiteful man and did not outline many valid reasons for censure. By the time he had arrived in Hispaniola the worst excesses were over, a certain stability on the surface had been established, and many of the chief Spanish malcontents had returned home. Also it was probably clear to the Sovereigns by this time that to be a successful governor of this first 'settlement' was a task which very few men would be capable of handling. Columbus put his case before them with all his customary ability, and they listened sympathetically in spite of his detractors 'who maligned this enterprise',* and he was to remember this for ever with an almost pathetic gratitude.

True, the Admiral had not much to show as a result of the

* 'Your Highnesses replied by smiling and telling me that I need not worry because they did not believe any of those who maligned this enterprise.' *Narrative of the Third Voyage*, Christopher Columbus.

seventeen-ship expedition which had sailed from Cadiz in 1493 with enormous expectation. There was no Cathay—though it was round the corner. There was no Grand Khan—though Columbus still hoped to call on him in the near future. There was no trading post, for there was nothing to trade—except slaves. There were no converts to Christianity, for the natives had shown themselves singularly obtuse to its advantages. But there was gold? Oh yes, there was gold, Columbus always insisted, again drawing attention to a few nuggets and precious stones which he could exhibit as a promise of things to come. And at this point a fortunate confirmation of his assertions was forthcoming from an unexpected quarter. A certain Pero Alonso Nino, one of the Admiral's captains, announced his arrival in Cadiz with a quantity of gold 'in bars' on board his ship. This news was received with great enthusiasm by everyone, while of course the relief of Columbus was unbounded. But then it appeared that Pero Nino was merely having his fun. The gold 'in bars' was only represented by the Indian slaves who composed his cargo, whose present captivity was secured by bars, and whose future sale was to furnish gold. The mortification of this, the ridicule it exposed him to, and the criticism inherent in the deplorable joke, must have struck deep into the heart of Columbus.

The incident seems well authenticated, there is no reason to suppose that it is an invention. It is certainly strange. It argues a truly extraordinary lack of respect as between subordinate and Admiral; and since it appears that he received no punishment, it argues an even more extraordinary lack of authority on the part of Columbus who must have wished—as who would not?—to destroy him utterly. It is not known why the captain played this trick. Did he do it because of some overpowering private grudge or from some high motive of moral outrage? Idle questions now; but the thing is very puzzling, very sad, and also notable in the justice of the vast rebuke.

If we are inclined to focus upon this incident, the extent to which the King and Queen focused upon it, or even knew much about it, is another matter. They had so many things to think about, there were all the affairs of state apart from the Admiral's 'affair of the Indies'; and apart from the political crises ever at play for any monarchs at any time, they were busy strengthening the royal house by the marriages of two of their daughters making an alliance with the House of Burgundy. But they did not lose sight of the main fact in front of them regarding Hispaniola. It was plain that the 'colony' could not now be abandoned. The Portuguese continued to cast a shadow which threatened the overseas activities of the Spanish; while Henry VII of England, excited by Cabot's voyages, was said to be planning a Columbian voyage of his own. Any day now they might hear news of a Portuguese arrival at India via the Cape of Good Hope; and as yet no one in Europe really knew where India was in relation to Cathay—they still thought it was next door.

The reason Ferdinand and Isabela continued to support Columbus in spite of the complaints made against him was chiefly because they had no geography. Their Admiral was a marvellous man who said he could find places, and in the teeth of all scepticism he did find them. They had no idea what constituted the Indies, and when he came before them then, so convincing in his convictions, and assured them that he had found the mainland of Asia together with seven hundred islands along the coast (for he counted every cay as an island), they had no grounds for disbelieving him. He told them that if they sponsored another expedition and he investigated a more southerly latitude, he would find more lands, and that every portent suggested more gold in the equatorial regions.

There was another consideration, of no small importance, especially to the Queen. This was the religious aspect. The Catholic motif in this affair was of the utmost moment. There was just one path to salvation: belief in Jesus Christ. More important than the appropriation of territory or the acquisition of gold, was the bringing of the knowledge of Christ to all mankind. This was also the opinion of Las Casas. But in his view slavery was totally inadmissible, and colonization inadmissible unless it meant salvation of souls through knowledge of Jesus Christ. And where did Columbus stand in this matter? We know, and Las Casas knew, only too well, that he had no objection to slavery and in fact urged it in lieu of gold when the necessity arose. But he contrived to feel that he was really doing them a good turn if at the same time he brought the Gospel to them. We can hardly apply the charge of hypocrisy to him since he was as completely sincere in his Christian devotions as he was completely blind to his unchristian activities. But he certainly could be shrewd, and when he spoke to the Queen now asking for a third voyage he was careful to stress the religious aspect of the enterprise and once again give voice to his long-cherished dream of first converting the natives of the East to

Christianity and then, with the help of the discovered gold, to wrest Jerusalem from the infidels.

The Queen listened, and when a third voyage was sponsored a clause in the instructions emphatically stated: 'You will take to the Indies a number of monks and ecclesiastics who are men of virtue, in order that they may administer the Sacraments and attempt to convert the Indians to our Holy Faith'. Simple words, and sober. But the Sovereigns, weak on geography, were still more in the dark as to what was really happening to the inhabitants of Hispaniola. They had not the least idea of the forces they had set in motion. Nor had Columbus. A simple soul, he had never expected things to become so complicated and disagreeably violent. He often loved the natives in a simple human way quite foreign to the character of a Hojeda or a Margarite, of a Bobadilla or an Ovando or a Roldan, or of any of the hidalgos, just as his love of wild nature was three hundred years in advance of the times.

Yet in another mood, in another context, he could advocate slavery without the slightest notions of mercy. The time was to come, as his life was drawing to a close, when he would fall into melancholy meditation on the remembrance of things past, and try to lay some unction upon his unhappy heart and excuse his merciless deeds. Shortly before his death he wrote: 'When I sent a great number of Indians to Castile to be sold, I intended that they be given instruction in our faith and customs, and then be sent back to their homeland so that they might teach the others'. Too late, and quite useless: for deeds cannot be undone with words—especially if those deeds have been proposed in words set down for all to see. 'From these two products,' he had written in 1495, referring to slaves and brazilwood, 'it seems to me that one could make a profit of forty million *maravedis*, so long as there is no lack of ships to sail here. . . . Although the Indians perish at present, this will not always be the case, for this is what happened to the Blacks and the Canary Islanders at first.' Those words, if they came from some other man of the period, could be read without much surprise or shock. But that they should have come from Columbus, 'the Christ-Bearer', does bother us a little. They bewildered Las Casas. 'It is beyond all belief,' he wrote, 'that a man whom I can call naught but good and well-intentioned should prove so blind to so clear an issue.'

II

Early in 1497 Columbus had triumphed in his negotiations with Ferdinand and Isabela. A third expedition was authorized. He had temporarily silenced his enemies and overcome his critics. He had been confirmed in his privileges. He had been granted new favours. His brother Bartholomew was officially appointed as Adelantado of the Indies. His two sons were made pages to the Queen.

The royal ordinances and instructions were drawn up in careful detail for the new voyage which the Admiral was to undertake. He was granted six ships this time, to be outfitted at the Crown's expense. 'You are to select 333 persons made up of: 40 gentlemen volunteers, 100 foot soldiers, 30 able seamen, 30 ship's boys, 20 gold-sluicers, 50 day labourers, 20 artisans, and 30 women' (these last to take the pressure off the treatment of the native women by the Spaniards). Added to this a strong group of monks to attend to conversion. Also, 'You will take a physician, an apothecary, a herbalist, and musical instruments for the diversion of those who establish themselves there'.

This was all right on paper. But in fact there was now the same difficulty that occurred when recruiting for the first voyage—there were too few volunteers. This fact speaks louder than the official complaints of interested parties: it was now apparently plain that Hispaniola was not a paradise where one picked up shovelfuls of gold from off the land, but a hell where, asking for a piece of bread, you were given a lizard. It was found necessary to tap the gaols again, and the Sovereigns offered a free pardon to all prisoners (with a few specific exceptions among whom murderers were not included) who would enlist. Obviously many such prisoners then, as now, and as at all times, were no worse or better than anyone else, but there must have been some prime ruffians among them, and the Grand Admiral of the Ocean Sea may have regarded them with a gloomy eye, and wondered to what extent they would be influenced by the musicians enlisted to divert them, and what standard they would set to the natives as exemplars of the Christian way of life.

However, there was the temporary advantage that the prisoners thus freed were in no position to claim salary in advance. But the rest of the crew did demand payment, and this was difficult, for the sum of money which had in theory been put aside for the enterprise was not immediately forthcoming since the royal exchequer had been much depleted by war and weddings. At least that was the reason given by those in positions of legal and financial power who wished to thwart the Admiral and delay the expedition. They resented the favours bestowed upon his sons and his brother, and especially the Queen's agreeable attitude towards him. Both esteem and affection are indicated in a missive she wrote him after an occasion when he had advised her with regard to a dangerous storm which might have' caught the Sovereign's future daughter-in-law on her way to Spain. The Queen said:

I saw your letter and opinion on the voyage of the Archduchess, my very dear and beloved daughter; and it is very good and as a learned man who has much experience of matters of the sea . . . I am grateful to you and hold it a special obligation and service, both for your timeliness in sending it (as your warning and advice was most useful to us), as for having tendered it with true goodwill and affection which have always been known in you; and please believe that all is received as coming from a special and faithful servant of mine.

Those are not insincere words. There would have been no object in writing thus if she did not feel it. It throws light upon the pleasing impact which Columbus could sometimes make— and note that none of this had anything to do with the Columbian enterprise. But it was this fact, as much as any other, that he, a Genoese, was received so well at the Spanish Court, that increased his enemies. He was thwarted at every turn, embroiled with officials, put off from week to week and from month to month with bickerings over equipment and food-stuff prices and so forth. All the dateless phenomena of delay by virtue of red tape were brought to bear upon him. Bishop Fonseca, the most powerful of his enemies, who made it a point of honour to oppose anyone of importance or distinction, openly mocked at Columbus's 'Affair of the Indies' as something laughable in contrast with the urgent affairs of state.

One of the officials who set out to obstruct him most was called Ximeno, the Royal Paymaster. He really enjoyed himself. A universal kind of personage. Slightly colder than a fish, and just as slippery, a man with a stiff upper and lower lip, and with the best interests of all parties at heart. The small man in the key financial position can always frustrate the plans of big men dependent upon finance. On what was practically the last day, he came on board the Admiral's ship, nosing around, looking into 'the necessity of this', or inquiring about the 'price of that', or demanding a receipt for something else. He was taking it easy, lounging about, asking his questions more for the sake of holding up proceedings than anything else, totally unaware of what was coming to him, and of the receipt he was going to have.

Columbus had been impeded from embarking for nearly two years by characters of this kind. He could bear it no longer. Prudence, restraint, the lack of courage which is often a concomitant of caution, generally ruled his actions. But there is always a point at which such a man will break out. Not spontaneously, though; not on the spur of the moment. He will nurse his fury, bide his time, and choose the right moment to launch an attack with a sudden extremity of violence. So it was now. The ship was loaded and ready to embark, and here was this man Ximeno insolently sauntering about on board with a view to holding things up, and now he wandered up onto the quarterdeck and asked in an offensive manner for a statement of certain purchases. To his amazement and terror Columbus suddenly attacked him, knocked him down, tore his hair, kicked him, and yelled at him, 'Take this for your receipt!'

It is with great pleasure that one reads about this episode—which seems well authenticated. With admiration also; for when it is not habitual with a man to let loose his temper, it requires a great effort to do so deliberately. The crew, perhaps equally frustrated with the delays, must have been delighted—and noted it, too, with a wary respect for their captain. But in the battle of public life, prudence, restraint, and caution are the best weapons if we look to the future. The other approach—such as this scene—brings only immediate satisfaction. It did Columbus much harm with the Sovereigns; for the insulted Paymaster could and did report the incident with as much exaggeration and carefully detailed mendacity as ever he chose, after the fleet had sailed.

CHAPTER NINE

The Third Voyage

I

THEY SET SAIL on May 30th, 1498. Three of the ships were to
go direct to Hispaniola, while with the other three the Viceroy,
true to form, went off on another voyage of discovery. He had
formed the idea that the nearer to the equator you went the
more likely you would be to find gold, and he planned now to
go south as far as the supposed latitude of Sierra Leone where
the Portuguese had found Guinea gold, and then strike out due
west. Accordingly he sailed down to the Cape Verde Islands
before launching out into the Atlantic. Meanwhile the other three
vessels sailed from the Canaries, taking the 1493 route again.

It was on July 4th that Columbus left the Cape Verde
Islands. Nine days later the decision to take this more southerly
route seemed disastrous. The wind failed. They were brought to
a halt. The heat became appalling. They had never had any
experience of such a thing. All the rumours they had heard
about being burnt alive were evidently about to be verified.
Their own particular brand of savage insanity—the wearing of
smelling woollen garments in tropic climes—drove them frantic,
while it never occurred to them to cool themselves in the water
all around them! A brief description of their plight is very
clearly presented in Columbus's entry for July 14th in his
journal on the third voyage:

> The wind failed and he came into such great, vehement, burning
> heat that he feared that the ships would catch fire and the people
> perish. So suddenly and unexpectedly did the wind cease and the
> excessive and unusual heat come on, that there was no one who
> would dare go below to look after the casks of wine and water
> which burst, snapping the hoops of the pipes. The wheat burned
> like fire. The bacon and salt meat roasted and putrefied. This heat
> and fire lasted eight days.

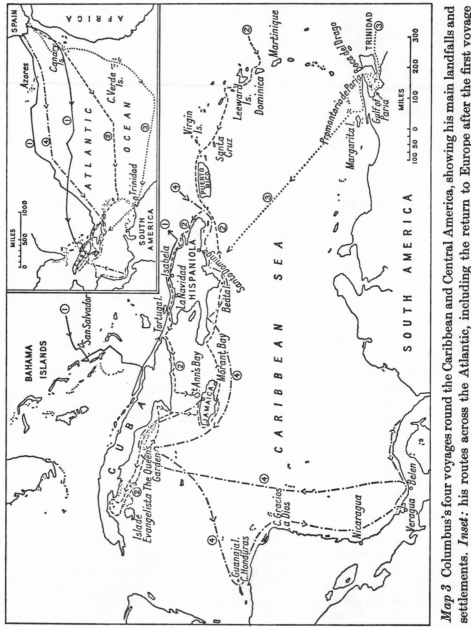

Map 3 Columbus's four voyages round the Caribbean and Central America, showing his main landfalls and settlements. *Inset*: his routes across the Atlantic, including the return to Europe after the first voyage

By good fortune a wind then sprang up and swiftly wafted them away from the hell in which they had expected to rot or to burn, and by the end of July they sighted three mountain peaks. As Columbus had placed this voyage under the special protection of the Holy Trinity he named this new island Trinidad, which it is called to this day. It is the most southern of the Leeward Islands.

Their most pressing need was water, and having replenished their casks at the first opportunity, they sailed round and entered the Gulf of Paria. And now at last Columbus could behold the mainland—the coast of Venezuela in South America. But just as previously he had insisted that Cuba was the mainland, and had made his crew swear a solemn oath to that effect, so now he insisted that Venezuela was an island, and named it Isla Santa—Blessed Isle. The great discoverer hated discovery. He had the greatest objection to discovering any continent except Asia or any sea except the Indian Ocean. The important thing was that his geographical conceptions should be proved correct. Hispaniola must be Chipangu: Cuba must be Cathay—he would not have it otherwise! And as Venezuela was not in the right place to be China, it must be another island. In all his career he gave no clearer example of the tenor of his mind.

During that terrible time in the doldrums many of the crew had been in such mental agony that it had affected them physically—in some cases injuring their eyesight. And Columbus, apart from the sleeplessness that now so often afflicted him even when vigilance was not especially called for, at this time suffered from a serious malady of the eyes. Some of his biographers have held that this malady caused a greater ardour in him than normal, even an exaltation of spirit, when, seeing so much with his inner eye in his monomanic imagination, he gave it all an outer habitation and a name. It could be so. At any rate he entered now into a period of marvellous hallucination. Gazing upon the coast of Paria he became convinced that he was now close to Paradise, the very Garden of Eden of the Old Testament. As late as the middle of the sixteenth century there was a tendency to regard those who denied the existence of the terrestrial Paradise as heretical. Columbus was the last person to deny this. His studies had convinced him that it was on an island in the Indian Ocean where he thought he now was. Surely he had found it here on the coast of Paria. It had to be high up, of course, so as to have escaped the Flood.

He could see it all so clearly in his mind's eye. He found himself in a sort of inland fresh-water sea, circumferenced by the many mouths of the great Orinoco delta and Trinidad, with a way to the ocean through two narrow channels. Now, in maintaining that the Garden of Eden was still to be found on earth, the Christian authors even gave it an exact location on their maps at some remote point in the Far East, on a high mountain beyond reach of the Flood, in a hot region near the equator, and with four great rivers flowing from it. The mouths of the Orinoco were just right to answer the requirements of Columbus, and this filled him with something akin to exaltation at this time.

But there was no high mountain anywhere near! This did not worry him.

> I do not believe that it is a steep mountain [he wrote]. The earth must rise gradually, beginning in regions far from here. Paradise is situated in a place which no one can reach except by Divine consent. It has the form of a mountain-top that resembles the thin end of a pear, or a ball topped with a protuberance like the nipple of a female breast; the earth swells up into this nipple and approaches Heaven. These are the sure signs of Paradise, which agree exactly with the descriptions given us by the saints and learned theologians.

We have here a man who can comfortably believe whatever he chooses, and give a biblical gloss. In such a state of illusion he is in no danger of disillusion. Thus, the Gulf of Paria had been described in the Book of Genesis. The rage of water in the narrow channel, when the fresh met the salt savagely as in a bore, and swelled terrifyingly above them, had been rehearsed in the Psalms of David and called The Dragon's Mouth—which name the Admiral now gave to the gorge in Paria.

Yet Columbus was not altogether easy in his mind about all this biblical geography. Doubts did occur to him. 'If this river does not flow from out of Paradise,' he wrote, 'it must come from an immense land to the south, whereof no one till now has had any knowledge.' As it could not be Marco Polo's territory, it would have to be another world altogether. The idea of such a discovery did not appeal to him, and he was unwilling to put it to the test. Not yet, at any rate. He would look into the matter later on; or send his brother Bartholomew to do so. Meanwhile, comforting himself again with the sayings of his 'authorities', with Aristotle and Seneca and Pliny, with Pierre D'Ailly and Esdras, with Petrus Comestor and Francisco de Mayrones, he set sail for Hispaniola, declaring that he must tarry no longer on account of the provisions which he had on board for the settlement.

It is sad to reflect that only a few miles away on the coast of Venezuela there were extensive pearl fisheries which were later found and exploited by others. This would have been an enormous asset for Columbus, and would have brought him the prestige he sorely needed. But it was always in the pattern of this man's life to seek for treasure where it could not be found, and to turn away when it came within his reach. It was as if some impurity of aim doomed him to this destiny, fatally impeding him from this chief implement of power.

So he set sail for Hispaniola. And at once changed character. It is really so. Now he becomes the great navigator again. We must never forget this about Columbus. Indeed we cannot forget it as we closely study his story. He was now completely off course; he had to find his way by dead reckoning from the Gulf of Paria to Hispaniola—and he never goes wrong, never falters in a navigational decision. Over and over again throughout his history one is struck by the Admiral's skill, and delighted to behold the practical nature of the man when on the waves, superseding the illusioned cosmographer and the incompetent viceroy.

II

On August 21st they reached Beata Island, which is the most southern point of Hispaniola, and from there proceeded in eight days to St Domingo—the town built by his brother, Bartholomew, to take the place of Isabela. Though by this time the Spaniards were in control of the island at the north in the environment of Isabela, and at the south in the environment of St Domingo, there was one part of the country which they had not penetrated—the long southern limb called Xaragua. The subsequent Spanish operations here may fittingly be taken as an example of the Christians' activity on the island.

The chief of Xaragua was called Bohechio, whose sister, Anacaona, was the wife of the great and betrayed Caonabo. 'She was a very remarkable woman,' says Oviedo, 'very prudent, very gracious and courtly in her speech, ways and movements', who exercised much authority. Don Bartholomew invaded the kingdom with a hundred men and found himself confronted with an army of Indians many times outnumbering his own force. He declared that he came peacefully, and peacefully he was received and indeed magnificently entertained by dancing and jousting. Nevertheless, when the festivals were over, Bartholomew demanded tribute—that is, a tax on the people who lived in the land which the Christians had invaded. Realizing that his forces were no match for the usurpers, Bohechio said that while he could not pay tribute in gold he would do so in cotton and in cassava-bread. And it seems that they parted on good terms.

But a less prudent chief called Guarionex (the same who had made that sensible agricultural suggestion to Columbus three years earlier), hearing of this, contrived a rising of the Indians, which was instantly quelled by Bartholomew, and Guarionex was taken prisoner. His subordinates were executed, and he was still kept captive. However, he managed to escape to the territory of Maiobanex, the cacique of a hardy tribe in the adjoining region. Don Bartholomew pursued the fugitive. After some fighting in which the Spaniards were victorious, the Adelantado (as Bartholomew was usually called) sent a messenger to Maiobanex saying that he did not seek war with him but that he must deliver up Guarionex—otherwise his villages would be destroyed with fire and sword. The reply of Maiobanex has come down to us. He declared that 'Everyone knew that Guarionex was a good man, endued with every virtue, wherefore he judged him to be worthy of assistance and defence; but that the Christians were violent and bad men, and that he would have neither friendship nor commerce with them.'

Thereupon Don Bartholomew burnt down a number of villages and advanced upon the camp of Maiobanex. His people became frightened and did not relish being destroyed just for the sake of Guarionex. But the noble Maiobanex insisted that

Guarionex was a good man, and deserved well at his hands, for he had given him many royal gifts when he came to him, and had taught him and his wife to join in choral songs and to dance, of which he made no little account, and for which he was grateful; wherefore he would be party to no treaty to desert Guarionex, since he had fled to him, and he had pledged himself to take care of the fugitive; and would rather suffer all extremities than give detractors a cause for speaking ill, to say that he had delivered up his guest.

Guarionex, hearing of this, felt constrained to leave the territory on his own account. But this did not save Maiobanex who, with his family, was surprised and taken; and eventually may have shared the same prison as Guarionex.

This is a story in a far away land, at a far away time. Yet, as Arthur Helps truly says, it is a story which had it 'been written by some Indian Plutarch, and the names had been more easy to pronounce, might have taken its just place among the familiar and household stories which we tell our children, to make them see the beauty of great actions'.

The Spaniards were faced with the necessity of conquering the natives as the only way to avoid a second La Navidad. Don Bartholomew had proved himself able enough and ruthless enough to accomplish this to a large extent, while also displaying his executive capacity in getting St Domingo built in the south to take the place of Isabela as headquarters. But this did not mean that he had been able to establish either solidarity or harmony in his own camp. As a brother of the unpopular Viceroy, and a Genoese, it would have called for a good deal of tact to have got on with the Spaniards. But he appears to have made no effort in this matter; on the contrary after he had been successful in the field he began to give himself airs and think it proper to tighten up discipline! It is put clearly enough by Oviedo: 'After the Adelantado had obtained these victories, it seemed as if his character had changed, for he proved very exacting towards the Christians from then on, to such an extent that some of them could not bear him'.

Columbus had not improved the situation by appointing a supposedly trustworthy household supporter called Francisco Roldan as Chief Justice, expecting that he would support his brother. He did nothing of the sort. He supported the Adelantado's enemies and even led an insurrection. Apart from the unpopularity of the Adelantado, there were two grounds for disquiet and unrest—illness and hunger. The illness came chiefly in the form of syphilis, made much worse by the lack of food. The planners of the enterprise had made the truly fundamental blunder of failing to include in the expedition enough farmers and bakers. Had there been a platoon of first-rate cooks and keen agriculturalists, the entire situation would have been different. As it was, the intense unrest and sheer physical misery of the Spaniards made it easy for Roldan to carry out a rebellion against Don Bartholomew and his few supporters.

It was with this that Columbus was now faced on his return to the island in August 1498. He was at a loss how to deal with Roldan. He did not know with what resolution he should meet this resolute man. He could not rally supporters around him and inspire them by fiery eloquence. His eloquence—which could be considerable—was always on the plane of cosmographical surmise linked with biblical overtones. In this man-of-action context he was weak. Yet, we may pause to ask, what exactly is a strong man of action? He is often, so very often, though of course not always, a chap with a few simple ideas in terms of 'conquest' or the like, and is enabled by some catch-phrases to command the obedience of hosts of simple souls whose consequent activities are little better in the eye of history and the calendar of nature than a plague of locusts or a pest of beetles. Anyhow, Columbus considered, no doubt rightly, that he could not meet Roldan with a sufficient show of force, and would have to negotiate with him. There was prudence in this. There was also an element of cowardice. Confronted with aggressive men, Columbus generally felt nervous and timid—for men with great gifts are often cowardly in this respect. The manly men of the world look down upon them, while they themselves, receiving little support from people in general, cannot feel indifference to the contempt of those very men who yet seldom possess that other species of courage which stands by inspiration in the face of all neglect and calamity and calumny.

But the Admiral had insisted upon being Viceroy, for which position he was unfitted. He was no match for the scheming Roldan, and after a whole year's parleying with him, gave ground all along the line. In the end the rebel was restored to office as Chief Justice, with extra powers, and all charges against him were proclaimed baseless. This so undermined the authority of the Admiral that he sent a message by the next ship returning to Spain to ask the Sovereigns for a trustworthy official to be sent out, learned in law, to look into the affairs of Hispaniola, and as the representative of their Majesties, to be superior to any Chief Justice such as Roldan. Presently this was granted, as we shall see, with interesting results.

The Admiral was unaware of the extent to which he had lost favour at Court. He had made a number of envious and formidable enemies, chief of whom was Fonseca, a specialist in enmity to eminence, who was later to be as implacable against Fernando Cortez as he now was against the 'Genoese upstart', Columbus. There were many ex-settlers in the country now loud in their complaints against the Admiral and his brothers, who were accused of harshness and cruelty towards salaried Spaniards; of refusing food to those who displeased them; of exclusiveness within a narrow circle almost entirely of blood relations. Many of these disgruntled Spaniards appeared at Court giving voice to their grievances. The Admiral's son, Fernando, gives an emotional account of this.

> When I was at Granada at the time the most Serene Prince Don Miguel died, more than fifty of them [returned settlers], as men without shame, bought a great quantity of grapes, and sitting down in the Court of Alhambra, uttered loud cries, declaring that their Highnesses and the Admiral made them live in this poor fashion on account of the bad pay they received, with many other dishonest and unseemly things which they kept repeating. Such was their effrontery that when the Catholic King came forth they all surrounded him and got him into the midst of them, crying—'Pay! pay!' and if by chance I or my brother who were pages to the most Serene Queen, happened to pass where they were, they shouted to the very heavens, saying—'Look at the sons of the Admiral of Mosquitoland, of that man who has discovered the lands of deceit and disappointment, a place of sepulchre and wretchedness to Spanish hidalgos!'

He was accused of having made a private hoard of pearls instead of openly declaring them for the benefit of the Sovereigns. He was even accused of treason. His manner of speaking about 'my Indies' gave colour to the accusation that he was planning to hand over the territory to a foreign nation, the absurdity of which idea in no way impeded a list of reasons being given to 'prove' that he was disloyal. With material of this kind it was not difficult for Fonseca and his minions to prepare to bring about his downfall.

We must add to this the fact which undermines our sympathy for the Admiral in his troubles: his error in judgement and lapse in humanity by seeking to retrieve the financial failure of the colony by a calculated slave trade. At the very time when his qualifications for remaining as Viceroy were being called in question, five ship-loads containing hundreds of slaves arrived in Spain! There were six hundred of them in all, and they made a pitiful spectacle, having crossed the ocean under most inhuman conditions. This made a deplorable impression at Court. The Sovereigns—both of them—were absolutely opposed to this method of raising money.* They had said so before, and now they said so again. They declared that they did not wish their Indian 'vassals' to be slaves, and they ordered that those who had survived the hardships which had been inflicted on them—a mere twenty-one—should be set at liberty and returned to Hispaniola.

It had at last become clear to the King and Queen that their Admiral was not capable of acting as Viceroy. And according to Las Casas, that sudden physical assault upon their deputy, Ximeno, just before he sailed on this third voyage, proved especially damaging to him now. This is surprising, since the other charges preferred against him would seem much more serious than loss of temper in relation to a monarch's creature; but no doubt Ximeno and Fonseca made the best of the incident—its simplicity and definiteness being a great advantage—and built it up into a proof that the Viceroy was as unable to control himself as to control others. The Sovereigns now decided that they would do just what he had himself requested; they would send a man to look into the affairs at Hispaniola: they would do more, they would send him to assume the reins of power. It could all be done in a smooth and agreeable manner so that their Admiral and discoverer, whatever his faults, could retire from his difficult assignment with dignity.

They chose a man called Francisco de Bobadilla to whom they felt they could entrust this task. He appeared to be just the right man for so delicate a job of transference. He was a true gentleman, says Oviedo, 'an old member of the royal household, a man very honest and religious'. Bernaldez describes him as 'a great gentleman and loved by all', while Las Casas says of him, 'He must have been a simple and humble man of nature and character; I never heard him accused of any dishonest thing or anything savouring of cupidity, in those days when he was discussed daily; on the contrary, all spoke well of him'.

Nevertheless he was not sent out to Hispaniola before a year had elapsed. That proved unfortunate for Columbus, because

* Salvador de Madariaga gives convincing chapter and verse proof of this. *Christopher Columbus: Part VI*, p. 341.

during that year he had managed to preserve a reasonable harmony among the settlers, but in the spring of 1500 there was bad trouble. A certain hidalgo who had kidnapped the daughter of a chief had been imprisoned by Roldan, whereupon another hot-headed hidalgo, called Adrian de Moxica, attempted to raise a rebellion against both Roldan and Columbus. The latter, as usual, wavered between severity and timidity, but Bartholomew, generally consistent in ruthlessness, persuaded him to take stern measures. Adrian de Moxica was condemned to death, and proving unbearably insolent, was thrown from a tower without benefit of clergy. The ferment became dangerous, and more Spaniards were hanged. And it happened that the first thing which Bobadilla saw on arriving at Santo Domingo were gibbets from which hung the corpses of six men.

The sight of those Spaniards hanging there gave Bobadilla a very sombre first impression. On that day when he set foot on shore both Columbus and Bartholomew were absent from Santo Domingo, and only Diego was present. This was unfortunate, for Diego, incompetent at all times, now surpassed himself in tactlessness. When Bobadilla said how shocked he had been on arrival by the spectacle of six Spaniards hanging in front of him, Diego replied with relish that five more were due to be hanged next day; and when Bobadilla (who had come with his Letter of Credence from the Spanish Sovereigns investing him with supreme power) forbade the executions, Diego replied that he only took orders from his brother, the Viceroy. This seems to have thrown Bobadilla off balance, and caused him to behave in a manner which was uncharacteristic of him. He had built up a reputation for acting with a wise restraint at critical moments—and suddenly committed so enormous an error that it created one of the most scandalous incidents in history.

The insolence of Diego's declaration that he only took orders from the Viceroy, made him lose his temper and order Diego to be thrown into prison. Then he set up his headquarters in the Viceroy's house, took possession of the official buildings, released the condemned Spanish prisoners, and confiscated the Admiral's property, his weapons, his horses, his silver plate and collection of gold objects, his letters, books, and papers and everything valuable to him as Viceroy. Having promised to pay all those whose salaries had fallen in arrear, he then sent a message to Columbus, who was in the Vega Real, demanding that he come to Santo Domingo forthwith. The astonished

Admiral, who had expected 'a legal and learned adviser' to come out, protested that Bobadilla had no right to make such demands or attempt to usurp his place. But Bobadilla, having suddenly acquired a heady taste for power, and having embarked upon a course from which he could not easily retreat, and fearing armed resistance, acted swiftly and ordered the Admiral to be put in irons and thrown into prison, along with Diego, and also Bartholomew.

This was done. The man who had had the courage to sail out into the unknown and had discovered new lands, and then sailed again in command of seventeen vessels, was now treated by a court official as if he were an enemy of Spain or a common criminal. Bobadilla did not even grant him an interview. No doubt he feared to face him. When the moment came for the irons to be put on the Admiral, everyone hung back, says Las Casas. Who could dare, who would wish to inflict such an indignity upon such a man? At this point an almost Shakespearean character steps forward, one of those marginal characters whom we find in, say, *Measure for Measure*. A subordinate cook belonging to the household advanced, and saying with shameless impudence, 'Allow me, Your Excellency', slipped the fetters on him with 'as much self-assurance as if he were serving him some savoury dish'.

The three brothers were imprisoned in a secret cell for as long as two months before they were permitted by Bobadilla to take ship for Spain, and all that time they were held in suspense as to what was going to happen to them, for they were completely powerless. Indeed, on the day when they were taken out they heard such yells from the mob (for Bobadilla had been zealous in advertising accusations) that Columbus thought they were being led to execution! He was reassured by a courteous equerry who explained that they were being taken on board ship.

Thus it was that in October 1500 the Very Magnificent Lord Don Cristobal Colon Grand Admiral of the Ocean Sea, who had changed the cosmographical conceptions of the Middle Ages, was brought back to Spain in irons because he was an inadequate administrator of the lands he had discovered. 'This occurrence,' says Wassermann, 'monstrous from any point of view, was later on used by most biographers as an excuse for romantic exaggerations and theatrical effects. It does not need such aids. The fact is irrefragable and suffices for a gloomy judgement on human intelligence and gratitude. . . . Austere critics say that Columbus paid the due penalty for his criminal weakness. But such a phenomenon as this, apart from the fact that it is beyond all social categories, stands out a melancholy memorial for ever, and is to be judged by other than temporal and moral standards: it is something beyond the scope of all transitory conceptions, and every attempt to analyse or describe it can only be the faintest adumbration.' Columbus, however, was equal to the situation, and met it in his own inimitable style. The courteous equerry who had brought him on board could not bear to see the Admiral on a ship—in chains. This man, whose name was Villejo, together with the captain of the caravel, whose name was Andreas Martin, was moved and distressed. Both offered to remove the chains. But the Admiral would not hear of it. He rose to the occasion in his own sombre fashion with unerring instinct for high comedy, paradox, and hyperbole. This situation was really perfect. It was just what was needed. The very thing. These were not chains: they were garlands. This was his finest accolade; here was the proof of his greatness; now all men could read his signature upon the tablets of immortality. No longer aloft upon a vessel guiding his century into a new era, but his head bent down upon his fettered wrists, covered in the four-fold black cloth of captivity, degradation, humiliation, calumny—his spirits rose. Now his stature must be evident at last. Had he not thrust his arm into the ocean sea and plucked up new worlds? Were not empires and islands 'but as plates dropt from his pockets'? Had not the Lord guided him, and untied the winds that would waft him all the way to Asia? Had he not hearkened to the counsels of Esdras and fulfilled the prophecies of Seneca? Had he not held ever before him the ideal of spreading the message of Christ across the seas to people who had not heard the news, and was he not preparing to expel the infidel from Jerusalem and rescue the Holy Sepulchre? It was absolutely in keeping with the composition of the world that such a man should be persecuted and reviled, for God in His merciless mercy had at all times prepared a path of stones for those who served Him best, that they might be numbered among the martyrs and named among the saints. Oh no, these were not chains but garlands. He cherished them. He wore them throughout the voyage. He wore them when he landed in Cadiz. He wore them when he arrived in Seville. He kept them on a mantelpiece in his house. He ordered that they be buried with him in the tomb.

III

The Admiral also knew of course that sticking to his fetters as long as he could was not only good theatre but good business. On his return from his second voyage, in order to shield himself from humiliation, he had adopted the garb of humility in Franciscan mode. Now he could do even better. The chains put him at an immense advantage. If he could hang on to them long enough he would be in an enormously stronger position than if he had been treated with courtesy. It gave him such a powerful initial ground of complaint that the complaints preferred against him would lose a good deal of their effect. If the discoverer of a country is brought back in irons from the country he has discovered simply because he has encountered difficulties in administration, it cannot fail to create a scandal.

Meanwhile, during his imprisonment, he had prepared the way by making use of his greatest ally. That ally was the pen—which has been wielded well by quite a few mariners. He composed an elaborate letter. It was not addressed directly to the Sovereigns but to the 'Governess of Don Juan of Castile', knowing that it would immediately be sent to and read by Ferdinand and Isabela. And in the event it was sent to them and read at once.

It is the most famous letter he wrote. Though it contains some striking phrases and powerful passages, it is extremely bad: confused, bombastic, mendacious, whining, and inconsistent. He had here a great chance to write a brief, dignified, and not over-emphatic general statement as to what he had done, and what Bobadilla had done to him in the name of the King and Queen. But he was far too insensitive to see this. Nevertheless, the letter in whatever terms it was written could not fail to be effective. The Sovereigns saw at once that Bobadilla, by exceeding his instructions, had put them in a very awkward position. They sent word that Columbus must come to Court to make his own explanations, and in the meantime he was to be released and treated with the respect due to their Admiral.

It is this meeting with the King and Queen which has sometimes been romanticized. Las Casas says that at first the Admiral was so overcome that he wept and could not speak for some time; and that the Queen also wept. Since Las Casas was not present, this is hearsay, and very suspect—though it could

have been so. His son is markedly brief about it, simply saying,

> As soon as the Sovereigns heard of the Admiral's arrival and his
> imprisonment, they sent orders, on December 17th, that he
> should be set at liberty, and summoned him to Granada where he
> was received by their Highnesses with smiling faces and
> affectionate speeches. They told him that his imprisonment had
> not been their will or command. On the contrary, it had much
> displeased them, and they would see that those guilty of it were
> punished and that this wrong should be redressed.

Such is Fernando's guarded account. Of course the meeting
may have been slightly theatrical as made out by Las Casas,
or there may have been something undignified in his father's
behaviour which the son preferred to omit. What the interview
was actually like no one will ever know.

The Sovereigns recalled Bobadilla and appointed Don Nicolas
de Ovando to take his place, who in due course (February 1502)
sailed with a fleet of thirty ships, carrying 2,500 soldiers, sailors,
and colonists—for, whatever the shortcomings of the Viceroy,
the enterprise of the Indies was regarded as of the greatest
importance. The question was, what to do with Columbus?
They could apologize for his treatment and restore to him his
property and most of his titles. But not the title of viceroy.
That was obviously out of the question, for the Admiral was not
endowed with administrative ability; he was not a governor
but a navigator, and in the latter capacity they could always
support him. They were diplomatic about this, intimating that
his recall was but temporary while things were sorted out in
Hispaniola, but he had the sense to realize that he would never
be installed there again.

He could easily have accepted the offer of an estate and
dukedom in Spain, and lived in retirement there as the
acknowledged chief explorer of the century. But that was not
at all to his taste. This was not his illusion of grandeur. He was a
restless spirit. Ease and leisure meant nothing to him. Nor
comfort. Nor domestic life. He was by nature a lonely wanderer
above all else, and could never rest on land for long at any
place. 'What was the cause of this profound unrest? What was
it that drove him again and yet again beyond the sea?' asks
Wassermann while puzzling over the third voyage. 'Was it the
fact that it was *his* world, his very own, a world that he had

found? Or was he one of those so tragically deceived by destiny who do not recognize their object when they grasp it in their hands? He was a figure without mercy: he knew nothing of inward peace: the mighty deed he had accomplished had marked him, as a murderer is marked by his guilt. Blindly he sailed the seas, and trod inviolate lands, ever thinking of something other than what the hour demanded, helpless before a present necessity, knowing no human face, master of no human heart, buried in his own dark self, a joyless exile.' Yes, indeed, he must wander; it was his nature to do so; and always it must be upon the sea. Even as a boy it was his own natural element, never the land. It was his destiny to wander eternally, not like Ahasurus the everlasting Jew doomed to pace perpetually the iron lands of earth, but across the oceans of the world. Here only could he be at ease: here only was he master. When at times he was brought low, when his darkening fortunes and his blackened name became too apparent, and when even his own motives grieved him, he would take a caravel and seek the solace of the sea away from the hated and hating world of men. Then, far out, shoreless, alone on his forecastle, he found rest. Then, with just the sky above him, the heaving dunes around, the cries of the circling sea-birds, and each wind-ruined wave renewed in endless riot, his spirits would rise, and he would hear, or think that he heard, a voice from heaven address him in admonishment and comfort.

Indeed, as his monomania grew upon him, he became increasingly lavish with his account of messages he had received from the Lord—never more so than when he was addressing the Sovereigns. The most striking instance which he gives of a voice from heaven exhorting and encouraging him, was on an occasion when he had taken a caravel out to get away from his problems and enemies at Hispaniola, in late December 1499.

Our Lord came to my help, saying: *O man of little faith, have no fear. It is I. Have courage; be not dismayed, and fear not. I shall see to all. The seven years' limit for gold is not over; and in that as in everything else I will set things aright for thee.*

We may wonder at the words, 'The seven years' limit for gold is not over'. How could gold come into a heavenly exhortation? It seems absurd. But it really fits. At bottom, Columbus did not want gold just for himself. Enough of it yes, to give him 'golden spurs' and personal equipage; but not gold in terms of comfort and a wealthy life. It was gold for his mission. Mountains of gold were what he needed for his mission, and that was to drive the Saracen from Jerusalem and ransom the Holy House. If, as some think, Columbus was the progenitor of Don Quixote, we must admit that at times he was more extravagantly enslaved by delusion. He would cross the western ocean and land at Chipangu. He would there meet and make friends with the Grand Khan who would give him sackfuls of gold in exchange for beads and baubles. He would return to Spain, and then by virtue of this gold would drive the Infidel from the holy streets.

Now, in 1501, he outlined this programme again. The fact that he was cold-shouldered at Court and denied his viceroyship in the Indies in no way diminished his sense of mission. On the contrary, his schemes became ever more grandiose and his claim as appointed saviour ever more emphatic. The threat of a Turkish invasion was again imminent, and Pope Alexander VI was urging another crusade. Columbus wrote a letter to this Pope telling him about his past voyages and the one he was now planning for 'the exaltation of the Christian religion', and he informed His Holiness that if 'Satan had not defeated my every effort' he would already have had one hundred and twenty bushels of gold for the crusade, and he declared that the affair of the Indies had as its aim the ransom of the Holy House of Jerusalem. 'From the moment that I found these lands, I wrote to the Sovereigns saying that seven years hence I would give them the sum needed to pay 50,000 foot-soldiers and 5,000 knights.'

It so happened that just at this time Vasco da Gama had reached India by going east round the Cape of Good Hope. In fact he had reached Calicut. And at last the hope of trading with 'the land of spices' by an eastern sea-route had become a reality to the Portuguese. This was disquieting news for the Spanish Sovereigns. It did, however, support the claim made by Columbus that there really was 'a land of spices' out there. The Portuguese had gone east, the Spaniards had gone west; the thing now would be for Columbus to find the strait which Marco Polo had used in order to enter the Indian Ocean. Thus, even if the Portuguese could now trade with India by making the immense journey down the coast of Africa and round the Cape, the Spaniards could do it much more easily by going west across the Atlantic and then, passing through Marco Polo's strait leading to the Indian Ocean, arrive at Calicut in no time. It would be sound policy, therefore, to send Columbus on a fourth voyage to find this passage.

What passage, what strait are we talking about? Quite simply, the only way by which Marco Polo could return home by sea—namely, the passage between Malaya and Sumatra, called today the Strait of Malacca, in the East Indies.

At the risk of being too elementary for the reader, let me attempt to clarify the extreme lack of geographical clarity in the mind of Columbus, his non-facts in relation to the actual facts.

We have to remember that there were two different errors under which he laboured. The first error is easily grasped: that he thought that the Americas constituted Asia, and that the islands which we now call the West Indies were the islands which we now call the East Indies.

The second error is more complicated. Indeed we are dealing with such a shambles of error that it will be a job to clarify the lack of clarity which prevailed. When Columbus reached the West Indies (to him the East Indies), he thought he was quite close to Japan—and in fact had hoped to land there.* For, apart from the fact that he was not in the right continent, he was hopelessly misled as to the geography of the continent he thought he had reached. His idea of his relation to Japan when he was at San Salvador was as if he were a few miles from New York (which is approximately on the same parallel as Japan). And he continually talked about Chipangu, Cathay, Mangi, India in the same breath as if they were all bunched together, and he quite close to them. During his second voyage while sailing along the coast of Cuba he still referred to Mangi and Cathay and the territories of Prester John. On his third voyage when he went further south and reached Venezuela, this was to him a more southerly island in the East Indies. Nevertheless, since that 'island', which he called 'Blessed Isle', was not more than four hundred miles from Hispaniola, it was still reasonably near Chipangu—which is like saying that Venezuela is near New York.

Columbus at no time gave any indication that he was aware that the distance between Japan and Singapore—for him between Chipangu and the Blessed Isle—was approximately

* On October 6th, 1492, during the first voyage, Pinzon and Columbus feared they had missed Chipangu by going too far north!

2,700 miles. He would have guessed approximately 700 miles. For not only did he think that the West Indies were the East Indies, but that the East Indies were the outshore islands of Japan and China. In his reckoning San Salvador would have been facing the north part of the East China Sea. Where was India then in his conception? Perhaps somewhere near Hanchow? The Indian Ocean between Shanghai and Ningpo? I put it crudely like that as another way of saying that the Admiral had no conception of the size of India or where it stood in relation to his Cathay—let alone any idea that it was some 2,000 miles distant from Peking.*

King Ferdinand took his geography from the Portuguese and from Columbus. The existence of the Ganges appears to have been known from the Portuguese, who had begun to conceive the true outlines of India. It remained to be seen whether Columbus could make his way into the Indian Ocean and the Bay of Bengal from the other side. It would be well worthwhile, he considered, to clear up this matter of the strait. He declared that he would be ready to sponsor a fourth voyage, and he requested Columbus to take care to be civil to Vasco da Gama if he came across him in the Indian Ocean!

King Ferdinand, having conceded the idea of the voyage, then in the manner of monarchs pressed by other duties and present crises became dilatory in the matter of providing the necessary equipment and funds, and began to talk about 'the empty coffers of the Treasury', and so forth. This waiting was very trying for Columbus, for he was always hearing of greedy adventurers setting out on their own. 'They all made fun of my plan in the past,' he said bitterly, 'now even tailors wish to discover!' It behoved him to remind the King of the urgency and importance of the new enterprise. He would approach from the religious angle. He made haste to compile (with the help of Father Gorricio) an anthology of biblical references and prophecies concerning the 'recovery of the Holy City of Zion and the conversion of the islands of the Indies and all nations'. He called it *The Book of Prophecies* and sent it to the Sovereigns reminding them of his mission as discoverer—'Our Lord opened my understanding, as if He had touched me with His own hand: I suddenly understood that it was possible to sail from here to the Indies'. He goes on to point out how God had further plans for him. 'Through the success of this voyage He

---

* Amazingly, Marco Polo had failed to clear this matter up.

wished to make a miracle manifest, in order that I, and many others, might take heart in so far as that other enterprise is concerned: that of the Holy House of Zion.' Completely forgetting what he owed to his own constant study of cosmography for years, he added: 'In the affair of the Indies, neither reason, nor mathematics, nor world-maps were of any avail; it was necessary rather that the prophecy of Isaiah be fulfilled'. He reminded them of the twelfth-century hermit, Joachim of Floris, whose works held great interest right up to the sixteenth century, who had predicted that humanity was about to enter a 'third stage', in which the whole world would be brought under the rule of the eternal Gospel, while the Mohammedan sect would disappear, and that 'he who would repair the Ark of Zion would come from Spain'.

An anthology of prophecies relating to some specific event is never difficult to compile, and always makes an impact even when some of the prophecies are extremely vague, such as, in this case (from Isaiah LXVI, 19), 'And I will set a sign among them, and I will send those that escape of them unto the nations, to Tarshish, Pul, and Lud, that draw the bow, to Tubal, and Javan, to the isles afar off, that have not heard my fame, neither have seen my glory; and they shall declare my glory among the Gentiles'. Or from Isaiah LX, 1–3, prophesying that Gentiles will come in great numbers to the capital of Zion—'Arise, shine, for thy light is come and the glory of the Lord is risen upon thee. . . . And the Gentiles shall come to thy light, and kings to the brightness of thy rising'. One might suppose that such blown-up phrasing would be difficult to apply to any event whatsoever, but Columbus persuaded himself that it applied to himself and his enterprises. Then comes the climax to the whole thing, the prophecy that the end of the world is swiftly drawing near. In fact, after careful calculation from St Augustine's ruling, it was due in one hundred and fifty-five years. And that therefore it behoved the Sovereigns to delay no longer.

The influence of the Catholic Church upon the Columbian enterprise was very great from the start, though it is difficult for us to realize the extent of this; and the present approach of the Admiral, whose fervent sincerity and convictions somewhat obscured the emptiness of his bombast, did make an impact. At all events, Ferdinand, whether impressed by the urgency of the prophecy, or by the progress of the Portuguese, or by the importance of disposing of Columbus (who this time might fail to return), now delayed no longer, and the Admiral was granted the means of setting out as soon as possible on a fourth voyage—with just two injunctions: that he would not visit Hispaniola; and that he would bring back no slaves.

CHAPTER TEN

The Last Voyage

I

ONCE THE KING had authorized the expedition there was little more delay, for Ferdinand now showed every evidence of being anxious to hasten the departure of Columbus, and in a matter of weeks four caravels (of poor quality as it turned out) were at his disposal, and he made for open sea from the Grand Canary on May 25th, 1502, on his last journey during which desperate hardships were to be endured for months on end, when all the facets of this strange Admiral's character were made manifest as never before.

He was accompanied by Bartholomew, who was persuaded into going, though much against his will, for by this time he was full of grievances, having been demoted from his position of Adelantado at Hispaniola when his brother was relieved of his viceroyship. And Fernando, the Admiral's son, who later went on to write the biography of his father, joined the ships at Cadiz.

Taking the same course as on his second voyage, Columbus arrived at Martinique in the Lesser Antilles in three weeks. After a few days' rest he continued through the chain of islands discovered on the second voyage—for no apparent reason, since he could not have expected to find the supposed strait into the Indian Ocean anywhere there. Could it be in the vicinity of Santo Domingo? That could not have seemed likely to him, knowing as he did only too well the position of Cuba. Anyway, instead of keeping clear of Hispaniola, as he had been asked to do by his Sovereigns, he actually stood off it on June 29th and sent a message ashore to Ovando. It was tactfully worded, and it contained a request and a warning. The request was (and it seems reasonable in the light of what was to happen eventually) that he might exchange one of his vessels, which was faulty as a light sailing ship but was all right for cargo. The warning was about an imminent hurricane. Columbus had somehow received information that Ovando was about to despatch a fleet home, and he warned him about the danger, at the same time asking refuge for himself and his other ships.

Ovando rebuffed both the request and the warning. He was no more than a Court official with a record which suggested that he might do well as a governor (which proved to be a bad misjudgement). He knew nothing about navigation or meteorology. Yet he made sarcastic remarks about the Admiral, one of the most skilled mariners in the world, referring to him as a preposterous soothsayer, and he sent the ships off the very next day. The hurricane occurred just as Columbus had predicted. There were thirty vessels in that fleet. Nineteen sank with all hands. Six others were lost leaving some survivors; four made harbour in a sinking condition. One got back to Spain.

Repulsed from his own doorstep, as it were, Columbus and his small fleet had to face the tempest as best they could. They found a lee just west of Santo Domingo, and though the vessels were of poor quality they all came through successfully in the end. But it was a terrible occasion.

> Any man, not excluding Job himself [wrote the Admiral], would have been ready to die of despair on the spot in the situation in which I found myself. I was in fear for my safety and even more for that of my brother and my son, and for all my following. And to think that I should have been barred from that land and that harbour that I had won for the King with God's help, and sweating blood in the deed.*

Fair enough. But he had no business to be in the storm at all. One of the two conditions made by the Sovereigns when sponsoring this fourth enterprise was that the Admiral should not visit Hispaniola. Moreover, Ovando did not purposely keep him in the hurricane. It was a quiet evening when he was approached. After the tempest had burst out and destroyed his ships he was powerless to help Columbus who should have sought the harbour at once, since the lives of his crew were more important than the displeasure of Ovando—who in any case would have been too shamefaced to complain, not to say

* This and all other quotations from Columbus in this chapter are taken from his letter from Jamaica. *The Four Voyages of Christopher Columbus*, trans. J. M. Cohen, Penguin, 1969.

fearful of the King's reprimand at sending the ships into a hurricane.

The ships which were lost were laden, we are told, with the gold that had been extracted from Hispaniola. There is the usual discrepancy in estimations as to the amount, but reference is always made to one famous nugget of gold weighing thirty-two pounds. It all went down to the bottom of the sea. Other things went down also: notably Bobadilla and Roldan, and other enemies of Columbus. He was not terribly sorry about this. Seeing himself always as God's chosen instrument, he was not slow to draw appropriate conclusions. Another thing interested him also. The one ship which got through was the vessel which contained his own personal fortune in gold and pearls which the Sovereigns had instructed to be returned to him. This was surely significant.

His next step, presumably, was to seek out the right place to find that strait leading into the Indian Ocean. So, after he had gone as far as the row of islands he had named 'The Queen's Garden', he turned south and sailed in the direction of Honduras. 'I sailed as soon as I could to the mainland', he says in his journal. To the mainland? That is what he calls South America now. The mainland of his Asia. Previously Cuba had been the mainland and South America (Venezuela) an island. Consistency is not to be looked for. And it is hard to trust the accuracy of his statement that it now took them sixty days before they made land (that is, from The Queen's Garden to Honduras). They met with storms 'so continuous that it seemed the end of the world', the three ships with their 'sails torn, anchors, rigging, and cables lost, and also the boats and many stores'. The crew, he says, were sick and terrified and repenting and confessing their sins. He declares that no storm he had ever known had lasted so long or been so terrifying.

> The distress of my son (Fernando) who was with me, racked my soul, for he was only thirteen and he was not only exhausted but remained so for a long time. But the Lord gave him so much courage that he cheered the others, and he worked as hard in the ship as if he had been a sailor for eighty years. He comforted me, for I had fallen ill and was many times on the point of death. I directed the course from a little shelter which I had erected on the deck. My brother (Bartholomew) was in the worst ship, which was in the greatest danger, and this distressed me greatly, especially as I had brought him against his will.

They made land in August 1502 on the island of Guanacca, off the coast of Honduras. While they were there something happened which could have changed the life of Columbus now from frustration into renewed glory. They came upon a party of natives in an unusually long canoe containing a great variety of merchandise which plainly came from a more sophisticated race than any of the tribes they had yet encountered. The range of the cargo revealed costly cloaks, highly-coloured coats and shirts, hatchets for wood-carving, crucibles for smelting, swords, copper axe-heads, and so forth. This was not Columbus's idea of Chinese merchandise, though certainly exciting. But at the moment he did not want to go into the matter very thoroughly. After all, he was on the coast of Malaya (was he not?) and at any moment he must find the Strait of Malacca just as Marco Polo had done, and that strait would be found if he went a little further east, he argued. Had he steered towards the west, a few hours would have brought him to the coast of Yucatan—and then the marvels and riches of Mexico would have been revealed to him.

He stood on a road in his life where one sign pointed to the West, and another pointed to the East. To have gone in one of those directions would have brought a dramatic change in his fortunes. His prestige would have been restored. Once more he would have been recognized as the marvellous explorer, the magical discoverer who could point to worlds unrealized. To go in the other direction meant terrible and interminable tempests, hunger, disease, fearful hardships, shipwreck, desertion, treachery, hatred and despair, and almost total loss of power.

But as Columbus stood upon this road he did not discern these signs. He turned his face away from the reality which was so full of promise and light, and clinging to false geography he hastened his decline and made way for the rising star of Cortez. It is not too sad. For it was just that kind of narrowness of vision which had given him the force to be the only man in Europe to open the gateways of the West.

So he turned east, and again in so fierce a turmoil of storm and thunder that the crew declared that they were 'bewitched' (a view which Columbus solemnly declared to be 'heretical'). It took twenty-eight days of this beating to windward before they came to a bend which Columbus named 'Cape Gracias a Dios' ('Thank God'). Sometimes, after a long day, they ended up opposite the very place on the coast where they had been in the morning, only thankful that they had not gone backwards.

Turning this corner they sailed down the coast of Nicaragua and Costa Rica, achieving some three hundred miles in ten days. They took a rest at a place called Lima off Caraia. The natives seemed well-disposed towards them, and sent out two girls to the Admiral's ship. They were extremely young—not more than eight and fourteen respectively. Fernando records: 'They showed great courage and exhibited neither grief nor sorrow but always looked pleasant and modest; hence they were well treated by the Admiral, who caused them to be fed and clothed, and sent them ashore'. However, they have gone down to history on account of what the Admiral said. He had become convinced that in the district there were 'very terrifying magicians who would have done anything to prevent my remaining there an hour. On my arrival they sent me two magnificently attired girls, the elder of whom could not have been more than eleven and the other seven. Both were so shameless that they might have been whores, and had magic powders concealed about them.' This comment would seem to throw more light upon the Admiral's state of mind than upon the girls.

The natives were equally scared by Spanish 'magic'. On one occasion in this vicinity the Indians attacked them and were repulsed by artillery. In the eyes of the natives this appeared as a species of thunder and lightning conjured up by the Spaniards. On another occasion when some kind of conference was being held with the Indians, the notary, Pordas, proceeded to lay out pen, ink, and paper to make a record. No sooner had he lifted the pen than the Indians fled in panic as from something that was indeed mightier than the sword. Presently they returned and carried out various mystic fumigations to act as counter-charms. This in turn alarmed the Spaniards who regarded them, as did their Admiral, as 'skilled sorcerers'.

In October, having gone further along the coast, they reached what seemed to be at last the Strait of Malacca. But it turned out to be only a lagoon—the Chiriqui Lagoon. Still, that strait could not be far off now because there was every sign that the riches of India were nearly within reach. The natives wore great discs of gold.

In the province of Ciguara [wrote the Admiral] which borders this sea there are, according to what these people tell me, great quantities of gold; the natives wear necklaces of coral and bracelets of gold, and cover their chests and tables with thick layers of gold; they have fairs and trading posts; the ships there are armed; the people are richly clad, and they are accustomed to waging war.

Then he heard rumours of an ocean that lay only nine miles from Chiriqui. That would be the Indian Ocean. Given the passage he was looking for, he would reach the Ganges in ten days, he declared. Presently he did come to just that part of the country where there was a strait. To be more exact: it was not yet a strait. That was to come: and it was to be man-made— though suggested by nature. He had reached the eventual site of the Panama Canal. He was then twelve miles from the Pacific Ocean. He was told about an ocean there. But he was still looking for a waterway, not a landway, not an isthmus— and he did not investigate. Thus it was left for Balboa to discover the Pacific, as it was left for Cortez to discover Mexico.*

If Columbus had had the curiosity, or the opportunity, to go that twelve miles on foot and come to the open sea, it would still have been for him the Indian Ocean. And if then he had been able to take another ship and once more sailed out into the west, what would he have made of it? Where was his India, his Cathay, his Chipangu?—for they were all clustered quite close together in his geographical conceptions. Supposing he had sailed north-west and come to the Hawaiian Islands. Is Oahu Chipangu? Is Quawai Cathay? No!—beyond them yet again a boundless sea, again the ringed horizon and the lost illusion! At last he would have had to abandon his cosmography. He might well have even abandoned the belief that the world was round. For what was this? An implacable void, the daunting deluge of the Flood's vast aftermath, an uncouth anarchy of waves as unchecked and alien as the endless ether. No crew would have been placated, no mutiny could have been subdued. Luckily he never had to face this, and could cling to his original ideas until the day of his death as one who had been confirmed in the geography according to the prophets whose ideas he had come to support, and he never allowed anything so outrageous to enter his head as that he had been privy to the discovery of two enormous continents and to an ocean mightier than the Atlantic.

* Balboa is supposed to have waded into the waters of the Pacific, waving his drawn sword and claiming the ocean for his emperor.

And so we see him, we see him now, on this his fourth voyage, beating up and down the coast of Central America for months. The crews became ever more restive, rebellious, and amazed. What did their Admiral want? What was he doing? He was looking for something that was not there. He was knocking at doors that could not open. His gaze was fixed upon lands five thousand miles away. But he would not give in, he would not swerve from his appointed task. Arthritis, gout, fever, insomnia, might assail him personally; hunger, privation, despair, might grip them all, but still he must pursue his fatal course.

From December 5th, for about a month, the caravels were buffeted up and down the coast in a series of appalling storms, and then the natural took on the aspect of the supernatural. For a strange form of fire seemed to surround them. The phenomenon of phosphorescence was at play inflaming the veils of vapour that flew from the wind-strewn waves.

Eyes never saw the sea so rough [wrote the Admiral], so ugly and so seething with foam. The wind did not allow us to go ahead or give us a chance of running, nor did it allow us to shelter under any headland. There I was held in those seas turned to blood, boiling like a cauldron on a mighty fire. The skies had never looked more threatening. For a day and a night they blazed like a furnace, and the lightning burst in such flashes that every moment I looked to see whether my masts and sails had not been struck. They came with such terrifying fury that we believed the ships would be utterly destroyed. One cannot say that it rained, for it was like a repetition of the deluge. The crews were now so broken that they longed for death to release them from their martyrdom. The ships had already twice lost their boats, anchors, and rigging and were stripped bare of their sails.

That was not the worst of it. It was probable that at any moment one of the ships would be sucked up by a waterspout. 'This waterspout drew the water up into the clouds,' says Fernando, 'in a column larger than a water cask and twisted it like a whirlwind'. A waterspout does not spout from the water and go up: it comes down from the sky. It is like an inverted cone descending from the ink-black canopy of the storm clouds. It is like a gigantic skewer gyrating a thousand times a minute, reaching the water and pulling it up. It is like a supernatural elephant's trunk with suctional power of apocalyptic dimension. When it appears on land—and is then called a whirlwind or tornado—its suctional updraught can transport cars and horses and cows and trees and even houses to a distance of eight miles. If a column descends directly upon a ship, then in a few seconds that ship would be lifted up and cast down elsewhere a splintered wreck. These sailors now saw for the first time in their lives a waterspout quite close to them, as an apparition from the gates of hell. Huddled together on the deck they listened to the Admiral in a loud clear voice reading from the Gospel of St John; and then holding the Bible in one hand and a sword in the other he traced a great cross against the sky.

Only one man in all the world and through all the centuries might have rendered visually that scene. Only the supernal power of Turner could have placed it before us to ponder on for ever. As it is we can but brood and reflect how strange it is that the most sublime moments in a great man's life come when least expected: not at the hour of triumph, not when receiving an accolade in the public place or in the palaces of kings—but at the moment of failure. So it was now. Pride, folly, ignorance, misjudgement, perversity, were driving Columbus to destruction; all had gone wrong and his way of life was falling to the sere and yellow leaf. Then, suddenly, the moment of sublimity. All unexpected, he casts a spell upon us, and lifts up the scene of man's life on earth. He becomes larger than living men, larger too than an Ahab or a Lear in their own tempests, even far outstripping Quixote, as, striding the blast, holding in one hand the Bible and in the other a sword, he calls upon his God to rebuke and exorcise those surges.

II

They did manage to survive that storm, and two days of calm followed, when the ships were surrounded by such a quantity of sharks that it was frightening. 'These beasts,' recounts Fernando, 'seize a person's leg or arm with their teeth and cut it off as clean as with a knife, because they have two files of saw-like teeth.' He says they found a turtle in the belly of one shark, the former still alive and continuing to live on board ship. They found a big shark's head in another shark's belly. However, the Spaniards did well, they ate the sharks instead of being eaten by them. By this time they needed fresh food very badly. The biscuits had turned into a kind of porridge half composed of worms. Fernando gives us a horrifying picture:

What with the heat and the dampness even the biscuit was so full
of worms that, God help me, I saw many men wait until nightfall
to eat the porridge, so as not to see the worms; others were so used
to eating them that they did not bother to pick them out, for they
might lose their supper by being too fastidious.

They could not rely upon getting food from the natives.
They never knew how they would be received on shore. Indeed,
it is one of the interesting things arising from all the accounts
of these voyages, that the inhabitants in this part of the world
differed widely in their characteristics and mores: some were
gentle and welcoming, some so fearful that they ran away, some
most aggressive in brave opposition. At a place in Veragua,
according to Fernando, on November 23rd, 1502, Columbus
attempted to be conciliatory with the inhabitants, but meeting
with no friendly response 'the Admiral in order to temper their
pride and teach them not to scorn the Christians, commanded a
shot to be fired at a group of Indians on a hilltop, and the ball,
falling in their midst, let them know that this thunder concealed
a thunderbolt.' They were, in fact, thunderstruck, and hardly
dared to peep out from behind the hills. But the Spaniards were
ill-advised to draw conclusions from this incident, and to think
that they could easily subdue the tribes in these parts. Indeed,
as we shall see in a minute, they were to pay dearly for this
mistake, and would be obliged to sail away ignominiously
from these shores.

The search for the strait, though doomed to failure, brought
Columbus in touch with the gold possibilities of Veragua. After
some landings on the coast he became convinced that he had at
any rate reached his second great goal—that of finding gold.
He became excited about this, and he wrote, 'I have found
more signs of gold in this land of Veragua than I found in
Hispaniola in four years. The chieftains are buried, I am told,
wearing their gold ornaments.' And once again he brings in
Solomon and his expedition to the mines in Aurea. 'I maintain
that the mines of Aurea are the very mines of Veragua.' King
Solomon's Ophir had once been Haiti: now it is Veragua! He
really thinks he has done it at last, for the lure of gold that
had dazzled and doomed him through his first, his second, and
his third voyages, loomed before him still as if he were the
principal in a fairy tale or the symbol in some pathetic parable.
He declared that what he had hitherto acquired in the island of
Hispaniola was 'naught by comparison with the mines that I

have now brought beneath the dominion of your Majesties'. Gold is so much more valuable than anything else, he insists, that Genoese and Venetians will barter any pearls for it: 'Gold is most excellent; of gold is treasure made, and with it he who has it does all he wants in the world, and can even lift souls up to Paradise'—for he was still thinking of his proposed crusade in the Holy Land.

He decided to establish a colony, or trading post, at a place which he called 'Belen' (after Bethlehem) where there was a river and natural harbour. There was a bar at the mouth, but there were seven feet of water and the caravels were able to get across where the river formed a basin with plenty of deep water. They were safe from storms. Here they remained till the spring when Columbus decided to leave Bartholomew in charge of the colony while he returned to Spain for more ships and provisions. But the natives were rising against them now. The behaviour of some members of the crews had stirred up enmity against the Spaniards, who then with a maximum of indiscretion captured a chieftain (who escaped), and made prisoners of others (who hanged themselves).

In spite of the hostility around them, that colony, or fort, or trading-post (what was the trade?) was actually built, consisting of a dozen palm-thatched houses—the unit being named Santa Maria de Belen. This was a frightful mistake, hardly to be credited to the decision of a sane man. But Columbus was scarcely sane at this time. He was utterly worn out by his sufferings and his anxieties, as is obvious from the confusion, the inexactitude, the inconsistency, and hysteria of his own account, in the course of which he also represents himself as weeping for himself instead of for others, and of hearing voices instead of giving orders. The situation is by no means wholly clarified by the apologia of his son Fernando, or by the boastfulness of Diego Mendez (who claims that the Admiral gave him the command of the colony), while the silence of Bartholomew becomes really as intolerable as the loquaciousness of his brother.

It was a terrifying time for all of them, but so complicated in incident as to be tedious to read or to relate in detail. The main facts may be stated briefly. The Spaniards, by their loose behaviour when they came on shore, by their folly in capturing the chieftain who escaped and in taking as hostages those natives who hanged themselves rather than remain in captivity, had clearly displayed themselves as unwelcome visitors to Veragua. In plain words, for the first time since coming to these parts, the Spaniards met with natives who, neither regarding them as gods nor fearing them as men, considered that the proper thing to do was to throw them back into the sea—and did so. On April 6th, 1502, four hundred of the inhabitants attacked the so-called fort at Belen, and were temporarily repulsed by Bartholomew and Diego Mendez; but presently a whole boatload of Spaniards who had gone upstream to fill water-casks, was attacked and all except one of the crew were killed. It became clear that Belen was not a good place in which to set up a settlement of any sort.

The extraordinary thing is that Columbus appears to have been unaware of this. He still thought that he could leave his brother holding the fort while he went back to Spain, in spite of the example of the fate of the garrison at La Navidad. However, eight days after that battle at Belen and the massacre of the boatload of Spaniards, he changed his mind and considered that he should further consult Bartholomew. But there was a difficulty about this. His brother was behind the bar with one of the ships, the remaining three being on the open side. On account of certain weather conditions, or of tides and currents, it was not always possible to cross the bar—and so it was now. But an intrepid hero called Pedro de Ledesma swam across the bar, reached Bartholomew and asked what he desired. The answer was swift and clear—'Let me and my company get out of this and join the other ships!' He managed to do this largely through the help of Diego Mendez who had a genius for improvisation in moments of crisis. Bartholomew's ship was abandoned, and all the crew and most of the gear and provisions were got across the bar by canoe.

Could they now sail back to Seville? Not a hope with these ships. They were honeycombed by the work of the terrible toredos, or shipworms. These are very remarkable creatures who having made cavities into the wood then expand their bodies and split the hardest hulks. Unwise before the event, we would not readily suppose that these creatures of darkness, these eyeless, toothless, earless pieces of squirming flesh have yet the power to torpedo the mightiest armada—yet so it is. And these ships of Columbus were particularly fair game, one of them being now so hopelessly holed that it had to be abandoned. Could he, by means of continuous baling with kettles, basins, and jugs, get the remaining two ships as far as Hispaniola and once more ask Ovando for help in this dire extremity? They were unable to make it. They even contrived to have another calamity—by colliding with one another, and doing further damage. They just managed to reach St Ann's Bay, on the north coast of Jamaica. At a comfortable distance from the shore on the sand, the ships were lashed together to keep them on an even keel, making a single unit, a house-boat and fort, where they could stay, pending further developments. And there the Spaniards did stay for a whole year—and the ships for ever. As the years passed they gradually sank from the surface of the water into the sand below.*

III

Thus housed, and solidly fortressed into the bargain, the mariners were in a good position to take a well-earned rest after their truly frightful sufferings, and enjoy themselves. As for food, they were surrounded with it, and could have as many meals a day as they wished. They could stretch their limbs at last and relax and exercise themselves boating and swimming and racing and fishing, and no doubt laughing and singing and inventing games and perhaps stories and ballads to beguile the lotus hours. Nowadays a handsome sum of money would have to be raised, and gladly raised, for such an opportunity.

Yet it was not so. They elected to make themselves miserable, and the year that they passed in Jamaica was a torment to them. Truly there was no food problem. There is nothing better to eat than fresh fish, and that sea (in which their house-boat stood) contained masses of fish. And the natives, who turned out to be very friendly, supplied them with cassava-bread and other things. But apparently these sailors had not heard of fishing. That would also have provided them with a perfect kind of work, together with good exercise in a glorious climate. But they were evidently incredibly lazy or stupid to the point of imbecility. And perhaps it is doubtful if they could have enjoyed themselves, since these Spanish half-wits probably wanted all the time to keep themselves fully clothed in the blazing sun-

---

* In recent years an attempt has been made to discover and bring up the remnants of these wrecks. In fact in the *Jamaican Journal* for December 1968, Mr Robert F. Marx claimed to have found certain relics of the two ships; but the hollowness of these pretensions was easily exposed by the distinguished mariner and archaeologist, Mr Charles Cotter, who pointed out that on account of sediment encroachment into St Ann's Bay, the site of the wrecks would now be some distance inland. Since miners rather than divers would thus be required to locate the wrecks, further exploration has been abandoned.

shine, no doubt believing that their filthy rags made them superior to the natives.

There is no document, no detailed account of any sort regarding how the Spaniards spent the day-to-day life. All that is known are a few general facts and what nowadays we call highlights. And I propose to frame them into as brief a space as with propriety I can command.

Food was procured from the natives* who were quite happy at first to supply it in exchange for the baubles of which—amazingly—there was still a supply, though not inexhaustible. The question was—what was to be done? They were stuck there with no possibility of being rescued by any passing ship, not even by an 'illegitimate' adventurer, because Jamaica had no reputation for gold. They were too narrow, too vicious, and too unadaptable to make friends with the other human beings on the island, and share their skills with them. The only thing to do was to get someone to reach Hispaniola and inform the Governor of their plight. But they were all afraid to go.

All except Diego Mendez. He stands out from the rest of the Spaniards on the expedition whose names we know. An educated man, a scholar whose favourite author was Erasmus. A man of striking personality and address, with boundless energy and a cool intelligent audacity that was quite astonishing. Indeed his courage was of the kind that so surprises the enemy that the hero goes unharmed. Once when in Veragua with just one companion, surrounded on all sides by hostile natives threatening him with death, he simply sat down—and had a hair-cut. He took from his pocket a comb, a scissors, and a mirror, and asked his companion, Escobar, to comb and cut his hair. This so amazed the raging natives that they became calm and friendly and asked for similar treatment, and the barber did such good business that they were allowed to go free, laden with food and presents.

Mendez could be rash—as when in Veragua he took prisoner that chieftain who then escaped—but he was the one man whom Columbus could rely upon to get them out of a tight corner, and the one man he could trust besides his brother.

* That food did not consist of any of the indigenous produce we associate with modern Jamaica: no bananas, coconuts, sugar-cane, breadfruit, achees, almonds, tamarinds, cinnamon. (It was Captain Bligh who introduced most of these things.) The Arawaks fished extensively, and they gathered shell-fish, turtles, crabs, and manatee (sea-cows), and relied a great deal upon cassava plants.

Mendez wrote an interesting account of the fourth voyage. He is somewhat boastful and gives himself a good press—but we feel glad that he does, and we are convinced. The trouble is that Columbus, unconsciously, ingenuously, gives himself a bad press almost always when he takes up his pen. He conceals his great qualities by bombast, so that we cannot see the giant that was really there. It is good to note that Diego Mendez respected and honoured him, he was always 'the great Admiral', 'his lordship'. It is important to realize this. And to realize how much Columbus honoured Mendez, and prized him. On more than one occasion, when returning to Columbus after some feat, Mendez says that the Admiral was highly delighted 'and repeatedly embraced me, kissing me on both cheeks, in gratitude for the service I had done him'. One feels sure that this was true; and it brings Columbus to life for us in a way which unfortunately Fernando never does.

This was the last man that the Admiral could afford to part with in Jamaica. He had already proved his additional gift of being able to establish friendly relations with the natives, the Arawaks, and thus organize the food supply. However, only Mendez, and one comrade called Fieschi, would volunteer to make the attempt to reach Hispaniola. They set out with six Indians who had been persuaded by Mendez to man the oars, but were captured by another tribe just as they were about to make for the open sea at the most easterly point of the island at Point Morant. This did not deter Mendez. He and his party escaped and then tried again.

It was not more than a hundred miles from there to Hispaniola. That may not seem very much to us today when great men—and they are great men—sail and even row the oceans single-handed. But the modern costly boats are designed to be almost unsinkable, and they go with all the advantages of communication and geographical exactitude of knowledge. All Mendez could command was a keelless canoe, with no compass or chart or warning of climatic conditions. Nevertheless—to cut the story to the essential—he made it in four days. Then he had to go three hundred miles down the coast—and then two hundred miles on foot to reach the place where Ovando was to be found. His physical endurance was indeed exceptional.

The Governor received him with a show of civility. He was delighted with the intelligence that the Admiral was marooned in Jamaica. The last thing that Ovando desired was to rescue him and welcome him to Hispaniola where he might be tempted to usurp his governorship, or at any rate stir up trouble. So, while not exactly refusing to do anything, he did nothing for nine months—until, shamed by disapproval from some quarters, he sent out a scout-ship to check the situation.

In the meanwhile the position of the Admiral and his company at St Ann's Bay had deteriorated and became critical. Since they were incapable of engaging themselves in any activity, not even in the attempt to grow a few vegetables, or do a bit of fishing, or organize something that would engage their energies, the congestion in their ship-house became intolerable, and the sexual tension—always a sailor's problem— reached a climax, which was not surprising since a disciplinary rule had been imposed preventing them from going on shore to seek native women, and thereby causing catastrophic resentment.

After Diego Mendez had been absent for six months a point was reached when Francisco de Porras, supported by forty-five men, declared outright rebellion against the Admiral who was confined to his cabin with an attack of gout. On January 2nd, 1503, Porras burst into Columbus's cabin and shouted, 'It seems to us, Sir, that you do not want to go to Castile, and that you will keep us here for ever, lost!' Columbus, lying defenceless on his bed, tried to expostulate and point out that he wanted to get away as much as they did. But Porras cut him short rudely, declaring that idle speeches were useless, and turning his back on the Admiral, shouted, 'I am going to Castile with those who wish to follow!' A number of rebels answered his call, and seizing ten canoes which the Admiral had managed to acquire from the natives, 'took to sea with as much elation and joy as if they were landing in Seville'.*

All this is somewhat curious—though authentic as given by Las Casas. Not one of these men had the courage to accompany Mendez in a bid to reach Hispaniola. And now they are setting out for Seville in a few canoes, very angry with Columbus for not having suggested it earlier. And one wonders why Columbus should have had any desire to detain them. It would have been quite in order if he had replied: 'As you observe, gentlemen, I lie here prone, afflicted with gout, and would not at the moment find it terribly easy to take to the open sea in a canoe. But you are more than welcome to make the attempt— with my permission and with my blessing.' And he could be

---

* *Historia de las Indias*, B. de Las Casas, bk. II, vol. 64, pp. 163–4.

pardoned for secretly hoping that they might be kind enough
to drown themselves.

They nearly did drown themselves. Having pressed Indians
into their service and plundered them for food, they set out,
only to be faced with such heavy seas that they had to throw
their plunder overboard, and then savagely threw the Indians
overboard also, on the ground that they were savages. After
three abortive attempts they gave it up, and made their way
back, living off the country, to St Ann's Bay.

It was the manner in which they plundered the natives while
returning that now brought on a food crisis. The Jamaicans
had already begun to get tired of supplying food to the
Spaniards in exchange for the diminishing baubles. They now
declined to do so any more. The situation became very
serious—even critical to the point of life or death.

However, this was a problem which Columbus could handle
much more effectively than anyone else could have done. Just
as he was always extremely shrewd with regard to his
finances and privileges, keeping careful memoranda of the
rights and royal stipulations granted to him, while at the same
time claiming to be a special instrument of the Almighty, so
also he had a discerning eye open regarding any scientific fact
which might serve him to impress simple people. Nothing
pleased his dark humour more than theatrical mendacity. And
now he was about to stage a scene which, though not unusual
in the setting of African magician-priests, was unique in the
context of a European stranded on a tropical island. We can
be very sure that no such scene had ever before or would ever
again be staged at St Ann's Bay, Jamaica.

He had on board his ship at this time the astronomic calendar
of Johannes Muller, known as *Regiomontanus*, in which he
learnt that there was to be a total eclipse of the moon on
February 29th in 1503, a leap year. This food crisis occurred
near the end of February. When the 29th drew near he made it
known that he had an important announcement to make to the
people. They were to come down to the shore and he would
speak to them through an interpreter—for there was one
native whom he had trained to understand him, half by signs
and by some simple words. Calculating to a nicety (he could so
easily have fumbled this) the exact time when the eclipse
would come, he prepared the theatrical effects. He made a chief
gather the people together and he stood high on the ship facing
this unique auditorium. It came naturally to him to speak as

one who had special relations with the Deity, and this was an occasion which really suited him. He explained in sonorous and full-lunged terms which were then interpreted to the rapt audience that he had come as a representative of the God of all mankind, and must tarry for a short time on this shore before passing to other lands. He explained that if they refused to give him and his people food they would suffer the displeasure of God, and that as a sign of this displeasure He would remove the moon from the sky—and after that He might even remove the sun also the next day.

Columbus did not know much about the religion of these natives of Jamaica, but it was obvious that if he could seem to have the ability to make the moon disappear he would be taken for a being with supernatural powers. Nor do we, however learned in comparative religion, know much about their worship; but we may be sure that at the very least the moon would have been to them the Queen of Heaven when the King had gone to rest, her benign lamp's beam shining as the fairest jewel in night's crown. Consider the scene. It was a quiet evening, the full moon's light laid upon the listening earth, and in the shadows of the trees the flickering of the fireflies in their soundless chase; and, as always in the tropics, the multitudinous muttering of those creatures which had set up their everlasting line long before the trampling of any feet; the harsh insistent cry, the ceaseless senseless song of the cicadas. No other sound, save perhaps the lapping of the ripples in the ruined hulks: an aeon-old refrain. Standing aloft there, the tall figure of the Admiral with the pale, sad countenance and the unsmiling lips.

Carefully watching his hour-glass, he explained the situation. He had been constrained to confer with God, and regretfully God had decided to remove the moon as a sign of His displeasure. All his audience did not necessarily believe him, there are always the doubters, and even here a few would have laughed a little, if uneasily. Then the great moment. The moon begins to shrink, bit by bit it narrows, and finally fades into the blackness of night. Then again the Admiral, now a prophet on his mountain, speaks out. He tells the petrified assembly that he will retire and confer again with the Almighty, and ask Him for a reprieve if the food should be restored. Again timing to perfection the term of the eclipse he steps out before the people to say that God has listened to his entreaty and on those conditions will give them back the moon. Even as he speaks, a shining arc appears, then the wider sickle, and soon the circle.

The panic was turned to rejoicing; and to gratitude towards the Admiral. And from then on there was no more trouble about obtaining food.

After eight months had passed since Diego Mendez set out for Hispaniola, a small caravel suddenly appeared at St Ann's Bay. It was in the nature of a scout-ship to ascertain whether the report made by Mendez was true and that Columbus really was stranded in Jamaica. Discourtesy could scarcely go further. But it did go further. Not only did the captain of the ship refuse to take anyone back with him, but he didn't even go on board the Admiral's wrecked ships. However, he brought a gift: one small cask of wine and a ham—that is to say a single glass of wine for each man and a thin slice of ham. Even after nearly five hundred years it is with something akin to indignation that we contemplate such treatment accorded to the discoverer by his mere successor at Hispaniola.

The captain of that caravel nevertheless did give a message from Mendez promising that he was doing all in his power to have a rescue ship sent across as soon as possible. But when this scout-ship had departed and was seen to pass from the horizon, there was a general feeling of despair. It made the rebellious faction still more discontented and mutinous. In fact there was shortly another mutiny, if that is the right word. What the rebels hoped to gain in such a situation is really a mystery. Anyway, a severe battle occurred between these rebels and those who were loyal to Columbus—and it is important to realize that the Admiral always did have loyal supporters. These supporters needed a strong leader, and they found this leader in Bartholomew. He never sang his own praises in any written record, but in deeds his stature stands out very clearly. He overcame the rebels, who surrendered. All were pardoned except their leader, Porras, who was secured in chains.

Another three months followed before Mendez was at last successful in sending over a rescue ship with Ovando's permission, and all were taken on board—about one hundred—and brought to Hispaniola. This ship was of poor quality—a sprung mainmast, rotting sails, and a foul bottom—and leaked so badly that there was fear of foundering. It actually took six and a half weeks to reach Hispaniola—as against the four days taken by Diego Mendez, and the thirty-one days taken by Columbus from the Canaries to San Salvador.

On arrival, Columbus, true to character, displayed no outward signs of indignation. He sent a courteous letter to Ovando,

considering then, as nearly always, that restraint and prudence
are superior weapons to expostulation and abuse. There are
indications that he never in his life forgot the interests of his
crews, or on the whole failed to master them—how otherwise
can we account for their loyalty to him during this terrible
fourth voyage in which they had no real interest? And now he
thought of them as much as of his own dignity. Thus Ovando
was constrained to give them all a show of welcome—though,
in order to display his power of jurisdiction, he demanded that
the chained Porras be released.

It was well over a month before Columbus could obtain a
vessel which would bring him back to Spain with those
members of his crews who wished to join him—which of
course included Bartholomew and Fernando. It was not an easy
journey home. It took nearly three months battling against a
sea of troubles. Twice his vessel nearly foundered. Twice her
masts were broken in successive tempests. But again Columbus
rode it out. It seems that there were no conditions on the ocean
that he could not ride.

IV

We do not know why he was detained so long in Hispaniola,
since this could not have been in the interests of Ovando who
could not have been glad to let anyone inform Columbus
concerning the details of his governorship. But since Columbus
was there for over a month, he would have heard a good deal.
He had said once, 'Whenever I think of Hispaniola, I weep'.
He certainly would have had cause to do so now if he had learnt
the whole truth.

If under his own rule the Indians had been shamefully
treated they were worse off under Bobadilla, who took a
census of the natives and assigned them all as slaves to the
colonists, many of whom were composed of the scourings of
Spanish prisons, and they treated their wretched victims with
terrible cruelty. But when Ovando came to take his place he
made haste to surpass his predecessor in what was cruel and
base.

Some biographers have professed a slight disdain for Las
Casas because of 'unbalancing' his history by too often
rehearsing the wickedness of the slavery in the Indies. How do
you balance a thing like that? Scarcely by leaving it out. One
of the factors which made it possible for Ovando to behave

worse was the large number of men who came over with him
in his thirty ships. This time there were no convicts but a great
many speculators and fools who expected to make a fortune in
a very short time, 'thinking that the gold could be picked up
easily and quickly like apples from a tree',* and when they
found that it was hard to win, they went to every extremity in
exploiting the Indians to sift the gold grains from the soil. It
makes a strange spectacle in the mind's eye: masses of simple
and bewildered men sifting for bright grains of metal in which
they had hardly the slightest interest; and standing over them
civilized men literally crazed by those same pieces of metal.

Since the whole purpose of the colony was to extract gold,
Ovando allowed every Spaniard thirty Indians for the
exploitation of the 'mines'. The men were taken from their
families under threat of the whip and made to work many miles
away. If they hadn't got their own food they starved; and if
they ran away they were hunted down by bloodhounds and
made to do their work in fetters. Most of them died in this
service. 'I have seen many dead lying by the way,' says Las
Casas, an eyewitness, not just an historian trying to be
'balanced'; and he adds: 'Those still alive had dragged themselves into the shade of a tree and were screaming as they
fought each other for bread'. Those who fled and managed to
get home found their homes abandoned for fear of the 'White
Terror'.

One tends to become unsophisticated when reading about
these things and to become unduly put out by the time-sanc-
tioned words, 'the colonies', when they so plainly mean 'the
burglaries'. Here you have your burglar who, having entered
the house, not only loots it but declares that it is legally his
house, and then sets all its occupiers to slave for him with dire
punishment if they fail to show satisfaction.

According to both Herrera and Las Casas the inhabitants of
Xaragua were superior to all the other natives in the graceful-
ness of their speech, the sweetness of their nature, and the
beauty of their persons, as also in policy and manners. Their
queen, Anacaona, was renowned for her beauty and personal
address. Now at this time some of Roldan's former partisans
were causing great trouble by their viciousness and banditry
in Xaragua. These Spaniards informed Ovando that the
Indians were planning to revolt. The Governor went there with

* *Historia de las Indias*, B. de Las Casas.

seventy horsemen and three hundred foot-soldiers, but represented himself to the queen as paying a friendly visit to discuss 'tribute'. Anacaona decided to receive them with all courtesy, and went out to meet him with a concourse of her subjects, and held festivities, singing and dancing, to make him welcome. This impressed Ovando, but the former followers of Roldan set about the Governor telling him that there would be or could be an insurrection, and the thing to do would be to quell it before it broke out. Thus they argued, says Arthur Helps, 'using all those seemingly wise arguments of wickedness which from time immemorial have originated and perpetuated treachery'.

Ovando, acting upon these conjectures, arranged to give a feast seemingly in return for the hospitality given to the Spaniards by the queen. There was to be a tournament during which there would be a mock battle between armoured men. At the same time, those not taking part in the tournament would surround the gathering and at a given signal, massacre them all. This was a role in dissimulation which came easy to Ovando. The poor queen fell into the snare prepared for her. She even told Ovando that the chiefs would like to see the tournament, whereupon he eagerly invited them to his quarters to explain the festivities to them. Meanwhile he gave his cavalry orders to surround the building.

He placed the infantry at certain commanding positions; and told his men that when, in talking with the caciques, he should place his hand upon the badge of knighthood which hung upon his breast, they should rush in and bind the caciques and Anacaona. It fell out as he planned. All these deluded Indian chiefs and their queen were secured. She alone was let out of Ovando's quarters, which were then set fire to, and all the chiefs burnt alive.*

The queen did not escape death. She was charged with high treason, tortured, then hanged upon a gallows especially erected for her. Deprived of their leaders, the Indians in this province could be easily exterminated. Las Casas was an eye-witness of this.

If it chanced that certain Christians, whether from kindness or greed of gain, seized upon an Indian child and took it away with

* *Christopher Columbus*, Arthur Helps, Everyman, 1910.

them on their horses, another rode up behind them and ran it through with his lance. A few Indians who escaped the blood bath of Xaragua fled in their canoes to the island of Zuanabo that was eight leagues away. They were condemned by the Governor to slavery for life, and any Spaniard was allowed to hunt them down and capture them. I have seen them burnt alive, torn to pieces, and put to all manner of elaborate torments. The tale of horrors is so long that I am not able to write it down. Only one thing will I say, and bear witness thereto before my God and my conscience, that the Indians gave not the smallest occasion for this treatment, they were innocent of the slightest guilt, and never committed any crime upon the Christians that deserved death. Indeed, only a few of them indulged in any vengeance or reprisals against such bloody devils as these Christians: I knew most of them very well and they were hardly wilder or more intractable than twelve-year-old boys. The war against them had no shadow of justice in it, but the Christians were so hellish cruel and unjust, more than any blackguardly tyrant that ever lived. All these things I saw with my own eyes, and I feared to repeat them because I could hardly trust myself, and was doubtful whether I had dreamed it all.

There was a neighbouring tribe called the Higneys, a warlike group from whom neither Bobadilla nor Columbus had been able to gather tribute. Ovando now decided to deal with them, and with this end in view he despatched a reliable captain called Juan de Esquibel to deal with them. Though they proved themselves extremely brave and showed a contempt for death which embarrassed the Christians, the captain was able to master them and root them out completely, old and young. With the help of bloodhounds he hunted them all down, including wives and children hiding in woods and caves. They were all slaughtered, impaled, mutilated and burnt by the hundred. They were forced to fly further and further into the mountains still pursued until a final band of six or seven hundred, driven to the edge of a rocky gorge, were forced over it to a man.

In order to celebrate the extinction of this tribe Ovando built on that site of blood and of tears a new town which he called The City of True Peace (La Villa de la Vera Paz), and the arms which he assigned to the new settlement bore a dove with an olive-branch, a rainbow, and a cross. We begin to understand more clearly why that dying native chief refused baptism on the ground that he might go to heaven and there meet only Christians.

So we come upon an awkward consideration. Columbus had not proved himself a good governor. But from almost any point of view, save the crassest savagery in cruel usurpation, his rule was superior to that of either Bobadilla or Ovando, his successors. Unfortunately the Sovereigns were not only ignorant as to where Hispaniola actually was, they had scarcely the faintest idea of what went on there in their name. Indeed it was not until three hundred years later, on the publication of Las Casas's *History of the Indies* in the nineteenth century, that the truth was known.

v

Columbus reached Seville on November 8th, 1504, after two and a half years' absence without any of his aims achieved. He had failed to discover the strait, since it did not exist. The promises of gold were once again unfulfilled. He was as far as ever from meeting the Grand Khan or seeing Cathay as from coming across Vasco da Gama in the Indian Ocean. All the King got from him (the Queen was dying) was an enormously long, incoherent, and tactless letter, written while he was in Jamaica.*

Whenever Columbus was in a tight corner he took to letter-writing if possible. In an extremity of catastrophe or crisis he would take to the pen as some other men take to drink or drugs; and, in his cups as it were, he would achieve flights of exaltation more satisfactory to him than fleeting ecstasies from the fumes of wine. Thus, on that awful occasion in Veragua at the bar of Belen, when all seemed lost, and it was doubtful if they would escape intact from the natives whom they had outraged, he writes,

> Tired out, I went to sleep moaning: I heard a very compassionate voice, which said—*O fool, man slow to believe and serve thy God, God of all! What more did He do for Moses or for David His servant? From thy birth, He always took great care of thee. When He saw thee of an age which satisfied Him, marvellously did He make thy name resound in the Earth. The Indies, which are part of the world, so rich, He gave them to thee as thine; thou gavest them to whomsoever*

---

* Drawn upon in this chapter. It purports to report his fourth voyage. Salvador de Madariaga quotes the whole of it, regarding it as a masterpiece. It is included in *The Four Voyages of Christopher Columbus*, ed. J. M. Cohen, Penguin, 1969.

*thou didst please and He gave thee power to do so. Of the shackles of
the Ocean Sea, which were bound with such strong chains, He gave
thee the keys; and thou wast obeyed in so many lands and didst win
such honoured renown amongst Christians! What more did He do for
the people of Israel when He led them out of Egypt? Nor for David,
whom from a shepherd He raised to be King of Judea?*

Learning, great practical skill, inspiration, genius—a man
may have all these and yet be very stupid in some respects. One
of the worst ways of being stupid is failure in tact—in other
words being lacking in simple psychology. Columbus suffered
from this particular form of stupidity throughout his career, and
at no time more so than when he wrote this famous letter in
Jamaica. 'The Indies . . . He gave them to thee as thine; thou
gavest them to whomsoever thou didst please, and He gave thee
power to do so.' Doubtless he sincerely believed in his voices,
which would have been in accordance with the spirit of the age,
but to have included that particular passage in a letter
addressed to the Sovereigns who had sponsored no fewer than
four voyages, is carrying an audacity of insolence even beyond
the madness of monomania. But at the same time—more
accurately, when he returned to Spain—he expected the
Sovereigns to ratify his privileges and financial rights. Of course
it is not unusual for men who speak in exalted terms about
their mission and God's guidance and so forth to keep a close
eye on their financial accounts, and indeed Columbus calculated
his assets and property privileges to the last penny, and worried
about them a great deal. But what is unusual, and really
extraordinary, is that Columbus did not hesitate to tell the King
that he could have given the Indies to anyone he chose, and yet
expect to be received immediately at Court on his return, and
have his rights ratified and all his financial demands recognized
and approved.

Yet that seems to be just what he did expect. On returning,
he spent much of the rest of his life—only one and a half years
to go—in demanding the fulfilment of the Capitulations of 1492.
On the whole the King was extraordinarily patient. True, he
kept the Admiral waiting for some time before he invited him
to Court, but then he offered him special travelling facilities,
welcomed him, flattered him, made handsome offers, and saw to
it that he should receive, through Deza, the executive of the
Sovereigns, the monetary obligations due to him. But Columbus
claimed that more was due (which would have made him one

of the richest men in Europe) and it is not easy to follow his assertions and claims at this time. What troubled him most was the fulfilment of the Capitulation which appointed his heirs as governors of Hispaniola. When the King said that Deza should act as arbitrator in this matter, Columbus refused, declaring that it was all or nothing. This stubbornness succeeded, for his son Diego did become the 'Second Admiral' as Governor of Hispaniola—though his father never lived to see this fulfilment of his demand.

That appointment is a pleasant thought, for Diego would have been no Bobadilla or Ovando. Pleasant also is the fact that Diego Mendez, the brave and the brilliant, and always so faithful to his Admiral, comes before us again.

One day when His Lordship, the Admiral, was in Salamanca, lying abed because of his arthritis [writes Mendez], I went to see him and said to him—Your Lordship knows full well the many things I have done in his service . . . I therefore ask Your Lordship to grant me some reward. The Admiral answered me with a smile, saying that I should tell him what I wished. I then begged him to grant me the office of Chief Constable in the Island of Hispaniola for my lifetime. He told me that he would grant me this willingly, and that it was small reward for my services. He asked me to tell this to his son Diego, who was most pleased and said that if his father gave me this with one hand, he gave it to me with both hands.

This is most charming and throws a little beam of light upon the three of them. Columbus did not spend all the time scheming for his own ends. He never ceased to plead with the financial authorities for worthy back-payment for his crews who had returned with him; and again we must not forget that if some of them staged mutinies at times, the majority supported him in spite of appalling privations and dangers.

There is another thing, which every chronicler has noticed. In his will, which he brooded over a good deal in these days, he enjoins Diego to give a share of his revenues to poor relatives, and other shares were to go to his young brother and his uncles. And there is a special clause regarding Beatriz Enriquez. It runs: 'I order my son Diego to provide the necessary funds for her to live a comfortable life. May he do so in order to unburden my conscience, for this matter weighs heavily upon my soul. It is not seemly that I write herein the reason thereof.' We know nothing about this, and we never shall. Yet again a small light plays upon his character here; as it also does when he writes to Diego at this period engaging him to treat his brother Fernando with respect: 'Ten brothers would be none too many. I have never found better friends than my brothers'. That tells us a good deal about himself; and about his brothers—especially about the silent Bartholomew who seems to have put the interests of Christopher always before his own, even when this meant the extremity of hardship and the likelihood of death.

We cannot say that Columbus got any kind of raw deal during his lifetime—still less after his death. Only one thing hurts us—that the New World should have been called America instead of Columbia. As we are all perhaps a little weak on our facts about Amerigo Vespucci, I venture a brief word of explanation here. Vespucci, a Florentine, made two journeys to the American continent, one in 1499, the other in 1503.* The account of the second expedition, published in Strasburg in 1505, brought him a sensational reputation (for he was a very clever and articulate man) and was the cause of the New World being called America. This was Central America, discovered by Columbus in 1498 (the coast of Paria). Now, Vespucci's adherents, for some dark motive, dated this discovery of Vespucci as 1497. This fraudulent alteration of the date was made clear when Diego Columbus was granted his hereditary privileges. One of the many witnesses was Alonzo de Hojeda who had taken part in Vespucci's voyages. He emphasized in court the priority of Columbus, and stated that he had seen the map of the ocean which the Admiral had sent to their Majesties—and that it was not till then that Vespucci had ventured to set out in the company of himself and Juan de la Cosa.

It is ironic enough. For if Columbus had not been so enslaved by his own cosmography he could have proclaimed the truth instead of insisting that Paria was an island somewhere off Asia. Yet again, I suppose, we must not be too sad about this. Without his tremendous error no one would have heard of Columbus—and who knows or cares much about Amerigo Vespucci?

The Admiral's body had been so battered by these voyages that he had now little strength left to keep alive. And he was not buoyed up mentally or spiritually. There was a division in

* See G. R. Crone's *The Discovery of America*, ch. 10, for an illuminating account.

him, as if a clear line were drawn separating two zones: exalted idealism, and insatiable greed. He wanted to believe that his lust for gold had been in the service of his God: he knew that it was not so. He knew that his singleness of purpose was not allied with purity of heart. He had done wrong by the Indians. When at last he realized this, suggests Wassermann, 'he fell for ever into irredeemable melancholy which thenceforth hung over him like a mortal sickness'. That could be so. He had professed to lift them up: he had cast them down. He tried to justify his actions saying that 'in the name of the Holy Trinity' he had brought Indians to Spain to be converted: yet he knew that you cannot enslave human beings in the name of the Father and of the Son and of the Holy Ghost. He was not in the least like so many of the powerful men involved in the enterprise of the Indies—happy in their evil wholeness. He was unhappy in the division of his soul, declaring with St Paul—the good that I would I do not, the evil that I would not that I do.

He did not die in discomfort or neglect—nor wholly un-honoured. The masses may have forgotten him in the usual way, just as the masses would later celebrate an immortal in the usual way. He had his brothers. He had his sons. And there were always those who, without guessing the abysmal terrors and dark splendours of his story, could discern his essence. It is said that one day shortly before his death on May 29th, 1506, he was approached in a street in Valladolid by a young stranger. 'Sire,' said the young man, gazing with bright-eyed awe upon the Admiral with the arthritic limp and tempest-torn coun-tenance, 'Permit me to touch the hand of the greatest man of our time, and true Emperor of the East.'

It is not known what Columbus replied, moved as he must have been, as all men are, however famous, by a stranger's word of kindness or of praise. And at once we recall how Cervantes on his last ride from Esquirias to Madrid was met by a student who expressed how thrilled he was to meet 'the hero of the maimed hand, the famous author, pride and joy of the Muses'. When taking leave of the young man the aged author said gently: 'My life is slipping away, and by the diary that my pulse is keeping, which at the latest will end its reckoning next Sunday, I must close my life's account. You, Sir, have met me at an uncouth moment, since there is not enough time left for me to thank you for the good will you have shown me.' It is an uncouth hour when any man goes towards the scene of his death, but that discord may be turned into harmony and that sorrow into beauty when a few such words as those fall to the ground. Don Quixote could not, like his creator, always command the phrase when needed; but Don Columbus, conscious to the end when his hour came, joined in the prayers for the dying, repeating with his last breath, *'In manes tuas, Domine, commendo spiritum meum'*.

Appendix

THE NORSE CONTROVERSY

A LUDICROUS VIEW was put forward in 1972 by Mr J. R. Enterline in a book called *Viking America,* supported in an epilogue by the celebrated Mr Thor Heyerdahl. They seem to think that it is interesting to speculate whether Columbus or Leif Eiriksson first discovered America. No doubt Leif Eiriksson reached those northern regions first—though the famous 'Vinland Map' is now found to be a forgery! But in any case the question is terribly tiresome, for the point about Columbus is that he crossed the Atlantic from the Canaries to the outskirts of Florida, and by so doing closed the door of the Middle Ages and changed the history of the world. For all the immediate effect which Leif Eiriksson had in impinging his deeds upon the consciousness of Europe, he might just as well have been a polar bear, and his colonies of Christians in Greenland a company of penguins. To equate Columbus and Eiriksson as supposed rival heroes in the imagination of mankind may serve in a thesis, but it remains claptrap.

Even more strange is the claim that Columbus must have obtained special information, in fact a chart, from the Norsemen which enabled him to know exactly where to sail and how long it would take to reach the mainland of 'Asia'. This hypothetical chart could only have been in relation to the north, but Columbus had not the smallest interest in the northern regions; he had no desire to have breakfast on a glacier or sing hymns in pastoral huts on Greenland's icy mountains: his gaze was turned towards the warm golden lands of Chipangu and Cathay where he hoped to convert the Grand Khan to Christianity and obtain boundless wealth by means of which he would rescue Jerusalem from the Saracens. The only chart that could have helped him would have been from the Canaries to San Salvador and he could only have received such a chart from someone who had been that way before, but preferred to remain anonymous!

199

Bibliography

The number of books written about and around Columbus during the centuries since his death is naturally formidable. It seems to me that the most helpful thing I can do here is simply to give a selected list of the volumes which have been most helpful to me, and some of which, at least, are easily accessible to the reader.

I   *Source Materials*
Christopher Columbus: the Journal of the First Voyage to America, introduction by Van Wyck Brooks, Jarrolds, 1925. Includes two letters from Toscanelli to Columbus.

The Log of Christopher Columbus's first voyage to America in the year 1492, as copied out by Bartolomé de Las Casas, W. H. Allen, 1944.

Three of the famous 'open' letters of Columbus:

1.   *Letter of Columbus to Various Persons Describing the Results of his First Voyage and Written on the Return Journey.*
2.   *Letter Sent by the Admiral of the Indies to the Governess of Don Juan of Castile in the year 1500, in which He was Brought from the Indies a Prisoner.*
3.   *Letter Written by Christopher Columbus, Viceroy and Admiral of the Indies, to the Most Christian and Mighty King and Queen of Spain, Our Sovereigns.*

These letters are included in *The Four Voyages of Columbus*, trans. J. M. Cohen, Penguin, 1969. Also included are:

1.   *A Digest of Columbus's Log-Book on his First Voyage Made by Bartolomé de Las Casas.* (This can be compared with the fuller volume listed above—Cohen's translation is the more skilful.)
2.   Extracts from Captain Gonzalo Fernandez de Oviedo, Book II, ch. 2–4.
3.   *Letter from Dr Chanca to the City of Seville.*
4.   Account by Diego Mendez of incidents during the fourth voyage.

5. Seven extracts from the *Life of Columbus* by his son, Fernando. Fernando's complete volume—*Life of Christopher Columbus*—is translated and annotated by Benjamin Keen, Folio Society, 1960.

Historia de las Indias, Bartolomé de Las Casas.

II *General Studies*

Crone, Gerald R., *The Discovery of America*, Hamish Hamilton, 1969. One of the most helpful of up-to-date books in English on the whole Columbian context.

Hay, David and Joan, *No Star at the Pole: a history of navigation from the Stone Age to the 20th century*, Charles Knight, 1972.

Helps, Arthur, *Christopher Columbus*, Everyman, 1910. Helps was one of the most distinguished of the literary lesser lights of the nineteenth century. Far from up-to-date, of course, but compelling, and particularly illuminating on the Portuguese discoveries under Henry the Navigator.

Hovelaque, Emile, *China*, trans. Mrs Laurence Binyon, Dent, 1923.

Irving, Washington, *The Life and Voyages of Christopher Columbus*, John Murray, 1828.

Kimble, G. H. T., *Geography in the Middle Ages*, Methuen, 1938. This covers also much of the ideology of the Middle Ages.

Lewis, C. S., *The Discarded Image: an introduction to medieval and Renaissance literature*, Cambridge U.P., 1964.

Mahn-Lot, Marianne, *Columbus*, trans. Helen R. Lane, Evergreen Profile Book, no. 33, Grove Press, New York, 1961.

Madariaga, Salvador de, *Christopher Columbus: being the life of the Very Magnificent Lord Don Cristobal Colon*, Hollis & Carter, 1949. A profusion of factual detail and a formidable display of scholarly reference. The case for Jewish origin persistently pursued, and yet also the Don Quixote element continually stressed.

Morison, Samuel E., *Christopher Columbus, Admiral of the Ocean Sea*, Oxford U.P., 1942. Admiral Morison followed Columbus's voyages in the Caribbean and South American coast in his own ship.

Mandeville, John, *The Travels of Sir John Mandeville*, Macmillan's Library of English Classics, 1900.

Nunn, G. G. E., *Geographical Conceptions of Columbus*, American Geographical Society, Research Series no. 14.

Polo, Marco, *The Travels of Marco Polo*, introd. John Masefield, Everyman, 1906.

Wassermann, Jacob, *Christopher Columbus: Don Quixote of the Seas*, trans. Eric Sutton, Martin Secker, 1930. Though sometimes reckless with regard to both fact and chronology this is a compelling impression by a great artist.

Index